THE CONSTITUTION OF BRAZIL

This book offers an original and comprehensive analysis of Brazilian constitutional law and shows how the 1988 Constitution has been a cornerstone in Brazil's struggle to achieve institutional stability and promote the enforcement of fundamental rights. In the realm of rights, although much has been done to decrease the gap between constitutional text and constitutional practice, several types of inequalities still affect and sometimes impair the enforcement of the ambitious bill of rights laid down by the Brazilian Constitution. Within the organisation of powers, the book not only describes how its legislative, executive and judicial functions are organised, but above all else, it analyses how a politically fragmented National Congress, a powerful President and an activist Supreme Court engage with each other in ways that one could hardly grasp by reading the constitutional text without contextual analysis. Similarly, the book also shows how the three-tiered federation established in 1988 has undergone a process of centralisation led not only by the central government but also by the Brazilian Supreme Court. In addition to chapters on organisation of powers, fundamental rights, federalism, and the legislative process, the book also presents an overview of Brazilian constitutionalism with a special focus on the transition from authoritarianism to democracy, which led to the enactment of the 1988 Constitution. In the conclusion, the author argues that part of the Constitution's transformative potential remains to be realised. Enforcing the Constitution, not changing it, has been the real challenge in the last three decades and will continue to be for many years to come.

Pictorial Narrative

Amazon, anthropological heterogeneity: *Constituição da República Federativa do Brasil*

An architectural juxtaposition of the iconic Three Branches Square (Praça dos Três Poderes) which unites, in a single square, the seats of the Legislative, Executive and Judiciary branches, is the heart of the composition. The synthesis serves as an allegory of the separation of powers. 1822 honours Brazil's independence, while 1988 commemorates the promulgation of the current constitution. The structure is suffused in an intense yellow triangle beam representing the public gaze on accountability. At the apex is a constellation of the Southern Cross, highlighting a compelling feature in the Brazilian national flag. A rendition of the Amazon occupies the top left, illustrating the important natural landscape of Brazil. A single 'onça pintada' – the Brazilian jaguar – signifies the fragility of the Amazon. On the opposite side, a spinning football celebrates Brazil's iconic national sport. Three portraits of anonymous faces, black, indigenous and white, represent Brazil's unique history of diversity and a crowd of people gesticulating towards the sign 'Diretas Já' (direct elections now) commemorates one of the rallies in 1984, when more than one million people took to the streets to demand free elections in Brazil.

Putachad
Artist

Constitutional Systems of the World
General Editors: Benjamin L Berger, Rosalind Dixon, Andrew Harding, Heinz Klug, and Peter Leyland

In the era of globalisation, issues of constitutional law and good governance are being seen increasingly as vital issues in all types of society. Since the end of the Cold War, there have been dramatic developments in democratic and legal reform, and post-conflict societies are also in the throes of reconstructing their governance systems. Even societies already firmly based on constitutional governance and the rule of law have undergone constitutional change and experimentation with new forms of governance; and their constitutional systems are increasingly subjected to comparative analysis and transplantation. Constitutional texts for practically every country in the world are now easily available on the internet. However, texts which enable one to understand the true context, purposes, interpretation and incidents of a constitutional system are much harder to locate, and are often extremely detailed and descriptive. This series seeks to provide scholars and students with accessible introductions to the constitutional systems of the world, supplying both a road map for the novice and, at the same time, a deeper understanding of the key historical, political and legal events which have shaped the constitutional landscape of each country. Each book in this series deals with a single country, or a group of countries with a common constitutional history, and each author is an expert in their field.

Published volumes

The Constitution of the United Kingdom; The Constitution of the United States; The Constitution of Vietnam; The Constitution of South Africa; The Constitution of Japan; The Constitution of Germany; The Constitution of Finland; The Constitution of Australia; The Constitution of the Republic of Austria; The Constitution of the Russian Federation; The Constitutional System of Thailand; The Constitution of Malaysia; The Constitution of China; The Constitution of Indonesia; The Constitution of France; The Constitution of Spain; The Constitution of Mexico; The Constitution of Israel; The Constitutional Systems of the Commonwealth Caribbean; The Constitution of Canada; The Constitution of Singapore; The Constitution of Belgium; The Constitution of Taiwan; The Constitution of Romania; The Constitutional Systems of the Independent Central Asian States; The Constitution of India; The Constitution of Pakistan; The Constitution of Ireland; The Constitution of Brazil

Link to series website

www.bloomsburyprofessional.com/uk/series/
constitutional-systems-of-the-world

The Constitution of Brazil

A Contextual Analysis

Virgílio Afonso da Silva

•HART•

OXFORD • LONDON • NEW YORK • NEW DELHI • SYDNEY

HART PUBLISHING
Bloomsbury Publishing Plc
Kemp House, Chawley Park, Cumnor Hill, Oxford, OX2 9PH, UK

First published in hardback, 2019
Paperback edition, 2019

A catalogue record for this book is available from the British Library.

Library of Congress Cataloging-in-Publication data

Names: Silva, Virgílio Afonso da, author.

Title: The Constitution of Brazil : a contextual analysis / Virgílio Afonso da Silva.

Description: Oxford, UK ; Chicago, Illinois : Hart Publishing, 2019. | Series: Constitutional systems of the world | Includes bibliographical references and index.

Identifiers: LCCN 2018061355 (print) | LCCN 2019000537 (ebook) | ISBN 9781509929672 (EPub) | ISBN 9781849465359 (hardback)

Subjects: LCSH: Constitutional law—Brazil. | Brazil. Constituicao (1988) | Constitutions—Brazil. | Constitutional history—Brazil. | Federal government—Brazil. | Executive power—brazil. | Brazil. Supremo Tribunal Federal. | Civil rights—brazil. | BISAC: LAW / Constitutional. | HISTORY / Latin America / South America. | LAW / Legal History.

Classification: LCC KHD2914 1988 (ebook) | lCC KHD2914 1988 .S553 2019 (print) | DDC 342.81—dc23

LC record available at https://lccn.loc.gov/2018061355

ISBN: HB: 978-1-84946-535-9
PB: 978-1-5099-3507-9
ePDF: 978-1-50992-968-9
ePub: 978-1-50992-967-2

Typeset by Compuscript Ltd, Shannon
Printed and bound in Great Britain

For Dora and Nuno

Acknowledgements

MY DAUGHTER WAS born four months after I signed the contract for this book. All of a sudden, my free time shrank; what was left completely vanished when my son was born less than two years later, exactly two months before the deadline to deliver the first version of this book. The world did not stop, and people still expected that I would be able to keep the agreements that I had voluntarily signed. And why shouldn't they? Still as a law student, I remember that I had learned that an important foundation of the law of contracts is the *pacta sunt servanda* principle. Since I know that there are exceptions to this principle, I simply assumed that having to take care of two children could be one of them.

Having said this, I first of all would like to thank everyone at Hart Publishing for their virtually endless patience with my continued delays. I would also like to thank the editors of the series 'Constitutional Systems of the World', Peter Leyland, Andrew Harding, Benjamin L Berger, Rosalind Dixon and Heinz Klug, for having accepted my manuscript to be part of this prestigious series. I would especially like to thank Ros and Heinz, who provided insightful comments on early drafts. I also would like to thank Grégoire Webber, former associate editor of the series, who firstly and kindly received the original proposal for this book.

I also would like to thank the following persons who have read and provided important comments on early drafts of this book or of some of its chapters. The order has nothing to do with the importance of their helping, it is alphabetical (Brazilian style, ie, by given name, not by surname): Adriana Vojvodic, Ana Laura Barbosa, Daniel Wang, Filipe Gaspari, Lívia Gil Guimarães, Luís Renato Vedovato, Octávio Ferraz, Orlando Villas Bôas Filho, Pedro Schrerer de Mello Aleixo, and Samuel Rodrigues Barbosa.

I also want to thank Putachad Leyland, who designed the cover of this book. Her patience with my constant new ideas was virtually endless. I am especially grateful that she accepted the suggestion of portraying three anonymous Brazilian people of different ethnic origins and genders, thus avoiding a picture in which only 'dead white men' have a place as well as the idea that constitutions are merely the product of some supposedly enlightened minds and not of the long struggles of an entire nation.

A considerable part of the bibliographic material I needed for my research was not in the library of the Faculty of Law but in the libraries of other schools. Since the Faculty of Law is located in the city centre of São Paulo, 15 km away from the main campus of the University of São Paulo, borrowing and returning the many books I needed could have been a nightmare. This was not the case thanks to the diligent help of the staff of the library of the Law School, and I would like to thank especially Rosangela Pupo and Mércia Fonseca.

The advantage of having written a book on the Brazilian constitutional system in Brazil is the opportunity to drink extremely good Brazilian coffee (Catuaí, Acaiá, Bourbon, Maragogipe, and Caturra, among other varieties). Brazilian coffee not only is the best in the world but also helps a lot when one has to work at night after an afternoon with two children whose energy seems endless. Thank you *coffea arabica*.

As with each and every one of my works, this book was written, and the research behind it was planned and organised, using only free and open-source software. I would like to thank everyone in the FOSS community both for their support and for the development of amazing software and platforms that make academic research even more interesting and less dependent on proprietary software.

I am proud that I need not finish these acknowledgements with the still frequent (and rather gender stereotypical) note, 'Kids, sorry that dad couldn't have been with you very much in the last few years, I was working hard … (but I am pretty sure that your mum took good care of you during my absence …)'. That is not to say that I didn't work hard. I think I did. But that does not mean that I was not there to change my children's diapers, cook for them, bathe them and put them to bed every single day and night, nor does it mean I took one minute less to read all the books in their fast-growing bookshelves, to watch *Bolek i Lolek* and *Reksio* for the 37th time (though I confess that I sometimes did doze off …), to play at Água Branca Park, to go to Álvaro Guerra Library, to build sandcastles and to learn how to surf on the beaches of Peruíbe, to play at the playground of the Horácio Sabino Square and to eat pizza on the way home (just like Basia), and to do everything else we did together in the last few years. At this moment, Magda, my wife, would surely say, 'Stop bragging about yourself, you only did your duty!' And she is probably right. Still, I will continue to argue (because that is all that jurists can do …) that sometimes it is perfectly acceptable to be proud of fulfilling even our most basic duties. Having said that, I would like to thank Magda for her patience with my endless arguing about everything and for her support all these years. Even though I have been doing half the job at home, she has done much more (it seems that raising children challenges even the most basic principles of mathematics …).

São Paulo, Winter 2018
(Yes, August, not January; São Paulo is down south!)

Table of Contents

List of Abbreviations

ACHR	American Convention on Human Rights
ADC	*Ação Declaratória de Constitucionalidade* (Declaratory Action of Constitutionality)
ADCT	*Ato das Disposições Constitucionais Transitórias* (Transitional Constitutional Provisions Act)
ADI	*Ação Direta de Inconstitucionalidade* (Direct Action of Unconstitutionality)
ADO	*Ação Direta de Inconstitucionalidade por Omissão* (Direct Action of Unconstitutionality for Omission)
ADPF	*Arguição de Descumprimento de Preceito Fundamental* (Allegation of Disobedience of Fundamental Precept)
ANVISA	*Agência Nacional de Vigilância Sanitária* (National Health Regulatory Agency)
BRL	Real (Brazilian currency)
CEDAW	Convention on the Elimination of All Forms of Discrimination Against Women
CNJ	*Conselho Nacional de Justiça* (National Council of Justice)
DRE	Direct-Recording Electronic voting system
EC	*Emenda Constitucional* (Constitutional Amendment)
ECR	*Emenda Constitucional de Revisão* (constitutional amendment passed during the Constitutional Revision 1993–1994)
HC	Habeas Corpus
IACHR	Inter-American Commission of Human Rights
IACtHR	Inter-American Court of Human Rights

IBGE	*Instituto Brasileiro de Geografia e Estatística* (Brazilian Institute of Geography and Statistics)
ICCPR	International Covenant on Civil and Political Rights
ILO	International Labour Organisation
INAF	*Indicador de Alfabetismo Funcional* (Index of Functional Illiteracy)
INCRA	*Instituto Nacional de Colonização e Reforma Agrária* (National Institute for Settlement and Land Reform)
LGBT	Lesbian, Gay, Bisexual, and Transgender
LIBRAS	*Língua Brasileira de Sinais* (Brazilian Sign Language)
MI	*Mandado de Injunção* (writ of injunction)
MS	*Mandado de Segurança* (writ of security)
OAB	*Ordem dos Advogados do Brasil* (Brazilian Bar Association)
OAS	Organization of American States
Rcl	*Reclamação* (Complaint)
RE	*Recurso Extraordinário* (Extraordinary Appeal)
RICD	*Regimento Interno da Câmara dos Deputados* (internal rules of the Chamber of Deputies)
RISF	*Regimento Interno do Senado Federal* (internal rules of the Federal Senate)
RISTF	*Regimento Interno do Supremo Tribunal Federal* (rules of procedure of the Brazilian Supreme Court)
STF	*Supremo Tribunal Federal* (Brazilian Federal Supreme Court)
STJ	*Superior Tribunal de Justiça* (Superior Court of Justice)
SUS	*Sistema Único de Saúde* (Brazilian Unified Health System)
UNDP	United Nations Development Program

Table of Cases

Brazilian Supreme Court (STF)

Brazilian Superior Court of Justice (STJ)

Brazilian Superior Electoral Court (TSE)

Brazilian National Council of Justice (CNJ)

Colombia

Inter-American Court of Human Rights (IACtHR)

Inter-American Commission of Human Rights (IACHR)

Table of Legislation

Germany

Mexico

United States

International

Introduction

Fundamental Rights – Presidential System – Federalism

Brazil is a country marked by the deepest inequalities. There are hardly any other countries in the world where inequalities are so ingrained. Although Brazil has the eighth largest economy in the world, in no other country does the wealthiest 1 per cent of the population possess a greater share of pre-tax national income.[1] Although more than 50 per cent of the population is non-white, it is hard to find any black or indigenous persons in positions of political or economic power. Racial democracy is and always has been a myth. If context matters – as the subtitle of each and every book in this series indicates – this is probably the most important information one should know before reading the text of the Brazilian Constitution, the decisions of the Brazilian Supreme Court (STF), or even this book itself.

In this short introductory chapter, I will present a very brief summary of the many aspects of the Brazilian constitutional system that will be analysed throughout this book. The next section begins with a formal overview of the structure of the Brazilian Constitution. The following sections present the main institutional features of the Brazilian constitutional and political system, which will be presented in more detail in the chapters that follow.

I. AN OVERVIEW OF THE 1988 CONSTITUTION

In the history of a country, political and institutional ruptures frequently coincide with constitutional breaks. Since its 1822 independence from Portugal, Brazil has been a monarchy and a republic and has experienced authoritarian and democratic regimes and both civil and military governments; it has experienced at least two coups d'état and several other institutional and constitutional crises. Brazil has already had eight

[1] Source: World Wealth and Income Database (http://wid.world/country/brazil).

constitutions, enacted in 1824, 1891, 1934, 1937, 1946, 1967 and 1969, and its current constitution, enacted on 5 October 1988.

The 1988 Constitution is divided into nine parts – called 'headings' (*títulos*) – which are divided into chapters, some of which are divided into sections (*seções*) and subsections (*subseções*). Additionally, there is a final, unnumbered heading for transitional provisions, called Transitional Constitutional Provisions Act (*Ato das Disposições Constitucionais Transitórias*, ADCT), which is mostly composed of rules for transitioning from the old to the new constitutional order. However, not every provision in this part of the Constitution is aimed at laying down rules for that transition. Some rules were included in the ADCT because they were aimed at regulating a single event in a given moment. Additionally, the transitional part of the Constitution has been used for a different type of transition, namely, that between the situation before and the situation after a given constitutional amendment.

The 1988 Constitution aims to do more than simply provide for freedom rights and establish the basic rules of government. It is a clear example of a constitution that aims to change the status quo by establishing goals to be pursued and defining the standards of public policies in different areas. In short, it is intended to be a transformative constitution. It is an example of what in the Brazilian tradition is called 'dirigiste constitution' (*constituição dirigente*), and it contains several programmatic provisions that depend on the execution of public policies to be effective.

By August 2018 – that is, 30 years after its promulgation – the Constitution had been amended 99 times.[2] There are several reasons for, and an unending debate on, the allegedly high number of constitutional amendments in Brazil. I will analyse this issue in more detail in chapter eight. The part of the Constitution that has been the most affected by constitutional amendments is that in which state intervention in the economy is regulated.[3]

In 1993, two events could have had a strong impact on the institutional and constitutional design established by the 1988 Constitution. Article 2 of the ADCT stipulated that a referendum on the government system (presidentialism x parliamentarianism) and the

[2] 105 times if one includes the six amendments made during the constitutional revision of 1993. However, these amendments do not follow the ordinary numbering of constitutional amendments.

[3] See ch 6.

government regime (constitutional republic x constitutional monarchy) should take place on 7 September 1993.[4] The results of this referendum maintained both presidentialism and the constitutional republic.[5]

The second event that could have had a relevant impact on the constitutional and institutional design defined in 1988 was the so-called Constitutional Revision. Article 3 of the ADCT provided that a comprehensive constitutional reform should take place five years after the promulgation of the 1988 Constitution. The most relevant procedural feature of this Constitutional Revision was related to the required majority to amend the Constitution: unlike the ordinary procedure, which requires a 3/5 majority in both chambers of the National Congress, during the Constitutional Revision, the Constitution could be amended simply by a majority vote of the members of the National Congress in unicameral sessions. Contrary to general expectations, however, lowering the required majority did not lead to comprehensive constitutional reform. Only six amendments were approved, almost all of them with rather minor impact.[6]

II. FUNDAMENTAL RIGHTS

The Bill of the Rights of the Brazilian Constitution is quite long. It encompasses freedom rights and political rights, as well as socioeconomic rights. In addition to their concise formulation in Heading II of the Constitution ('Fundamental Rights and Guarantees'), many of these rights are further regulated in other parts of the Constitution, especially in Heading VIII ('Social Order').

Enforcing this long list of rights in an unequal country such as Brazil has been a daunting challenge. The transformative ambition of many constitutional provisions is yet to be adequately realised. Still, much has been done since 1988. One of the most important challenges is surely the enforcement of the right to equality and other rights related to it, especially socioeconomic rights, such as the rights to health, education,

[4] In 1992, a constitutional amendment (EC 2/1992) anticipated this date to 21 April 1993.

[5] Considering only valid votes, the option to maintain a constitutional republic received 86.6% of the votes and the option to maintain presidentialism received 69.09% of the votes. For details on the plebiscite, see Javier Martinez-Lara, 'The Brazilian plebiscite of 21 April 1993' (1993) 12 *Electoral Studies* 403.

[6] The most relevant of these six amendments was amendment 5 (ECR 5), which reduced the presidential term from five years to four years.

and housing, among others. In this realm, an impressive body of literature has grown in recent decades that attempts to tackle the difficulties of conciliating policy and legal discourses and practices to foster the enforcement of this category of fundamental rights, which has long been neglected.

III. PRESIDENTIAL SYSTEM

Brazil adopted a presidential system of government in the 1889 proclamation of the Republic. The relationship between the President of the Republic and the National Congress – the core of this system of government – has varied considerably over these more than 100 years. The history of the Brazilian system of government in the twentieth century involved institutional instability, confrontation, deadlocks, revolutions, coups d'état, and even a very short experience with parliamentarianism between 1961 and 1963 (which was the result of one of these institutional crises).

Still, the core features of a presidential system – a directly elected president, who serves for a fixed term and does not need the confidence of the legislature to remain in office, along with a legislature that is also directly elected for a fixed term and cannot be dissolved early by the president – have been present in almost every Brazilian constitution since 1891.

Since at least 1988, the presidential system has coexisted with a highly fragmented party system. At the beginning of 2018, 27 parties had at least one representative in one of the houses of the National Congress. The association of a presidential system and a fragmented party system is usually blamed for institutional instability, crises and even democracy breakdowns. In Brazil, however, this has not been the case. In general, presidents have been able to build legislative coalitions that allowed them to advance their political agenda.

Nevertheless, some have argued that even if Brazil's so-called 'coalitional presidentialism' has usually worked well in recent decades, this functionality has come at a high price. Presidents must be willing to enter into almost any kind of compromise to be able to govern. Sometimes the price of a stable coalition is not only political but also financial, as several corruption schemes uncovered in recent years have made clear. Finally, coalitions that are difficult to tame may sometimes resort to the most drastic measures to get rid of a president: remove him or her from office due to the commitment of an (at least allegedly) impeachable offence. Since 1988, two presidents have been removed from office: Fernando Collor (1992) and Dilma Rousseff (2016).

IV. FEDERALISM

Brazil is the fifth largest country in the world, with an area of 8,515,759 square kilometres. Unsurprisingly, federalism has been an enduring idea since at least the declaration of independence in 1822 and a key feature of the Brazilian political system since 1889. The variations in Brazilian federalism have been many: dual in the beginning, merely nominal during authoritarian periods and potentially cooperative in others, and sometimes decentralised but usually displaying a strong trend towards centralisation.

Although the 1988 Constitution marked an attempt to restore a robust federalism after the highly centralised and authoritarian period under the 1969 Constitution, several variables have undermined the fulfilment of this task, including regional inequalities and the inflexible case law of the STF. As a result, although the Constitution provides for several shared powers among the constituent units of the Brazilian federation, which could potentially foster cooperation among them, the fact is that at least in several areas, the central government clearly has the upper hand.

V. A NOTE ON TRANSLATIONS AND REFERENCES

This book is written for an international readership, that is, for readers who do not speak Portuguese (Brazil's official language). Among other things, this means that references to works written in Portuguese with the sole aim of providing further readings about a given subject have been avoided. But whenever a given argument is based on a work written in Portuguese, that work is of course mentioned. In such cases, when a direct quotation from a text written in Portuguese is included, the translation into English is mine.

In this book, I frequently quote articles of the Brazilian Constitution, of which there are a few translations into English. I will not use a single translation; rather, for each quotation I will use the translation I deem the best. In some cases, the translation is my own. Nevertheless, it may be useful to recommend a single translation for further reading. For this, I recommend the translation by Keith Rosenn, available both in the project *Oxford Constitutions of the World* and in the *Constitute Project*.[7] There is also a translation by the Brazilian Chamber of Deputies.[8] Quotations from past Brazilian constitutions are mostly based on my own translations.[9]

Almost all the constitutions of the world are structured in articles. But, in addition to the general idea that articles are the internal divisions of a legal text, the precise meaning of the term 'article' may vary considerably across different constitutions. Furthermore, the manner in which those articles are subdivided varies even more. Some of the articles of the Brazilian Constitution are rather long and have several subdivisions, which may not be intuitive for a foreign reader. The main idea of an article is expressed in its head (in Brazil, the Latin term 'caput' is used). Every article, thus, has a head. The most important divisions are *incisos* and *parágrafos*. There are no standard translations for these terms. In this book, the former will be translated as 'clause' and the latter as 'paragraph'.

Paragraphs complement or establish exceptions to the head of an article; the number of a paragraph is always preceded by the symbol '§'.[10] When an article has only one paragraph, this symbol is not used and one refers to the 'single paragraph'. Clauses are employed for enumerations

[7] See oxcon.ouplaw.com and constituteproject.org.

[8] See livraria.camara.leg.br/direito-e-justica/constitution-of-the-federative-republic-of-brazil.html.

[9] For those interested in the full text of these constitutions in English, the following translations may be useful. For the 1824 Constitution: George A Glynn, *Foreign Constitutions* (Albany, Argus, 1894) vol 2/3, 65–105; for the 1824 and 1891 Constitutions: Herman G James, *The Constitutional System of Brazil* (Washington, Carnegie Institution of Washington, 1923) 237–52 and 221–36 (respectively); for the 1891 Constitution: Walter Fairleigh Dodd, *Modern Constitutions: A Collection of the Fundamental Laws of Twenty-two of the Most Important Countries of the World* (Chicago, The University of Chicago Press, 1909) 150–81; for the 1934 Constitution: Ernest Hambloch (tr), *Complete Text of the Brazilian Constitution of 1934* (São Paulo, Graphica Paulista, 1934); for the 1937 Constitution: 'The Constitution of the United States of Brazil' (1939) 346 *International Conciliation* 30; for the 1946 Constitution: Russell H Fitzgibbon (ed), *The Constitutions of the Americas (as of January 1, 1948)* (Chicago, The University of Chicago Press, 1948) 60–106; for the 1967 Constitution: General Secretariat of the OAS, *Constitution of Brazil 1967* (Washington, Pan American Union, 1967); and for the 1969 Constitution: General Secretariat of the OAS, *Constitution of Brazil 1967 (As amended by Constitutional Amendment No. 1 of October 17, 1969)* (Washington, Organization of American States, 1969).

[10] I am aware that in many English-speaking countries this symbol is usually read as 'section' and that the symbol for paragraph is '¶'. Still, translating *parágrafo* as section would have been confusing, especially because in Brazil 'sections' (*seção/seções*) are subdivisions of chapters, not articles.

and are numbered with Roman numerals. The best example is Article 5, which is a single article that encompasses the whole bill of individual rights of the Brazilian Constitution. It has no less than 78 clauses (I to LXXVIII). In a few cases, there may also be another subdivision, called an *alínea* (in this book translated as 'subclause'), preceded by lower-case letters. Subclauses are used for enumerations within enumerations.

Examples of the standard form for citing articles and their subdivisions are as follows: Art 5, § 2 (ie, the second paragraph of Art 5); Art 60, § 4, IV (the fourth clause of the fourth paragraph of Art 60); Art 101, single paragraph; Art 52, III, *a* (the first subclause of the third clause of Art 52); and Art 14, § 3, VI, *d* (the fourth subclause of the sixth clause of the third paragraph of Art 14).

References to court decisions in Brazil do not include the names of the parties. This book almost exclusively cites decisions of the Brazilian Supreme Court (STF), and references to these decisions will include three pieces of information: type of action, number and year of decision. For instance, ADI 3510 (2008) is a direct action of unconstitutionality (ADI) decided in 2008 and numbered 3510; HC 82424 (2003) is a habeas corpus action decided in 2003 and numbered 82424.[11] Actions in the STF receive a number when they are filed, not when they are decided. Therefore, decisions with higher numbers may sometimes be older than decisions with lower numbers.[12]

In Brazil, laws do not usually have a name (although some may have a nickname). Ordinary federal legislation is numbered sequentially, beginning with Federal Law 1, from 1946.[13] In this book, I will follow

[11] Sometimes there is a fourth piece of information indicated by suffixes – such as 'MC', 'AgR', 'ED', or 'QO' – to the case number (for instance, ADI 1434-MC, ADI 1254-AgR, Pet 1388-ED, or ADI 2344-QO). These suffixes indicate that the cited material is not the final decision on the merits of a case but rather a provisional decision (MC, *medida cautelar*), an internal appeal to a collegiate body against a decision made by a single judge (AgR, *agravo regimental*), an appeal for clarification of an alleged obscure aspect of a decision (ED, *embargos declaratórios*) or a decision concerning the decision-making process itself (QO, *questão de ordem*).

[12] The ADI 3776, for instance, was decided in 2007, while the ADI 907 was decided in 2017.

[13] There were other numberings before 1946. These numberings partially coincide with the constitutional periods since the first republican constitution of 1891. Thus, the numbering of ordinary legislation started anew in 1891, 1934 and 1946. Under the 1937 Constitution, the Legislature had never met and therefore there was no ordinary legislation. Since 1946 the numbering has been continuous despite constitutional changes and authoritarian regimes since then.

the standard formula for referring to legislation in Brazil, naming the type of law (federal or state, ordinary or complementary, among others), followed by the law number and the year of enactment – for example, Federal Law 9868/1999. Exceptions include the few laws that have names (whether an official name or a nickname) and codes. Although these laws also have a number and a year of enactment, in general the reference will be made simply by the name and, if necessary, the year. The Brazilian Civil Code, for instance, is an ordinary Federal Law, passed in 2002 (Federal Law 10406/2002), but in this case, the number/year formula is normally not used. The same applies, for instance, to the Elections Act (Federal Law 9504/1997) and the so-called Clean Slate Act (Federal Complementary Law 135/2010).

1

A Long and Winding Road to the 1988 Constitution

Political Organisation from 1500 until 1822 – Brazilian Constitutions before 1988 – Constitution-Making Process – Legitimacy of the 1988 Constitution

BRAZIL HAS BEEN an independent country since 1822. This means that politically, institutionally and constitutionally speaking, the history of Brazil as a sovereign state began in that year. The Portuguese arrived three centuries before, in 1500. Before their arrival, the Brazilian territory was populated by several indigenous ethnic groups, especially the *Tupi*, who lived primarily along the coast and spoke one of the *Tupi-Guarani* languages. A second, less homogeneous group lived mainly in the interior and spoke one of the *Macro-Je* languages.[1]

It remains unclear how many indigenous groups and in general how many inhabitants lived in the current Brazilian territory when the Portuguese arrived. Until quite recently, many still assumed that the scenario before 1500 had simply been of a virgin and almost empty land, with a few indigenous groups scattered in small clusters in an immense area. Still according to this view, the aboriginal peoples would have been hunter-gatherers, who lived in small groups displaying virtually no social and political organisation. The contrast with the Inca Empire – in the Andean region today occupied by countries such as Ecuador, Peru and Chile, which had a population of millions of inhabitants and displayed a complex social, political and economic organisation – has always cast the study of the organisation of the

[1] In addition to these two main linguistic families, there are several other families, the most important of them being the *Arawak* and *Karib*.

indigenous peoples of other regions of South America in a shadow. The oversimplified view according to which, especially if compared to the case of the Inca Empire, in the current Brazilian territory there had been only primitive tribes, organised exclusively on the basis to kinship relations, without any social and political differentiation, had prevailed for quite some time.

It is currently well known that the social, cultural and political landscape in the Brazilian territory before the arrival of the Portuguese was much more complex than what had usually been assumed. Although there is still much to learn about that period, it is nevertheless well established that there were far more indigenous peoples and that there was more contact among them than was supposed until recently, and that in some cases there was social stratification and political complexity.[2]

Although some indigenous civilisations probably achieved their zenith well before the arrival of the Portuguese, there is no doubt that the event that marked (negative and definitely) these civilisations was the arrival of the Portuguese and the colonisation process. Within a very short period of time, a considerable part of the indigenous population was decimated, especially due to the contact with previously unknown diseases. The Portuguese military conquests and the slavery of many natives have only completed this tragic destiny.

In the centuries that followed the arrival of the Portuguese – and, it could be argued, until the end of the twentieth century – the rights of indigenous groups to their land, culture, political and social organisation had been to a greater or lesser extent violated, ignored or, at best, tolerated insofar as they were compatible with the law of the settlers or, after Brazil's independence, with Brazil's official constitutional and legal system. Until recently, Brazilian legislation in this realm aimed – sometimes explicitly, sometimes implicitly – at integrating indigenous peoples into what has always been called (both in constitutional texts and in ordinary legislation) the 'national communion'. It is not a coincidence that constitutional texts and ordinary legislation have always referred to indigenous persons by the term *silvícolas*, that is, 'those who live in the jungle' or simply 'wild'. Real changes occurred only with the promulgation of the 1988 Constitution.

[2] See, for instance, Michael J Heckenberger and others, 'Amazonia 1492: Pristine Forest or Cultural Parkland?' (2003) 301 *Science* 1710; Michael J Heckenberger and others, 'Pre-Columbian Urbanism, Anthropogenic Landscapes, and the Future of the Amazon' (2008) 321 *Science* 1214; and Joana Bezerra, *The Brazilian Amazon* (Cham, Springer, 2015) 34–37. See also John Hemming, *Tree of Rivers: The Story of the Amazon* (London, Thames & Hudson, 2009).

I. AN OVERVIEW OF BRAZILIAN POLITICAL ORGANISATION FROM 1500 UNTIL 1822

The period ranging from the arrival of the Portuguese, in 1500, until the declaration of independence of Brazil, in 1822, may be roughly divided into three periods: (1) pre-colonial, from 1500 to 1530; (2) colonial, from 1530 until 1808; and (3) post-colonial, from 1808 to 1822.[3]

A. Pre-Colonial Period

In 1494, Portugal and Spain divided the world outside Europe into two. The Treaty of Tordesillas established a meridian 370 leagues west of the Cape Verde Island. According to the treaty, the lands to the east of this meridian belonged to Portugal and those to the west, to Spain. It is unclear what Portugal and Spain knew exactly about the lands divided by the Treaty of Tordesillas, especially about the eastern part of current South America. The fact is that the only relevant amount of land crossed by the meridian defined by the treaty is the current Brazilian territory. Thus, in 1500 only the eastern part of the current territory of Brazil belonged to Portugal. Until 1530, although there had been some Portuguese expeditions, there had not been systematic exploration of the new territory. The only relevant regular activity in this period was the extraction of the highly prized Brazilwood (the tree that eventually gave its name to the country).

Even though Portugal's main rival in the overseas exploration was Spain, the decision of King João III to colonise the new territory was a reaction against the threat posed by the French incursions in the new territory. As a matter of fact, France did not recognise the Treaty of Tordesillas and assumed the *uti possidetis* principle, according to which 'whoever effectively occupied an area owned it'.[4]

B. Colonial Period

The long colonial period can be divided into several different periods. From a political and institutional point of view, the most relevant

[3] The following subsections do not aim at presenting a history of Brazil before its independence, but rather at referring to some key dates and events related to the political organisation of that period.

[4] Boris Fausto, *A Concise History of Brazil* (Cambridge, Cambridge University Press, 1999) 11.

subdivision is that based on the different forms of administration during these almost three centuries. In the beginning, Portugal decided to occupy and govern Brazil by means of the so-called hereditary captaincies, which had already been used in the Madeira Islands. Portions of land were granted to private persons, the Captain Generals, who were responsible for exploring and protecting the new land.

In 1548, Portugal decided to establish a new administrative system, the Governorate General. Although the captaincies had been maintained, the colony was unified under the administration of the Governor General. The extreme decentralisation of the captaincies was abandoned in favour of a centralised administrative system. The city of Salvador was the capital of the colony.

In 1580, a crisis in the succession of King Sebastião of Portugal was the pretext for Spain to unify both crowns. During the Iberian Union, the administration of Brazil was again slightly decentralised. The Governorate General ceased to exist for the whole country and the territory was divided into two: the state of Brazil in the south and the state of Maranhão in the north. After several changes in the administrative configuration of these states in the second half of the seventeenth and first half of the eighteenth century, in 1774, they were merged again into the Viceroyalty of Brazil, with Rio de Janeiro as its capital.[5] This status was maintained until 1808.

C. A European Court in the Tropics

In 1807, the Napoleonic army invaded the Iberian Peninsula and in December of that year invaded Portugal. This event radically changed the history of Brazil. The prince regent of Portugal, João VI, decided to transfer the Portuguese court to Brazil.[6] For the first (and supposedly only) time in history, a European court transferred its seat to another continent. The capital of the Kingdom of Portugal was no longer Lisbon, but Rio de Janeiro.

The transfer of the court to Rio de Janeiro immediately and radically changed Brazilian history.[7] The colonial status could not be

[5] The capital of the state of Brazil was already transferred from Salvador to Rio de Janeiro in 1763.

[6] The prince João VI had governed Portugal on behalf of his ill mother, Maria I, since 1792 and was officially declared regent in 1799.

[7] See Kirsten Schultz, *Tropical Versailles: Empire, Monarchy, and the Portuguese Royal Court in Rio de Janeiro, 1808–1821* (New York, Routledge, 2001).

maintained any longer: first, because the Portuguese court now lived in Brazil, and secondly, because the British military protection was immediately 'paid' as soon as João VI arrived in Brazil: even before he arrived in Rio de Janeiro, he signed a decree opening the Brazilian ports to the 'friendly nations', that is, to Britain. If the colonial status was based on the so-called 'colonial exclusivity', that is, Brazil could only trade with Portugal, then opening the ports to Britain, which meant allowing direct commercial relations between Brazil and Britain, undermined, at once, the colonial status of Brazil.

Additionally, after the Portuguese court settled in Rio de Janeiro, several economic, educational and cultural activities that had been hitherto forbidden were eventually allowed. A Brazilian bank was founded, medical schools were created, newspapers and books were now printed in Brazil, among several other measures. In a few years, the economic, commercial, financial and cultural landscape in Brazil was radically changed.

In 1815, after Napoleon's defeat, João VI could have returned to Portugal. But he chose not to do so. He remained in Brazil and even changed the status of the relationship between Portugal in Brazil, now united within the United Kingdom of Portugal, Brazil and The Algarves. The old captaincies were converted into provinces of the new united kingdom, with Rio de Janeiro as its capital.

It can be argued that the territorial unity of Brazil, definitely consolidated only many years after independence, was considerably strengthened when João VI was in Brazil. On the other hand, however, the long absence of the king and the court, the economic and above all commercial crisis caused by the end of the colonial pact as well as the commercial privileges granted to Britain created the ideal atmosphere for a political revolution in Portugal. In 1820, the so-called Porto Liberal Revolution erupted, aiming above all at substituting a liberal constitutional monarchy for the *ancien régime*.

The election of a constituent assembly (called 'Cortes') and the ultimatum for the immediate return of the king and the court to Portugal were strong enough to convince King João VI to return to Portugal. Before returning, however, he issued a decree investing his heir son, Pedro, with the title of 'Regent of the Kingdom of Brazil'.

A very common interpretation of the objectives of the Lisbon Cortes was that it was part of a plan to recolonise Brazil. However, there is no evidence that there has ever been any such plan. As Barman puts it, '[a]t the worst, the deputies can be accused of setting the wrong priorities, of being blind to the realities of the situation, and so of taking for granted the unity of the Portuguese world'.[8] The lack of political tact of the Cortes therefore premeditated a separatist movement that was not inevitable.

In January 1822, Pedro decided to stay in Brazil and a few months later, in June, summoned a constituent assembly. The path to the independence of Brazil seemed to be definitely paved. On 7 September 1822, after having been informed that Portugal had revoked all his acts as prince regent, Pedro declared the independence of Brazil.[9] On 1 December 1822, he was crowned the emperor of Brazil: Dom Pedro I.[10]

The official historiography has usually presented the process of independence of Brazil as peaceful and without almost any kind of resistance. This version of history played an important political role in building national identity and unity. However, especially in the Northern provinces, the independence process was far more contentious than it has usually been presented, especially because many of these provinces did not recognise the legitimacy of the Rio de Janeiro government. That is, there was a resistance to the independence that was not necessarily linked to Portuguese interests, but to Brazilian local peculiarities and interests.

II. BRAZILIAN CONSTITUTIONS BEFORE 1988

Brazil had seven constitutions before the enactment of the 1988 Constitution. In the sections below, the main features of these constitutions as well as the contexts in which they were drafted will be presented. These sections offer only a simplified overview, and do not aim at presenting in detail the complex web of constitutional, institutional and social issues that led to a given constitutional design or to a constitutional breakdown. Thus, it is not a constitutional history of Brazil. Still, hints of

[8] Roderick J Barman, *Brazil: The Forging of a Nation, 1798–1852* (Stanford, Stanford University Press, 1988) 73.

[9] Although 7 September 1822 is considered Independence Day – a national holiday – and books and paintings depict what happened on that day, the process of independence, however, was inevitable before that. The summoning of the Constituent Assembly on 3 June and the decree of 1 August, which expelled the Portuguese troops from Brazil, are two of the most important pieces of evidence confirming this.

[10] A good account of the reasons why the title of emperor, instead of king, was used can be found in Barman (n 8) 98–102.

these constitutional, institutional, and social issues may be found in other chapters of this book.[11]

A. Brazilian Empire: The 1824 Constitution

As mentioned above, the prince regent and future emperor had summoned a constituent assembly in June 1822, even before the independence of Brazil. This assembly, however, began its work only in May 1823, and it did not last long. Soon the disagreements between the emperor and the members of the assembly – especially concerning the relationship between the legislative and the executive branches – became unbearable. The emperor wanted more control over the legislature than the members of the assembly were willing to grant. In November 1823, the emperor dissolved the Constituent Assembly, promising to summon a new one and to offer a constitution draft that would be 'twice as liberal' as the project that was being drafted by the assemblymen.[12] But he did none of these. In 25 March 1824, the 'Political Constitution of the Empire of Brazil' – this was its official name – was granted by the emperor himself.

Even though the 1824 Constitution formally complied with the major principles of the liberal constitutionalism of the early nineteenth century, especially the separation of powers and the guarantee of fundamental rights, it would be a mistake to consider the Brazilian constitutionalism under the 1824 Constitution a liberal one, at least for two reasons.

First, the separation of powers laid down by the Constitution was a very particular one: a quadripartite separation, supposedly inspired by the work of Benjamin Constant.[13] But Constant argued that the royal power should be a 'neutral power', separated from the other three branches and responsible for keeping the harmony among them.[14] But under the

[11] Furthermore, because the overview below attempts only to schematically show why an ensuing constitution replaced a previous one, there is a noticeable emphasis on the problems of each period, which may overshadow the many vibrant constitutional debates which took place in the previous constitutional periods. This was an unavoidable trade-off.

[12] Decree of 12 November 1823.

[13] The 1824 Constitution, art 10 stated: 'The political powers recognised by the Constitution of the Brazilian Empire are four: the Legislative Power, the Moderating Power, the Executive Power and the Judicial Power'.

[14] This separation was, according to Constant, 'the key to all political organisation'. See Benjamin Constant, *Réflexions sur les constitutions, la distribution des pouvoirs, et les*

1824 Constitution the emperor held both the neutral power – called 'moderating power' – and the executive power. This conflation mitigated the separation of powers under the imperial constitution.[15]

A second relevant illiberal character of the constitutional reality of the nineteenth century Brazil is related to the guarantee of fundamental rights. As Viotti da Costa argued: 'The Brazilian constitution stressed the equality of all before the law and guaranteed individual freedom. But the majority of the population remained enslaved and excluded from citizenship'.[16]

Brazil was the last country in the Western hemisphere to abolish slavery, only doing so in 13 May 1888. The 1824 Constitution was completely blind to this reality, even though the history of the Empire is marked by the shameful history of slavery in Brazil, which although abolished in 1888 left its marks in Brazilian society until today. As Joaquim Nabuco, one of the most prominent advocates of the abolition of slavery, put it at the end of the nineteenth century, slavery will remain for a long time as Brazil's national characteristic.[17]

The abolition of slavery is usually portrayed as a magnanimous act of a white enlightened elite in favour of the black population. According to this mainstream view, Princess Isabel, the daughter of Emperor Pedro II, took advantage of an international travel of her father and signed the so-called Golden Law (*Lei Áurea*), which definitely abolished slavery in Brazil. What is frequently overlooked is that this was only the last act of a long struggle that involved many actors, black and white, enslaved and free, anonymous and public.

The history of the nineteenth century is marked by the resistance of the Brazilian Empire to comply with the abolition of the slave trade and to give up slavery altogether. In the end, this resistance was one of the reasons of the demise of the Empire only one year after the end of slavery. A second reason was the deafness to the claims for more regional

garanties, dans une monarchie constitutionnelle (Paris, H Nicolle, 1814) 1: 'Some could be surprised that I distinguish royal power from executive power. This distinction, always overlooked, is very important; it is, perhaps, the key to the entire political organisation'. The same expression was reproduced by the Brazilian 1824 Constitution: 'Art 98. The Moderating Power is the key to the entire political organisation'.

[15] One of the most important opponents of the emperor at that time, Frei Caneca, wrote – paraphrasing Constant and the 1824 Constitution – that 'the Moderating Power is the master key to oppression'. Caneca was later jailed and executed.

[16] Emilia Viotti da Costa, *The Brazilian Empire: Myths & Histories*, 2nd edn (Chapel Hill, University of North Carolina Press, 2000) 60.

[17] Joaquim Nabuco, *My Formative Years* (Oxford, Signal Books, 2012).

autonomy, which grew very strong especially at the end of the 1880s. The federalist movement, already present at the beginning of the Empire, had become increasingly strong. Even though many supporters of the federalist ideas were at the same time also supporters of the monarchy, many of them eventually changed to the republican side when they realised that the federal form of state would never be a reality under the monarchy. On 15 November 1889, a coup led by Marshal Deodoro da Fonseca deposed the Brazilian monarchy.

B. First Republic: The 1891 Constitution

On the very first day of the First Republic, a decree was issued to transform the unitary state into a federation.[18] Simultaneously, a commission of five members wrote a draft constitution, which, with some minor modifications made by the provisional government, served as a draft for the Constituent Assembly, elected in September 1890. In 24 February 1891, the first republican constitution of Brazil was promulgated. This constitution laid down the foundation of the Brazilian constitutional system that remains today: presidential and federal systems, as well as judicial review of legislation.

However, despite the guarantee of fundamental rights, political representation, separation of powers, as well as a perfectly defined federalism and presidential system, the constitutional and institutional reality of Brazil at the end of nineteenth and in the first decades of the twentieth century was rather different: frequent declarations of a state of siege, a hypertrophy of the executive power, electoral fraud,[19] a federalism that coexisted with constant intervention from the central government into the weakest states, among other things. Just as was the case during the Empire, the liberal discourse during the First Republic was also detached from Brazil's constitutional, institutional, political and social reality. Despite the radical constitutional change – from a monarchical and unitary to a republican and federal system – the widespread perception was that a new group of elites simply replaced the old ones.

[18] Decree 1 of 15 November 1889.

[19] On the matter, see Paolo Ricci and Jaqueline Porto Zulini, 'The Meaning of Electoral Fraud in Oligarchic Regimes: Lessons from the Brazilian Case (1899–1930)' (2017) 49 *Journal of Latin American Studies* 243.

C. Vargas Era: The 1934 and 1937 Constitutions

In October 1930, Getulio Vargas started a movement – later called the '1930 Revolution' – aiming to prevent the newly elected president, Júlio Prestes, from taking office. The goal, however, was not only to seize power as such, but to change the oligarchical power structure in Brazil. The movement started in the states of Rio Grande do Sul (where Getulio Vargas was from), Paraná, Minas Gerais and Paraíba. Rapidly, several other Brazilian states joined and adhered to the movement. On 3 November 1930, Getulio Vargas was declared chief of the provisional government.

The so-called 'Vargas Era' changed the country with regard to several aspects. Social, economic, cultural, as well as legal changes rapidly took place. Brazil experienced a strong industrialisation period, with the creation of several state-owned enterprises, especially heavy and infrastructure industries (steel, mining, and electric power).[20]

In 1932, an electoral code was enacted and laid down the foundations of Brazilian electoral law that are still valid: proportional representation, universal suffrage and women's right to vote, among others. In July 1934, the third Brazilian constitution was promulgated. It marked the beginning of Brazilian socioeconomic constitutionalism. The 1934 Constitution, though not using the language of rights in the socioeconomic realm, had several provisions defining social goals as well as regulating the state intervention in the economy and conditioning economic freedom to the realisation of principles of social justice.

However, this constitution was very short-lived. Three years later, under the pretext of fighting a communist threat, Getulio Vargas suspended the 1934 Constitution and established a fascist-inspired, dictatorial rule. In the same day that he suspended the 1934 Constitution, Vargas personally granted a new constitution (10 November 1937). This new period of the Vargas Era – known as 'Estado Novo' – showed remarkable similarities to European fascist, anti-liberal and anti-parliamentary regimes of its time. According to Francisco Campos, the jurist who wrote the new constitution, the 'parliament's incapacity for the legislative function' and the 'defective parliamentary processes' led to a 'general movement throughout the world to remove from parliament

[20] The most important state-owned enterprises in these fields, however, were created only during the second, authoritarian, Vargas period.

the initiative of legislation and to increasingly extend the field of delegation of powers'.[21]

Even though in the second period of the Vargas Era there were important legal advances, especially in labour law (like the establishment of labour courts, the codification of labour legislation and the definition of a minimum wage), from the political and constitutional point of view, it was plainly a dictatorship. Federalism was completely undermined, the National Congress was never elected and fundamental rights were constantly violated.

In 1945, the regime was weakened, as Fausto argues, 'more from Brazil's entry into the sphere of international relations than … from Brazil's internal conditions'.[22] Vargas convened elections for president as well as for a new constituent assembly for December of that year. But he was forced to resign in October, putting an end to the *Estado Novo*.

D. Fragile Democratisation: The 1946 Constitution

The new elected constituent assembly was heterogeneous as never before and included representatives of parties that had never been allowed to run for election, like the Brazilian Communist Party. In September 1946, the fifth Brazilian constitution was promulgated. After eight years of dictatorial rule, it re-established the institutional design defined with the proclamation of the republic, that is, presidential government, federalism, and judicial review of legislation. Proportional representation, introduced in 1932, was also maintained.

The 1946 Constitution stayed in force less than 20 years, a period characterised by a fragile democracy and institutional instability. In August 1961, after less than one year in office, President Jânio Quadros resigned. The military did not want to let Vice-President João Goulart take office. A compromise was reached by amending the Constitution and introducing a parliamentary system of government, considerably reducing the powers of the President. Only in January 1963, after a popular referendum, was the presidential system reintroduced. But Goulart could not finish his term: on 1 April 1964, a military coup,

[21] Francisco Campos, *O Estado nacional*, 2nd edn (Rio de Janeiro, José Olympio, 1940) 52. Campo's views on the relevance of political representation could not be clearer: 'The halls of parliament now have the same importance for political decisions as the halls of a museum' (ibid 28).

[22] Fausto (n 4) 229.

strongly supported by the United States, extinguished the fragile democratic experience under the 1946 Constitution. A period of more than 20 years of authoritarianism, violence, torture, censorship and general lack of freedom began.

E. Military-Civilian Dictatorship: The 1967 and 1969 Constitutions and the Institutional Acts

Although it is common to refer to the period after the 1964 coup as the 'military regime' or 'military dictatorship', I will avoid these expressions in this book because they obscure the active participation of civilians in the authoritarian regime, as well as the support of part of the civil society and private corporations. It should also be stressed that in the legal realm, the authoritarian regime found strong support among judges, public prosecutors and scholars.[23] Many of them, including several constitutional scholars, provided important expertise by drafting the most authoritarian legal documents that aimed at legitimising the regime.

During the military-civilian dictatorship (1964–85), although there have been two constitutions, from the political point of view the most important documents were the so-called 'Institutional Acts' (*Atos Institucionais*, hereafter also 'AI'). The first one was issued on 9 April 1964 and aimed at legitimising the new authoritarian regime. Though maintaining the 1946 Constitution in force, this act authorised the commanders-in-chief of the army, air force, and navy to suspend basic constitutional rights for 10 years, to remove members of the Congress from office, among other things.

Other institutional acts followed, as well as several amendments to the 1946 Constitution, until January 1967, when the sixth Brazilian constitution was promulgated by the National Congress. The draft was presented by the military government and the Congress simply approved it. In many aspects, the 1967 Constitution was similar to most constitutions of democratic countries. As a matter of fact, democracy is mentioned four times as a value to be preserved. It maintained the separation of powers and guarantee of fundamental rights, as well as

[23] For an analysis of the great degree of civilian-military cooperation in Brazil, see Anthony W Pereira, *Political (In)Justice: Authoritarianism and the Rule of Law in Brazil, Chile, and Argentina* (Pittsburgh, University of Pittsburgh Press, 2005).

Constitution (EC 26) and summoned a 'free and sovereign' constituent assembly, to be elected in November 1986. This assembly started its work in February 1987.

Although EC 26/1985 summoned a 'free and sovereign' constituent assembly, it reproduced several provisions of the Amnesty Law, mentioned above. The message was clear: the amnesty granted by the authoritarian regime not only to its political adversaries, but also to the members of the regime, was not open to debate during the constituent assembly.

Unlike the case of previous constituent experiences in Brazil, the process of drafting the 1988 Constitution was not based on a preliminary constitutional blueprint. Although the President of the Republic had convened a commission to draw up such a blueprint in July 1985,[30] and although this commission, after almost a year of work, did present a constitutional blueprint to the President of the Republic, he decided not to send it to the Constituent Assembly. Also a considerable number of the members of the assembly did not want to have a project as a basis.[31]

For this reason, the work of the Constituent Assembly started from scratch. Among other consequences, this prolonged the work, which took more than a year and a half. The assembly organised its work based on a staggered task division. There were eight thematic committees,[32] each divided into three subcommittees with even more specific themes. In addition to these, there was a general systematisation committee. In a nutshell, the work progressed from the subcommittees to the thematic committees, and from these to the systematisation committee, and then to the floor of the assembly for voting in two shifts. The draft projects also received tens of thousands of amendments. There was also great popular participation, not only by means of the submission of 83 proposals of popular amendments, endorsed by millions of people,[33]

[30] See Decree 91450/1985.

[31] However, as Martínez-Lara puts it: although the President of the Republic buried the blueprint, 'the document entered the assembly through the back door and became in fact a sort of "semi-official" project to which many parliamentarians turned' (Javier Martínez-Lara, *Building Democracy in Brazil: The politics of constitutional change, 1985–95* (London, Palgrave Macmillan, 1996) 127).

[32] The subject-matters of each committee were: (1) sovereignty and the rights and guarantees of men and women; (2) organisation of the state; (3) organisation of powers and system of government; (4) electoral and party organisation, and protection of institutions; (5) tax system, budget, and finance; (6) economic order; (7) social order; (8) family, education, culture, sports, communication, science, and technology.

[33] In addition to popular amendments, for which 30,000 signatures were required, the Constituent Assembly also opened a more informal channel for popular participation, through which anyone could submit suggestions. Post offices throughout Brazil had printed

but also through the intense participation of agents of the organised civil society in the almost one thousand public hearings that were held within the thematic subcommittees.

Perhaps the most important consequence of the internal organisation of the Constituent Assembly – especially of the power of the committees as well as of the enormous power of the systematisation committee – was a noticeable discrepancy between the ideological profile of the members of the Constituent Assembly and the text they created. Although members of the Constituent Assembly were predominantly from the centre to the right on the ideological spectrum, the 1988 Constitution clearly does not match that profile. The key to understanding this discrepancy is precisely how the assembly worked. The party with the majority of seats, the PMDB (Party of the Brazilian Democratic Movement) was the successor of the only opposition party during the authoritarian regime, which brought together members of diverse ideological profiles. As the largest party, it had great power in choosing the members of the directing boards of the thematic committees and of the systematisation committee. As a result, the rapporteurs of all committees were chosen by the PMDB. The party leader in the Constituent Assembly, Senator Mário Covas, who had a centre to the left political profile, managed to appoint almost all rapporteurs more or less aligned with his ideological profile. Moreover, the most important committee, the systematisation committee, had a clearly centre-to-left bias compared to the profile of the Constituent Assembly.

After the presentation of the first draft by the systematisation committee, the conservative members of the assembly realised that, due to the way in which the decision-making process was organised by the rules of procedure of the Constituent Assembly, it would not be easy to change what they wanted to change on the floor of the assembly. An absolute majority of the assembly (280 out of 559 members) was required for each and every small change; otherwise, the text approved by the majority of the systematisation committee (only 47 of 93 members), or an alternative text proposed by the committee's rapporteur, would be maintained.

Confronted with this situation, a conservative coalition, known as the 'big centre' (*centrão*), supported among others by the incumbent President of the Republic, José Sarney, business corporations, and the military, was able to change the rules of procedure of the Constituent Assembly in order to make it easier for the floor of the assembly to

forms for this, which could be filled out and sent free of charge. Between March 1986 and July 1987, 72,719 individual suggestions were received.

amend articles of the draft produced by the systematisation committee. This group achieved some important victories, especially in regard to the economic order and land reform. The 'big centre' was also crucial for changes that directly interested the incumbent President of the Republic, especially by rejecting semi-presidentialism[34] and by assuring five years of term for him against attempts within the assembly to reduce it to four years.[35]

At the end of a year and a half of an almost Herculean task of systematising partial drafts made by separate and independent committees, and also of numerous compromises that the making of any constitution necessarily implies, it is possible to argue that the text of the 1988 Constitution is, despite countless voices in the opposite direction, a consistent text. As the President of the National Constituent Assembly, Ulysses Guimarães, said in his address to the floor of the assembly on the day of the promulgation of the Constitution, 'the Constitution is certainly not perfect'; nevertheless, it has guided Brazil's political, legal and social life with a certain degree of success in recent decades.

IV. THE LEGITIMACY OF THE 1988 CONSTITUTION

A final important feature of the making of the 1988 Constitution concerns the members of the Constituent Assembly. The Constituent Assembly was composed of 487 federal deputies and 72 senators. Hence, strictly speaking, it was not composed of 'members of the Constituent Assembly', but of 'deputies and senators'. This is, for several reasons, not only a question of terminology. First, the election of the Chamber of Deputies is based on proportional representation, while senators are elected by plurality voting. Secondly, the number of deputies tends to be proportional to the population of each state, while the number of senators is constant, namely three per state. Thirdly, since senators have an eight-year term and elections take place every four years, the 1986 elections renewed only part of the seats (two-thirds); senators elected in 1982 – ie, before the end of the authoritarian regime – were in the middle of their terms and nevertheless took part in the Constituent Assembly.

[34] Brazilian constitutional scholars still refer to the system of government that was adopted by the systematisation committee and later defeated on the floor of the Constituent Assembly as 'parliamentary'. This is not correct though. What the Brazilian Constituent Assembly nearly adopted was actually a semi-presidential, not a parliamentary system. For more details, see ch 3.

[35] For a very detailed account in English of these and other issues concerning the making of the 1988 Brazilian Constitution, see Martínez-Lara (n 31) 91–169.

Fourthly, deputies and senators functioned not only as members of the Constituent Assembly but at the same time as ordinary legislators. Fifth, and lastly, after the 1988 Constitution was promulgated, deputies and senators stayed in office until the end of their regular terms.

These five peculiarities of the constitution-making process of 1987–88 are used to label the Constituent Assembly as a 'non-exclusive constituent assembly' or as 'constituent congress', because of the lack of separation between ordinary legislature and constituent assembly. The decision for a non-exclusive constituent assembly and for the participation of the senators elected in 1982 was subjected to harsh criticism at that time. According to this criticism, a constituent assembly with those peculiarities lacked legitimacy for making a new democratic constitution. This criticism was later intensified due to the decision of the Constituent Assembly to not submit the new constitution to a popular referendum.

The aforementioned debate on the legitimacy of the 1988 Constitution was above all a procedural one. There is no doubt that some weaknesses could have been avoided. On the other hand, however, the constitution-making process of 1987–88 also had several undeniable merits, the most relevant of them being the massive popular participation during the whole process.

Independent of dispute on whether the merits outweigh the weaknesses or the other way around, the most relevant issue is whether the procedural legitimacy of the constitution-making process (or lack thereof) affects the legitimacy of the Constitution itself. Those who challenge the legitimacy of the constitutional document because of some problematic issues of its making process seem to mix up two different levels of analysis: the legitimacy of the constitution-making process itself and the legitimacy of the constitutional document. Though some weaknesses of the constitution-making process may negatively affect the legitimacy of a constitution, in the long run its acceptance as the supreme law of the land takes precedence in the assessment of its legitimacy. Comparative constitutional law provides several examples of constitutions whose process-making had obvious legitimacy shortcomings, which, however, did not negatively affect their legitimacy in the long run.

Thus, even if the criticism on the legitimacy of the Constituent Assembly were justified during the making of the Constitution – and it was – after decades of this founding moment many of these objections may have lost their strength. The enduring appropriation of the Constitution as a central argument for popular demands, both before the political powers and the courts, is a strong sign of its acceptance.

It may finally be argued that to a great extent thanks to the 1988 Constitution, Brazil has enjoyed decades of institutional and constitutional stability and an analysis of the legitimacy of the Constitution cannot ignore this fact. To be sure, Brazil has experienced several political crises since 1988. The deepest of them was without any doubt the one that led to the removal from office of President Rousseff in 2016 as well as to its aftermath: the continuous uncovering of several corruption schemes involving politicians of all major parties, a vice-president – Michel Temer – who was accused of having conspired against his running mate Rousseff but nevertheless took office, only to become the least popular president since 1988, and finally a party system perceived by many as completely exhausted. And yet, there is a consensus that this and other crises must be overcome following the rules laid down by the Constitution, not by overthrowing it.

FURTHER READING

Barman RJ, *Brazil: The Forging of a Nation, 1798–1852* (Stanford, Stanford University Press, 1988)

Bethell, L (ed), *Brazil: Empire and Republic, 1822–1930* (Cambridge, Cambridge University Press, 1989)

Bethell, L (ed), *Colonial Brazil* (Cambridge, Cambridge University Press, 1987)

Costa EV da, *The Brazilian Empire: Myths & Histories*, 2nd edn (Chapel Hill, University of North Carolina Press, 2000)

Fausto B, *A Concise History of Brazil* (Cambridge, Cambridge University Press, 1999)

Hemming J, *Red Gold: The Conquest of the Brazilian Indians* (Cambridge, Harvard University Press, 1978)

Martínez-Lara J, *Building Democracy in Brazil: The politics of constitutional change, 1985–95* (London, Palgrave Macmillan, 1996)

Pereira AW, *Political (In)Justice: Authoritarianism and the Rule of Law in Brazil, Chile, and Argentina* (Pittsburgh, University of Pittsburgh Press, 2005)

Schwarcz LM and Starling HM, *Brazil: A Biography* (New York, Farrar, Straus and Giroux, 2018)

Skidmore TE, *Brazil: Five Centuries of Change* (New York, Oxford University Press, 1999)

2

The Legislature: Bicameralism, Multipartism, and Ongoing Crisis

Organisation – Electoral System – Parliamentary Immunities – Removal from Office – Investigative Powers – Financial Control – Legitimacy Crisis

BRAZIL HAS HAD a bicameral legislature since the proclamation of its first constitution in 1824. Since the 1891 Constitution and the introduction of federalism in Brazil, the Senate has been called the Federal Senate, and senators have been elected for a fixed term, which is always longer than the term for deputies in the Chamber of Deputies. Since 1891 – with some exceptions – the bicameral body (Chamber of Deputies + Federal Senate) has been called the National Congress (*Congresso Nacional*).

At least according to the constitutional text, the Chamber of Deputies is composed of representatives of the *people*, while the Federal Senate is composed of representatives of the *states*. In reality, this difference is largely undermined by political practice and by the fact that the Chamber of Deputies and the Federal Senate have almost exactly the same legislative powers and almost every step of the legislative process is repeated in both chambers.[1] Research has consistently shown that senators from the same state almost never vote as a cohesive block, instead voting along party lines.[2]

I. COMPOSITION, SEAT, AND BASIC ORGANISATION

The Chamber of Deputies has 513 members and the Federal Senate has 81 members. The size of the Senate is defined by the Constitution

[1] For details on the legislative process (including constitutional reform), see ch 8.

[2] See Marta Arretche, 'Federalism, Bicameralism, and Institutional Change: General Trends and One Case-Study' (2010) 4 *Brazilian Political Science Review* 10.

itself. Art 46, § 1, stipulates that each state and the federal district shall elect three senators. In contrast, Art 45, § 1, provides that the size of the Chamber of Deputies shall be defined by complementary legislation 'in proportion to the population'. The current number of deputies (513) was established by Federal Complementary Law 78/1993.

Deputies[3] serve four-year terms and senators serve eight years. Candidates for the Chamber of Deputies must be Brazilian citizens and at least 21 years of age; candidates for the Senate must also be Brazilian citizens and at least 35 years of age. However, only Brazilian-born citizens may be elected president of the houses of the National Congress.

The seat of the National Congress is in Brasília (Federal District). Its building (*Palácio do Congresso Nacional*), alongside the presidential building (*Palácio do Planalto*) and the seat of the Brazilian Supreme Court (*Palácio da Justiça*), is located in the *Three Powers Plaza* (*Praça dos Três Poderes*). Created by architect and urban planner Lúcio Costa, it is perhaps the most concrete realisation of a constitutional idea: the separation of powers.

The basic internal organisation of both the Chamber of Deputies and the Federal Senate is similar. In each of the houses, the most important decision makers are the floor (*plenário*), the president, the directing board (*mesa*) and the committees.

II. ELECTORAL SYSTEM

With the exception of the Federal Senate, legislative elections in Brazil – at all three federal levels – are held according to the principle of proportional representation. For the Chamber of Deputies and state legislatures, the constituencies coincide with the area of the member states; for local legislatures, the constituencies are the municipalities.

A. Constituency Magnitude and Malapportionment

In the elections for the Chamber of Deputies, the constituencies coincide with the limits of the member states (and the federal district). Due to the enormous variation in population among the states, it is difficult to

[3] The members of the Chamber of Deputies are called federal deputies (*deputados* and *deputadas federais*) to differentiate them from the members of the state assemblies, which are called state deputies (*deputados* and *deputadas estaduais*).

achieve strict proportionality within the Chamber of Deputies. The state of São Paulo, for instance, has more than 40 million inhabitants, while the state of Roraima has less than 500,000.

The Constitution makes this task even more difficult by providing that 'none of the units of the federation may have fewer than eight nor more than seventy deputies'. Strict proportionality is therefore impossible to achieve. The state of Roraima has eight deputies and the state of São Paulo has 70. This means that the former has approximately one deputy for every 62,500 inhabitants, while the latter has one deputy for every 625,000 inhabitants. This is what the literature on electoral systems calls *malapportionment*.

Although usually considered a pathology because it violates the 'one person, one vote' principle, the fact that this malapportionment is established by the Constitution itself makes malapportionment a central element of the Brazilian political system. Its constitutionality has already been challenged before the STF, which decided that since the Constitution itself opted for disproportionate representation, the system cannot be declared unconstitutional.[4] Thus, the relationship between the Executive and Legislative branches and the federative balance within the National Congress are marked by a clear overrepresentation of northern states (especially the smallest ones like Roraima, Amapá, and Acre) and an underrepresentation of some southern states (especially São Paulo).

B. Party List and Ballot Structure

Candidates for the Chamber of Deputies must be affiliated with a political party. The number of candidates each party may present varies according to district magnitude. In the states with 12 or more representatives in the Chamber of Deputies, each party may present a number of candidates corresponding to 150 per cent of the seats; in states with less than 12 representatives, this number corresponds to 200 per cent of the seats to be allocated (Elections Act, Art 10).

These numbers are extremely high by international standards. Unlike the case of many countries that adopt proportional representation, party lists in Brazil are open and unranked. Parties cannot define a fixed

[4] ADI 815 (1996).

order of candidates in advance. Everything is decided on election day: not only how many seats each party gets but also who (which candidates) gets these seats according to their individual electoral performance.

This means that voters not only vote for a party but also choose a candidate within the party of their preference. This single fact – the personal vote – is probably the most important feature of Brazilian proportional representation. Initially, the personal vote partially explains why parties may present so many candidates: although an electoral campaign is to a considerable extent an individual matter, the votes cast for candidates of a given party increase the overall number of seats this party may win, so the more candidates, the better.

As will be explained in chapter five, several problematic consequences are attributed to personal voting, including the skyrocketing cost of campaigns and weakening party identification within the electorate.

C. Electoral Formula

The electoral formula used in proportional elections in Brazil works in two stages. First, the seats are distributed according to the Hare quota system (Electoral Code, Art 106); secondly, the remaining unallocated seats are distributed according to a modified highest average system (Electoral Code, Art 109).[5]

D. Electoral Threshold

In Brazil there is no legal electoral threshold. In other words, there is no legal minimum share of votes required for a party to secure a seat in the legislature. Art 13 of the Political Parties Act did establish a legal electoral threshold, which was declared unconstitutional by the STF.[6] This provision, however, did not follow the model adopted in several countries, since it did not aim to prevent parties that did not reach the threshold (5 per cent) from securing seats in the Chamber of Deputies.

[5] For details on the working of the electoral formula along with other variables of Brazilian proportional representation, see Jairo Nicolau and Julia Stadler, 'The Brazilian Electoral System' in Dana de la Fontaine and Thomas Stehnken (eds), *The Political System of Brazil* (Berlin, Springer, 2016).

[6] See ADI 1351 (2006) and 1354 (2006).

The consequence of not having reached the threshold (had this provision not been declared unconstitutional) would have been denying those parties the right to function as parties within the Chamber of Deputies. In this case, the party would not have offices, it would not have seats on committees, it would receive money from only 5 per cent of the public party fund, and it would not have a floor leader, among other things.

Until 2018, there was a factual, usually also called an effective, threshold. In many Brazilian states, this effective threshold was considerably higher than the usual legal threshold adopted in other countries (which usually varies from 3 to 5 per cent). Parties that did not reach the electoral quota were excluded from the allocation of seats, even when they could have enough votes to secure at least a remaining seat. In 2017, Art 109, § 2, of the Electoral Code was amended in order to allow all parties to participate in the distribution of remaining seats, even those that did not reach the electoral quota.

E. Party Alliances

The allocation of seats for the Chamber of Deputies (and for the state and local legislatures) has been based on the share of votes received by a given party or *party alliance*. Party alliances (*coligações*) used to be an essential feature of proportional representation in Brazil. Unlike the more widespread (especially in parliamentary systems) party coalitions, Brazilian party alliances are defined (and formally registered at the Electoral Court) before the elections.

When a party alliance is formed, two or more parties present a joint list and the allocation of seats is based on the votes the alliance receives as a whole. Especially for small parties, being in a party alliance has frequently been pivotal to reaching the electoral quota. Many parties that otherwise would not reach the electoral quota managed to elect representatives because they benefited from the votes cast for parties in the same alliance. In 2017, EC 97/2017 altered Art 17, § 1, of the Constitution to put an end to the possibility of forming party alliances for proportional elections. This change will enter into force in 2020. Although Brazilian multipartism has been at least partially fostered by the possibility of party alliances in proportional elections, the ban on this type of alliance will probably not have such a strong impact on the number of parties, because, as mentioned above, the rules governing seat allocation were also changed and now all parties participate in the distribution of seats, even those that did not reach the electoral quota.

F. Participation of Women

Although Brazil followed the international trend of adopting a gender quota (a 30 per cent quota is required by the 1997 Elections Act), the participation of women has increased only marginally since the adoption of this quota.[7] In the 1994 elections (the last before the adoption of the gender quota), women made up 6.24 per cent of the Chamber of Deputies, whereas after the 2014 elections, they were still merely 9.94 per cent.

There are surely several reasons for these low numbers, many of which are not related to the electoral rules but rather to a still-predominant perception in Brazilian society that does not recognise equal roles for women and men in the public sphere. Nevertheless, electoral rules matter, and the Brazilian electoral system may also be considered responsible for the failure of gender quotas. Since Brazil adopts proportional representation with open lists and personal votes, the success of a candidate for the Chamber of Deputies strongly depends on the number of personal votes she receives. Additionally, even if the electorate were willing to vote for women – which is not always the case – certain strategies may undermine the likelihood of women being elected. Parties often allocate less money to women candidates;[8] some parties only put women on the list to fulfil their legal duty (some women do not even campaign); and sometimes candidates even withdraw after the Electoral Court has approved the list, clearly demonstrating that parties use fake candidates to fulfil their quotas.[9]

G. Electoral System for the Federal Senate

Each state and the federal district have three representatives in the Federal Senate. Senators serve eight-year terms. Every four years either one or two-thirds of the seats are alternately allocated. Senators are elected by plurality (single majority) and may be re-elected indefinitely.

[7] See, for instance, Luis F Miguel, 'Political Representation and Gender in Brazil: Quotas for Women and their Impact' (2008) 27 *Bulletin of Latin American Research* 197.

[8] See, for instance, Kristin N Wylie and Pedro dos Santos, 'A Law on Paper Only: Electoral Rules, Parties, and the Persistent Underrepresentation of Women in Brazilian Legislatures' (2016) 12 *Politics & Gender* 415, 436.

[9] See Luciana de Oliveira Ramos and Virgílio Afonso da Silva, 'The Gender Gap in Brazilian Politics and the Role of the Electoral Court' (2019) 15 *Politics & Gender*.

III. EXCLUSIVE POWERS OF THE FEDERAL SENATE

Although both the Chamber of Deputies and the Federal Senate have similar powers in the Brazilian bicameral system, the Chamber of Deputies has a slight predominance within the legislative process.[10] However, beyond the legislative process, the Constitution grants more exclusive powers to the Federal Senate than to the Chamber of Deputies. The powers that are granted either to one or the other house are listed in Art 51 (Chamber of Deputies) and Art 52 (Federal Senate). The former has five clauses, while the latter has 15. The only noteworthy exclusive power granted to the Chamber of Deputies is the power to authorise the opening of legal proceedings against the President and Vice-President of the Republic and the ministers of the federal government. The other clauses of Art 51 primarily address the powers of self-organisation of the Chamber.

The list of exclusive powers granted to the Federal Senate is not only considerably longer but also more substantial and relevant. While the Chamber of Deputies may authorise the opening of legal proceedings against the President of the Republic, it is the Federal Senate that tries the President (along with several other authorities) for impeachable offences.

Additionally, the Senate is responsible for giving prior approval, after a public hearing, on the selection of judges of the STF; judges of other superior and high courts; members of the Federal Audit Court; the President and directors of the Central Bank; the Federal Procurator-General; and the heads of permanent diplomatic missions. The Federal Senate also has the power to suspend the enforcement of laws declared unconstitutional by a final decision of the STF.[11]

IV. PARLIAMENTARY IMMUNITIES

To ensure the autonomy of deputies and senators, the Constitution grants them some immunity. Two types of immunity are the most relevant: substantial and formal. The first type of immunity is related to opinions and speeches; the second type of immunity is related to criminal prosecution. Further, deputies and senators are always judged by the STF.[12]

[10] See ch 8.

[11] See ch 4.

[12] Art 53, § 1. In 2018, the STF limited the scope of this provision and members of Congress are now judged by the STF only if a crime is committed during their term and is connected with their office. See AP 937-QO (2018).

Art 53 provides that 'deputies and senators shall enjoy civil and criminal immunity for any of their opinions, words and vote'. This means that they are completely free to say and write anything in the houses of the National Congress and may not be held responsible in a civil or criminal court for their opinions. However, unlike in many countries, this immunity is valid not only within the National Congress, but everywhere. According to the case law of the STF, however, there is one relevant difference between speeches inside and outside the premises of the National Congress. In the first case, the freedom is unqualified; in the second case, only speeches related to one's activity as a member of the Congress are protected.[13]

In June 2016, however, in a very controversial decision, and reportedly for the first time, the STF accepted the indictment of a member of the Chamber of Deputies for the slander of a fellow deputy.[14] The alleged slander occurred during a speech on the floor of the Chamber of Deputies. The following day, the offence was repeated by the same deputy in a newspaper interview. Although the interview took place in the building of the Chamber of Deputies, the Court decided that it was not covered by parliamentary immunity, since it was published by a newspaper and its contents had no relation to parliamentary activity. It still remains to be seen whether this was an isolated decision made because of the very harsh, offensive and sexist content of the deputy's speech, or if it will become the standard for future cases.

Formal immunity aims to protect members of the National Congress from arrest. According to Art 53, § 2, members of the National Congress, from the date of the issuance of the certificate of electoral victory, 'may not be arrested, except in flagrante delicto for a non-bailable crime. In this case, the case records shall be sent within twenty-four hours to the respective House, which, by a majority vote of its members, shall decide on the arrest'. The first part of this provision seems to be unproblematic: if the members of the National Congress may only be arrested in flagrante delicto for a non-bailable crime, this means that in any other case, even if they are suspected of having committed a crime, they simply cannot be arrested.[15] Moreover – in the second part of this provision – even if they are arrested in flagrante delicto for a

[13] In the case law of the STF, see Inq 655 (2002), concurring opinion judge Nelson Jobim, and Inq 1710 (2002).

[14] See Inq 3932 (2016).

[15] In December 2015, in a unanimous but nevertheless controversial decision, the STF authorised arresting a senator in a case that did not involve flagrante delicto. After the case

non-bailable crime, the corresponding house (Chamber of Deputies or Federal Senate) may revoke the arrest warrant if the majority of its members so decide. It goes without saying that this immunity relates only to remand prison, that is, prior to a trial. If a member of the National Congress is sentenced and convicted of a crime, this immunity does not apply.

A different, albeit still formal immunity is related to criminal prosecution. The original wording of the Constitution established that deputies and senators could not be criminally prosecuted without the authorisation of their houses. In 2001, a constitutional amendment (EC 35/2001) substantially altered Art 53, which now stipulates that deputies and senators may be criminally prosecuted without the authorisation of their houses, even though the Chamber of Deputies and the Senate still may suspend the case before the STF.[16] One could argue that this amendment did not substantially change the immunity and that the possibility of suspending a criminal prosecution is very akin to the previous rule of 'no prosecution without authorisation'. However, this is not the case. Before 2001, a criminal prosecution could not even begin without prior authorisation of the appropriate house of Congress. Now, although the Chamber of Deputies or the Federal Senate may suspend prosecution, this can only happen if a political party so demands. It is a political burden not only for the demanding political party but also for the Chamber of Deputies or the Senate to suspend a criminal prosecution that has already begun.

V. REMOVAL FROM OFFICE

Members of the National Congress may only be removed from office in cases explicitly defined by the Constitution. One reason for removal from office is criminal conviction by a final (non-appealable) judicial decision. However, in 2013, a federal deputy was criminally convicted by a final (non-appealable) decision of the STF and the Chamber of Deputies kept him in office, although he sat in prison. This was possible because Art 55, §§ 2 and 3, set forth two different procedures for removing members of

records were sent to the Federal Senate, the arrest was confirmed. The Court argued that the crime was a continuous one and therefore the flagrante delicto should be considered continuous. See AC 4039 (2015).

[16] Art 53, § 3. The decision to suspend criminal prosecution automatically suspends the statute of limitation for the crime allegedly committed (Art 53, § 5).

the National Congress from office. According to this provision, in some cases, removal from office shall be *declared* by the Chamber of Deputies or the Federal Senate by absolute majority, whereas in other cases removal from office shall be *decided* by the directing board of the respective House. Removal from office due to a criminal conviction is one of the latter cases. Thus, the distinction between 'deciding' and 'declaring' has consequences that are more far-reaching than may appear at first sight. When the Chamber of Deputies or the Federal Senate must *decide* upon a removal from office, this happens by the vote of the absolute majority of the appropriate house. This implies that the Chamber of Deputies and the Federal Senate are free to decide otherwise. That is exactly what happened in 2013.

The popular outcry was huge and in the same year, the National Congress passed a constitutional amendment (EC 76/2013) changing Art 55. Since then, although the Chamber of Deputies and the Federal Senate still have the power to keep a deputy or senator in office even after his or her criminal conviction, this decision must be made by open (roll-call) voting. After this amendment, the same deputy that had been kept in office after his criminal conviction was removed from office for far less grave reasons (violation of parliamentary decorum).

This was not the first time that Art 55 was amended due to popular outcry against impunity involving members of the National Congress. In 1994, a constitutional amendment passed when the Constitutional Revision (ECR 6/1994) added § 4 to Art 55. According to this new provision, if the National Congress opens a disciplinary procedure that intends to remove (or that may lead to the removal of) one of its members, even if she or he eventually resigns, the Chamber of Deputies or Federal Senate may still decide to remove him or her from office. Before 1994, several members of the Congress had resigned to escape the consequences of being removed from office, especially the prohibition from running for other offices for eight years that applied in some cases.[17]

VI. INVESTIGATIVE POWERS

The Chamber of Deputies and the Federal Senate, either jointly or separately, may set up parliamentary committees of inquiry. According to Art 58, § 3, these committees 'have the same investigative powers as

[17] See Federal Complementary Law 64/1990, Art 1, I, b.

judicial authorities'[18] and are set up upon the request of one-third of the members of the Chamber of Deputies or Senate[19] to investigate 'concrete facts, for a given period of time'. Although such committees are usually set up to investigate alleged misconduct within both the Executive and Legislative branches, the Constitution does not limit their scope. This means that the Congress may establish committees of inquiry to investigate any concrete fact it deems relevant. In this sense, Art 35, § 1, of the internal rules of the Chamber of Deputies (hereafter, RICD) defines 'concrete fact' as 'event of major interest to the public life and to the constitutional, legal, economic and social order'.

Since 1988, several committees of inquiry have been set up both within the Chamber of Deputies and in the Senate;[20] moreover, there have been joint committees with members of both houses. The conclusions of many of these committees have been used as evidence in criminal prosecutions, for removing members of the Congress from office and for presidential impeachments.

VII. FINANCIAL CONTROL AND THE FEDERAL AUDIT COURT

One important feature of Brazil's checks-and-balances system is the financial control (also called 'external control') that the National Congress holds vis-à-vis the Executive. According to Art 84, XXIV, within 60 days of the opening of the legislative session, the President of the Republic shall render the annual accounts of the Executive to the National Congress.

This control is performed with the help of the Federal Audit Court (*Tribunal de Contas da União*), which (despite its name) is neither a court nor part of the judiciary branch. The Audit Court is composed of nine members, one-third of whom are chosen by the President of the Republic after approval by the Senate and two-thirds of whom are chosen by the National Congress. Among its other functions, the Audit Court issues

[18] It cannot, however, issue search warrants or tap telephone conversations, among other actions for which the Constitution explicitly demands a 'court order'. See, for instance, MS 23452 (1999).

[19] According to the STF, a request of one-third of the Chamber of Deputies or the Federal Senate cannot be rejected by the floor of the appropriate house. See MS 24831 (2005).

[20] See Argelina Cheibub Figueiredo, 'The Role of Congress as an Agency of Horizontal Accountability: Lessons from the Brazilian Experience' in Scott Mainwaring and Christopher Welna (eds), *Democratic Accountability in Latin America* (Oxford, Oxford University Press, 2003) 175–83.

an advisory opinion upon the accounts rendered annually by the President. The final decision, however, is made on the floor of the National Congress. Until 2015, this was done separately in the Chamber of Deputies and in the Federal Senate. The STF, however, decided that beginning in 2015, the final decision would be made on the floor of the National Congress (ie, in a joint session of both houses).[21]

Since 1988, the National Congress had not rejected the accounts of a President of the Republic. However, in 2015, the Federal Audit Court issued an advisory opinion that for the first time recommended rejecting the accounts of President Dilma Rousseff. The Congress has still not decided the matter. Nevertheless, this raises the question of the consequences of a rejection of the presidential accounts. Some have argued that this could lead to the impeachment of the President, but neither the Constitution nor the law that regulates the impeachment process supports this conclusion. The Constitution simply provides that the National Congress decides the accounts of the President of the Republic, but has no provision for the case of rejection. The only consequence of the rejection of the presidential accounts – and only in those cases in which the rejection was based on acts of purposeful administrative misconduct – seems to be the one established by the Federal Complementary Law 64/1990, namely, eight years of ineligibility for political office.[22]

VIII. ONGOING LEGITIMACY CRISIS (BUT STILL POWERFUL)

The National Congress has been experiencing a legitimacy and identity crisis almost since the promulgation of the 1988 Constitution. At the heart of the legitimacy crisis are constant cases of corruption involving deputies and senators, the inability of the National Congress to respond to social demands, an unintelligible electoral system for the Chamber of Deputies and an extremely fragmented party system (more than 20 political parties currently have representatives in the National Congress). However, this does not mean that the National Congress plays a marginal role in Brazilian politics. On the contrary, despite the continuous use

[21] See MS 33.729 (2015).

[22] Art 1, I, g, of the Federal Complementary Law 64/1990. This consequence applies to all cases of rejections of accounts, not only accounts rendered by the President of the Republic.

of the presidential provisional decree as a form of legislation, the law-making process still has its core within the legislative branch.[23]

Furthermore, although it is true that the extremely proactive roles of both the President of the Republic and the Brazilian Supreme Court (STF) seem to frequently cast the National Congress in a shadow, it is also true that the Congress is still a key (and sometimes a very strong) player in Brazil's presidential system, as will be discussed in the next chapter. The fact that within 25 years two Presidents of the Republic were removed from office by the legislature is a strong evidence of the power of the Congress.

FURTHER READING

Amorim Neto O, 'Presidential Cabinets, Electoral Cycles, and Coalition Discipline in Brazil' in S Morgenstern and B Nacif (eds), *Legislative Politics in Latin America* (Cambridge studies in comparative politics, Cambridge, Cambridge University Press, 2002)

Cheibub JA, Figueiredo A, and Limongi F, 'Political Parties and Governors as Determinants of Legislative Behavior in Brazil's Chamber of Deputies, 1988–2006' (2009) 51 *Latin American Politics and Society* 1

Figueiredo AC and Limongi F, 'Presidential Power, Legislative Organization, and Party Behavior in Brazil' (2000) 32 *Comparative Politics* 151

de la Fontaine, D and Stehnken, T (eds), *The Political System of Brazil* (Berlin, Springer, 2016)

Wylie KN, *Party Institutionalization and Women's Representation in Democratic Brazil* (Cambridge, Cambridge University Press, 2018)

[23] See Andréa Marcondes de Freitas, 'Unboxing the Active Role of the Legislative Power in Brazil' (2016) 10 *Brazilian Political Science Review* 1. For details on the legislative process, see ch 8.

3

The Executive: A Strong President and Coalitional Presidentialism

Election – Coalitional Presidentialism – Treaty-Making Power – Impeachment and Removal from Office – Emergency Powers

His Majesty, the President of Brazil is the title of a book published in the 1930s by a British observer of Brazilian politics who pointed out how powerful the President of the Republic seemed to be.[1] Indeed, many constitutional scholars in Brazil and specialists in comparative politics elsewhere still argue that the President of Brazil has too much power. It is undeniable that the list of constitutional powers the President of the Republic holds is long and comprehensive. Still, many conclusions that are drawn from this premise – especially those related to the executive-legislative relation – should be strongly mitigated, as will be seen in this chapter. The idea that the President of Brazil is almost an emperor works well in a book title, but falls far short of describing the dynamics of the Brazilian presidential system. Constitutional and political practices are sometimes different from what one may expect by reading the Constitution without considering the context.

Thus, even though comparative studies usually rank the Brazilian President as one of the most powerful among those of many current (and past) constitutional democracies, it would be naive to imagine that she or he could govern without any support from the National Congress. The fact that two presidents – Fernando Collor and Dilma Rousseff – were removed from office by the Congress within only 25 years should be strong evidence that overbearing governing may be a bad option for

[1] See Ernest Hambloch, *His Majesty the President of Brazil: a Study of Constitutional Brazil* (New York, Dutton & Co, 1936).

presidents. Hence, even if it is true that presidents can initiate the law-making process, including the process of amending the Constitution, that they have the exclusive right to initiate legislation in some areas (such as budgetary matters), that they have veto power, including a partial (line-item) veto, along with the power to issue provisional decrees with force of law, and that the judges of the STF and many other officeholders are nominated by them, it is also true that the bills they introduce or the provisional decrees they enact must be approved by the Congress, that presidents have no veto power over constitutional amendments, that the presidential veto (in ordinary legislation) may be overridden by the vote of the majority of deputies and senators, and that appointed STF judges and other officeholders must be confirmed by the Senate. Most importantly, the National Congress may remove presidents from office in some circumstances.

Therefore, even if the President does have a certain advantage in the law-making process, this advantage can be strongly mitigated if the President has no majority in the Congress. Due to the fragmented Brazilian party system, ever since the first election held after the promulgation of the 1988 Constitution, the party of the President has never held more than 20 per cent of the seats in the Chamber of Deputies. Thus, if presidents need the support of the Congress to implement their political agendas, they must build party coalitions to govern. One way of doing this is by offering ministerial positions (portfolios) to parties that wish to participate in the government coalition. Hence, the presidential system in Brazil functions in many aspects in a manner very similar to many parliamentary systems.

In addition to presenting and analysing the peculiarities of the Brazilian presidential system, analysis of the executive branch demands the study of other aspects, especially because the President is not only the head of Government but also the head of State, the head of the Federal Administration and the head of the Armed Forces. Additionally, legislation strongly depends on executive regulation for enforcement.

I. THE ELECTION OF THE PRESIDENT OF THE REPUBLIC

According to Art 77, the President shall be elected by an absolute majority of valid votes. If no candidate obtains an absolute majority of votes in the first round, a second round between the two candidates who obtained the greatest number of votes is necessary. Since 1988, the President and Vice-President have been elected together, that is, they run on the same electoral ticket. Although this seems to be an intuitive and almost natural rule, the electoral tradition in Brazil was different before 1988. In the 1960 elections, for instance, the elected Vice-President, João Goulart, was not the running mate of the elected President, Jânio Quadros.

The President and the Vice-President of the Republic serve four-year terms beginning on 1 January of the year following their election. Originally Art 82 provided for a five-year term, but that provision was amended during the constitutional revision of 1993–94 (ECR 5/1994).

The Brazilian constitutional tradition had always rejected the re-election of presidents for a subsequent term.[2] The 1988 Constitution originally maintained this tradition, but Art 82 was amended a second time by EC 16/1997 and the explicit prohibition on re-election was removed. Art 14, § 5, was also amended accordingly, to explicitly allow for re-election ('The President of the Republic … may be re-elected for only one subsequent term'). The amendment is clear in allowing the re-election of the heads of the executive branch (President of the Republic, Governors and Mayors) for a subsequent term, but created several incongruities within the regulation of ineligibilities, whose rules were defined before re-election was allowed.

II. REPLACEMENT, SUCCESSION, IMPEDIMENTS AND VACANCY OF OFFICE

The Constitution contains detailed rules concerning the replacement, succession and impediments of the President of the Republic, along with the vacancy of his or her office. According to the terminology adopted by the Constitution, impediments result from temporary impossibilities of discharging the duties of the office, caused by, inter alia, illness, vacation, and international travel. In contrast, vacancy of the office is the result of a permanent impossibility caused by death, resignation, removal from office after an impeachment process, if the President does not take office within 10 days of the date scheduled for the inauguration or if during his or her term, the President leaves the country for more than 15 days without authorisation from the National Congress.

[2] In other words, Brazilian constitutions have never prohibited anyone from being elected president twice or even three or more times. What had always been forbidden was re-election 'for a subsequent term'.

A second divide runs parallel to that of impediment/vacancy: replacement and succession. Art 79 provides that '[t]he Vice-President shall replace the President in the event of impediment and shall succeed him in the event of vacancy'. The Vice-President thus *replaces* the President, that is, becomes acting president, in any case of impediment, even in the case of very short international travels. If the office of the President is declared vacant, the Vice-President *succeeds* him or her and therefore becomes President, serving until the end of the term. The line of replacement and succession of the President also includes the President of the Chamber of Deputies, the President of the Federal Senate and the President of the STF. However, although these individuals may time and again replace the President (ie, become acting president), they do not succeed her or him. According to Art 81, in the event of vacancy of the offices of both the President and the Vice-President of the Republic, 'elections shall be held ninety days after the occurrence of the last vacancy'. However, this rule applies only if the vacancy occurs in the first half of the term; if it occurs in the second half, the elections shall be indirect, within the National Congress, 'within thirty days after the last vacancy occurred, as provided by law'.

Because the law mentioned in Art 81, § 1, still has not been enacted, there were deep controversies after the removal from office of President Rousseff in 2016, since a pending case at the Electoral Court could have led to the Vice-President's removal from office as well. These controversies were related above all (but not only) to who might run for the office of President and Vice-President of the Republic in such an intermediate election. However, since the Electoral Court ultimately acquitted the Vice-President,[3] those controversies have lost their importance for now. Nevertheless, they remain unsettled.

III. A STRONG PRESIDENT BEFORE A WEAK CONGRESS?

As is usual in presidential systems, the executive power in Brazil is unitary, as provided for by Art 76: 'The Executive Power is exercised by the President of the Republic …' The President is thus the head of State, Government, Public Administration and Armed Forces. Expressions of each of these spheres of power may be found within the 27 clauses of Art 84, which establishes the matters upon which the President of

[3] See TSE, AIME 761 (2017).

the Republic has exclusive powers. It is also worth noting that the final clause of Art 84 clarifies that the powers listed therein are not exhaustive: the President also exercises powers provided for elsewhere in the Constitution.

In their book on constitutional dynamics, Shugart and Carey list 10 legislative and non-legislative powers that they argue are crucial for assessing how powerful a president is.[4] These powers are as follows: (a) package veto/override; (b) partial veto; (c) power to issue decrees; (d) exclusive introduction of legislation; (e) budgetary initiative; (f) power to propose referenda; (g) cabinet formation; (h) cabinet dismissal; (i) censure;[5] and (j) dissolution of the assembly.

Powers (a) to (f) are legislative while (g) to (j) are non-legislative. They compared 46 (current and past) democracies that have had popular elected presidents, and the Brazilian president ranked as the most powerful in legislative matters among current[6] democracies and the third most powerful in non-legislative matters (behind only Paraguay and Chile).[7]

In addition to the presidential powers considered by Shugart and Carey, it is possible to add some other relevant powers, at least for the Brazilian case, such as the following: (k) to introduce constitutional amendment proposals; (l) to appoint judges of the Supreme Court, (m) to have standing to trigger abstract judicial review of legislation before the Supreme Court; (n) to declare or request the declaration of states of defence and siege; (o) to appoint persons to other positions in the judiciary and to other relevant offices, such as the President of the Central Bank (who in Brazil has no tenure and may be dismissed any time by the President); and (p) to run for re-election.

The picture of an almighty president seems even more realistic if one assumes, as does part of the comparative literature on the matter, that the Brazilian Congress is extremely weak due to peculiarities of the electoral and party systems and the profile and behaviour of federal deputies and senators. Sartori's assessment may summarise well this strain of thought: 'Probably no country in the world currently is as anti-party, both in theory and in practice, as is Brazil. Politicians … frequently

[4] See Matthew S Shugart and John Carey, *Presidents and Assemblies: Constitutional Design and Electoral Dynamics* (Cambridge, Cambridge University Press, 1992) 148–54.

[5] Censure is actually not a presidential power, but a power of the legislature of removing ministers. If the legislature does not hold this power, the power of the president is stronger. See ibid 153.

[6] At the time of the publication of Shugart and Carey's book.

[7] See Shugart and Carey (n 4) 155.

change party, vote against the party line, and refuse any kind of party discipline on the ground that their freedom of representing their constituency cannot be interfered with'.[8]

The association of a strong president with a fragmented party system has usually been considered problematic or even doomed to failure. As Melo and Pereira put it, 'experts on constitutional design considered strong presidents to be the black beasts of multiparty political systems'.[9] Presidents would either have incentives to bypass a weak legislature and impose their preferences unilaterally,[10] or if they do not want to or are unable to bypass the legislature, their government will be extremely unstable due to party fragmentation and especially a lack of party discipline.

Still, the Brazilian presidential system has worked well most of the time. Admittedly, after the political crisis that led to President Rousseff's removal from office, some started to blame the Brazilian presidential system for the cases of corruption that plague the country and to argue that the model is exhausted.[11] To assess whether or not the model is exhausted, it is necessary to present its basic features first.

IV. BRAZIL'S COALITIONAL PRESIDENTIALISM

The formation of government in multiparty parliamentary systems is based on party coalitions. The number of parties necessary to form a government coalition depends on how fragmented the party system is. The formation of government under the Brazilian presidential system does not differ considerably from this basic rationale. Presidents, regardless of how strong they are, need the support of the National Congress, otherwise they cannot advance their agenda. Since no President's party

[8] Giovanni Sartori, *Comparative Constitutional Engineering: An Inquiry into Structures, Incentives and Outcomes* (New York, New York University Press, 1994) 95. See also Scott Mainwaring, 'Politicians, Parties, and Electoral Systems: Brazil in Comparative Perspective' (1991) 24 *Comparative Politics* 21, 21: 'no other democracy grants politicians so much autonomy vis-à-vis their parties'.

[9] Marcus Andre Melo and Carlos Pereira, *Making Brazil Work: Checking the President in a Multiparty System* (Basingstoke, Palgrave Macmillan, 2013) 3.

[10] An assessment of the powers of the Brazilian President of the Republic based only on the attribution of scores for each one of the variables mentioned above – a form of analysis that has been common since Shugart and Carey's book – could lead to exactly this conclusion.

[11] See, for instance, Eduardo Mello and Matias Spektor, 'Brazil: The Costs of Multiparty Presidentialism' (2018) 29 *Journal of Democracy* 113.

has even come close to gaining an absolute majority in Congress since the first elections held after the promulgation of the 1988 Constitution,[12] there are two basic options for a President to get his or her bills approved in the legislature: negotiate with members of the Congress for each and every relevant vote or attempt to build a legislative coalition. The latter has been the preferred option of almost every president at least since the government of President Fernando Henrique Cardoso (1994–2002). The government of President Lula (2002–10) followed the same pattern. Both built legislative coalitions that allowed them to implement their political agenda.

The process of forming such a coalition is very similar to forming coalitions in multiparty parliamentary systems and is based above all on offering positions in the cabinet. The more seats a party has in the legislature, the stronger its participation in the cabinet tends to be. This model is known in Brazil as 'coalitional presidentialism' (*presidencialismo de coalizão*). In this model, the fact that the President of the Republic is strong is a strength rather than a weakness. Indeed, the ability to build coalitions is directly related to the powers of the President, and more specifically to his or her power to influence and even determine the legislative agenda. This agenda-setting power is based above all on legislative powers.

As Cheibub and Limongi argue, '[t]he concentration of legislative powers in the executive's hand, coupled with a highly centralized decision-making structure in the legislative chambers, explains the high degree of legislative success of Brazilian presidents – a success that is not much different from that obtained in parliamentary democracies'.[13] This does not mean, however, that the President imposes his or her will, but rather that he or she can strongly influence a legislative agenda that must be supported by those who have the last word, the members of the

[12] The party of President Collor (PRN) had 5.05% of the seats in the Chamber of Deputies; in his first term, the party of President Cardoso (PSDB) had 9.36%, in his second term, 18.32%; in President Lula's first term, his party (PT) had 11.11% of the seats, and in his second term, 15.79%. See Argelina Cheibub Figueiredo and Fernando Limongi, 'Political Institutions and Governmental Performance in Brazilian Democracy' in Dana de la Fontaine and Thomas Stehnken (eds), *The Political System of Brazil* (Berlin, Springer, 2016) 70. For an analysis of possible reasons for ticket-splitting in Brazil, see Barry Ames and others, 'Split-ticket voting as the rule: Voters and permanent divided government in Brazil' (2009) 28 *Electoral Studies* 8.

[13] See José Antonio Cheibub and Fernando Limongi, 'Legislative-Executive Relations' in Tom Ginsburg and Rosalind Dixon (eds), *Comparative Constitutional Law* (Cheltenham, Edward Elgar, 2011) 226.

Congress. Hence, the crucial role of a stable coalition. 'Unilateral action as a way of governing and setting policies contrary to preferences of the majority is simply not feasible',[14] and those who tried it – like President Fernando Collor – clearly failed. Therefore, none of the powers granted by the Constitution to the President of the Republic are enough to bypass the Congress, not even the power to issue provisional decrees with immediate force of law, which had long been considered by constitutional scholars as an instrument that the President could use to usurp the power of the Congress. Resorting to provisional decrees is the result of mutual coordination rather than of usurpation,[15] and they are primarily used to ensure that important matters will be timely discussed in Congress, thus mitigating the ability of minorities to postpone deliberation and decision.[16]

The final feature that makes the successful functioning of coalitional presidentialism possible is the previously mentioned centralised decision-making structure within the National Congress. Contrary to what some critics of the Brazilian party system have argued, empirical studies have consistently shown considerable party cohesion in the legislature: 'The decision-making process follows a centralized model, comparable to that found in most countries with a parliamentary system … The president and the party leaders are able to define what, when and how issues of their interest will be voted on'.[17]

The most evident sign of the functioning of coalitional presidentialism is the rate of dominance and the rate of success of bills proposed by the President of the Republic. The first (rate of dominance) is the percentage of bills introduced by the executive in relation to all approved bills; the latter (rate of success) is, among only those bills introduced by the executive, the percentage of bills that were successfully passed into law.

[14] ibid 228.

[15] See Figueiredo and Limongi (n 12) 74. This does not mean that the frequent use of provisional decrees never has a negative impact on the quality of democracy. As Negretto argues, decree powers may 'weaken mechanisms of horizontal and vertical accountability [and] affect the legitimacy of lawmaking in a democratic regime' (Gabriel L Negretto, 'Government Capacities and Policy Making by Decree in Latin America: The Cases of Brazil and Argentina' (2004) 37 *Comparative Political Studies* 531).

[16] See Figueiredo and Limongi (n 12) 67.

[17] ibid 75. See also Argelina C Figueiredo and Fernando Limongi, 'Presidential Power, Legislative Organization, and Party Behavior in Brazil' (2000) 32 *Comparative Politics* 151, 164. For a more nuanced view on the similarities between Brazilian coalitional presidentialism and parliamentary regimes, see Octavio Amorim Neto, 'Presidential Cabinets, Electoral Cycles, and Coalition Discipline in Brazil' in Scott Morgenstern and Benito Nacif (eds), *Legislative Politics in Latin America* (Cambridge, Cambridge University Press, 2002).

Both the rate of dominance and the rate of success are approximately 75–80 per cent,[18] which is similar to many parliamentary democracies. There seems to be no sign of the much-feared deadlock that supposedly doomed multiparty presidential systems in the past.

V. ATTEMPTS TO CHANGE THE BRAZILIAN PRESIDENTIAL SYSTEM

Presidentialism has been an enduring feature of the Brazilian political system since the proclamation of the republic in 1889. The charges against this system of government, along with proposals to replace it, are almost as old. Under the 1946 Constitution, there have been constitutional amendment proposals aimed at adopting a parliamentary system. In 1961, an amendment to the 1946 Constitution was approved, and parliamentarianism was adopted. In this case, however, the aim was primarily to reduce the powers of President João Goulart, who took office after President Jânio Quadros resigned. In January 1963, the presidential system was reintroduced after a popular referendum.

The enduring history of the Brazilian presidential system was most intensively threatened during the Constituent Assembly of 1987–88. The preliminary constitutional blueprint, drafted by the Interim Commission for Constitutional Studies, along with the projects drafted within the thematic committees and subcommittees and the projects drafted by the systematisation committee within the National Constituent Assembly, proposed the adoption of a semi-presidential system of government.

In Brazil, the dispute over the system of government during the National Constituent Assembly of 1987–88 has usually been portrayed as a dispute between presidential and parliamentary systems. However, this is inaccurate. The system of government that was proposed by the systematisation committee and nearly adopted in the final text of the Constitution was not a parliamentary but a semi-presidential system under any of the mainstream definitions of semi-presidentialism.[19] Although the draft projects did propose a system of government in which the head of government should be the Prime Minister, whereas

[18] Figueiredo and Limongi (n 12) 69.

[19] See, for instance, Maurice Duverger, 'A New Political System Model: Semi-Presidential Government' (1980) 8 *European Journal of Political Research* 165, 166; and Robert Elgie, *Semi-Presidentialism: Sub-Types And Democratic Performance* (Oxford, Oxford University Press, 2011) 22).

the President of the Republic would have been the head of state, an important feature of the proposed system clearly indicates that it was not a parliamentary system: the President of the Republic should be elected by direct elections. In addition to the direct election of the President of the Republic, the draft projects also provided for the responsibility of the Prime Minister and cabinet vis-à-vis the legislature.[20]

Both of these features are enough to characterise the proposed system of government as semi-presidential, at least according to Elgie's minimalist definition: 'Semi-presidentialism is the situation where a constitution makes provision for both a directly elected fixed-term president and a prime minister and cabinet who are collectively responsible to the legislature'.[21] However, even if one takes into account Duverger's slightly more demanding definition, which was already well known during the work of the Constituent Assembly, the proposed system should also be defined as semi-presidential. In addition to the two features Elgie mentions for defining a system as semi-presidential, Duverger argued for a third one: the president must possess 'quite considerable powers'.[22] Even though it is not clear exactly what 'quite considerable powers' means, the list of powers of the President of the Republic in the mentioned draft projects were quite comprehensive and included the powers to appoint the judges of the Supreme Court; to propose, approve and veto bills; to conclude international treaties; to declare war; to exercise supreme command over the Armed Forces; to declare a state of defence or siege; and to order federal intervention in a member state, among many others.[23] Thus, there is no doubt that the proposed system, with a powerful and directly elected president, was not a parliamentary but a semi-presidential system.

It could be argued that this is a minor, solely a terminological question, and the fact that the proposed system was semi-presidential, not parliamentary, was irrelevant for the discussion within the Constituent Assembly. This may be true. It is impossible to assess what could have been different if the advocates of the proposed system had made it clear that the changes in the Brazilian presidential tradition would have been less radical than many imagined. Besides, it is well known that the debate on the system of government (like almost all debates within any

[20] See Draft Project A of the Systematisation Committee, Art 101, § 1.
[21] Elgie (n 19) 22.
[22] Duverger (n 19) 166.
[23] See Draft Project A of the Systematisation Committee, Art 95, II, VII, VIII, IX, XIII, XIV, XVII, XXI, XXII, XXIII.

constituent assembly) has never been solely an abstract debate on what is best for Brazil.

Nevertheless, the debate on the system of government did not finish on 5 October 1988, the date of the promulgation of the Constitution. After having lost the battle on the floor of the Constituent Assembly, the adversaries of the presidential system managed to include an article into the ADCT providing that a plebiscite on the form and system of government should be held five years after the promulgation of the Constitution. At this moment, the conceptual issue may have had a relevant impact beyond the terminological discussion. Art 2 of the ADCT reads as follows: 'On September 7 1993, through a plebiscite, the electorate shall define the form of government (republic or constitutional monarchy) and the system of government (parliamentary or presidential) that shall prevail in the Country'. At least based on a strict interpretation of this article, semi-presidentialism was no longer an option. It may be argued that the conceptual confusion of the members of the Constituent Assembly sealed the fate of semi-presidentialism in Brazil.

It may be even argued that this conceptual confusion may have helped the presidential system to triumph once again. During the public campaign that preceded the plebiscite, in which supporters of presidential and parliamentary systems tried to convince the electorate of the advantages of each system, a running argument used by the supporters of presidentialism against the parliamentary system referred to one of the most important popular demands against the authoritarian regime (1964–85), namely, the demand to directly elect the President of the Republic. One of the most important moments of popular mobilisation in recent Brazilian history was the 1984 movement for direct elections (*Diretas Já*, ie, 'direct elections now') in which millions took to the streets to demand the right to freely choose the President of the Republic. In 1993, the supporters of the presidential system repeatedly argued that choosing a parliamentary system would necessarily mean losing the hard-fought right to directly elect the President of the Republic and that the President would be a merely decorative figure with only ceremonial powers. As clarified above, the semi-presidential system that was proposed and nearly adopted by the National Constituent Assembly of 1987–88 entailed neither the former nor the latter features. It was a system with a directly elected and powerful president. This system did not have a second chance in 1993. The conceptual confusion of the members of the Constituent Assembly prevented that from occurring.

VI. PRESIDENTIALISM UNDER ATTACK

After the victory both during the Constituent Assembly of 1987–88 and the plebiscite of 1993, it seemed that nothing would change the enduring history of the Brazilian presidential system. Moreover, the fact that both presidents Fernando Henrique Cardoso (1994–2002) and Lula (2002–2010) managed to build strong coalitions in the National Congress, which allowed them to advance their political agenda, has been frequently understood as the definitive argument in favour of this system of government.

Nevertheless, both the inability of President Rousseff (2010–2016) to build a stable coalition in Congress and the discovery of corruption schemes involving members of both the executive and the legislative branches, including many deputies and senators, re-opened the discussion on the system of government and provided fresh arguments to the critics of the Brazilian coalitional presidential model. Criminal investigations showed that the price to pay for attaining stable coalitions was not always a political price, but frequently also a monetary price, that is, the need to illicitly buy support from deputies.[24]

Since the difficulty in building a stable coalition is largely due to the fragmented party system (almost 30 parties have seats in the National Congress), some critics of the coalitional presidential model focus their objections on the electoral system. For them, no system of government can work with so many parties. The most important political reform is thus an electoral reform. For others, even though party fragmentation is the central issue, the presidential system should also be considered part of the problem. In this case, not only electoral reform but also a replacement of the system of government must take place. Again, semi-presidentialism has been one of the preferred alternatives.

VII. TREATY-MAKING POWER

As head of state and of government, the President of the Republic, with the assistance of the Ministry of Foreign Affairs (also called *Itamaraty*), is the major holder of treaty-making power. According to Art 84, VIII, the President of the Republic has the exclusive power to 'conclude international treaties, conventions and acts, subject to the approval of the National Congress'. In Brazil, the process of making and incorporating

[24] See Melo and Pereira (n 9) 64. See also Mello and Spektor (n 11).

treaties into domestic law has several steps. First, the political decision on whether to sign an international treaty falls within the exclusive power of the President of the Republic. Secondly, incorporation into domestic law depends on the approval of the National Congress by means of a legislative decree. Thirdly, after legislative approval, the ratification of international treaties falls again within the powers of the President of the Republic. Fourthly, after signature, legislative approval and ratification, an international treaty depends on the issuance of a presidential decree that promulgates it to enter into force.

The President of the Republic plays a prominent role not only in the process of making international treaties but also in the process of withdrawing from them. Although the Constitution does not contain any provision on the matter, it has always been understood that the President of the Republic has the power to unilaterally decide to withdraw from a treaty, that is, without the approval of the National Congress. However, this unilateral power has recently been challenged. An action challenging the unilateral decision of the President of the Republic to withdraw from Convention 158 of the International Labour Organisation (ILO) was filed before the STF in 1997.[25] The claimants argue that because the process of approval of international treaties depends on a decision by the National Congress, the process of withdrawal from them should also depend on the will of the Congress. Although this constitutional action was filed decades ago, several interruptions in its judgment have delayed a final decision.[26] The STF, however, seems inclined to change the old tradition of accepting unilateral withdrawals by the President of the Republic. If this tendency is confirmed, the result will be a clear decrease in the powers of the Brazilian President.

VIII. REGULATORY POWERS

In addition to being an important player in the legislative process, the President of the Republic also has the power to issue decrees and regulations for the proper enforcement of laws. Indeed, this is one of the most important powers of the President. These decrees and regulations contain provisions that lay down the necessary detailed rules for enforcing primary legislation. This means that, at least according to common

[25] See ADI 1625 (pending).

[26] For more details on the decision-making process in the STF and the possibility of interrupting judgment sessions, see ch 4.

understanding, this regulatory power is subordinated to primary legislation and therefore cannot establish rules that do not harmonise with the latter. As a result of this understanding, autonomous regulations are not allowed in the Brazilian constitutional system. In praxis, however, the boundaries between laying down details for the enforcement of primary legislation and creating new rules are not always easy to establish. The STF recognises this fact when it allows for judicial review of decrees and other types of subordinated regulations.[27]

Furthermore, the National Congress has the power 'to suspend normative acts of the executive that exceed its regulatory authority or the limits of legislative delegation'.[28] In other words, whenever the Congress understands that the President went too far in his or her regulatory power, it may suspend his or her actions. However, Congress does not have the final word in this realm either. If a President alleges that the boundaries of his or her regulatory powers had not been exceeded, he or she may challenge the decision of the National Congress before the STF.[29]

IX. THE VICE-PRESIDENT

With the exception of the 1891 Constitution, which provided that the Vice-President of the Republic was also the President of the Federal Senate, Brazil's constitutions usually have not paid much attention to the Vice-President. Under some past constitutions, such an office did not even exist (such as under the 1934 and 1937 Constitutions). Still, vice-presidents have often been pivotal players in Brazilian political history. This occurred almost exclusively on those occasions when vice-presidents succeeded (or were impeded from succeeding) presidents who died, resigned, or were removed from office.

Indeed, the provisions on replacement and succession, which have been analysed above, are virtually the only relevant provisions concerning the Vice-President. Other than replacing and succeeding a President, the Constitution grants no relevant function to him or her. It merely provides that 'the Vice-President of the Republic shall assist the President whenever called on by him for special missions',[30] but it is unclear what exactly this provision means, for instance, whether it allows the

[27] See ch 4.
[28] Art 49, V.
[29] See ADI 748-MC (1992).
[30] Art 79, single paragraph.

Vice-President to represent the President of the Republic on international missions. Additionally, the same single paragraph of Art 79 states that other powers may be granted to the Vice-President by federal complementary law, but no such law has ever been enacted. The Vice-President is also a member of the Council of the Republic and the Council of National Defence.

X. THE MINISTERS OF STATE

As a presidential system, the 'cabinet' is a concept that is not used in Brazilian constitutional law. The members of what could be called a cabinet – the ministers of state – are freely appointed and may be freely dismissed by President of the Republic. Due to their auxiliary function, the Constitution has very few provisions concerning ministers of state.

The head of Art 87 defines who may be appointed as a minister of state: 'Brazilians over twenty-one years of age and in possession of their political rights'. This general rule has one restrictive exception: to be appointed minister of defence, one must be a native-born Brazilian.[31] Notwithstanding the separation of the executive and legislative branches that is characteristic of presidential systems, members of the National Congress may be invested with the office of minister of state without losing their legislative office.

Although ministers of state are freely appointed and may be freely dismissed by President of the Republic without any interference from the other branches, in recent years the Judiciary has unduly interfered with the President's discretion. The most controversial case of such interference occurred when President Rousseff appointed former President Lula as her minister. Political opposition parties filed writs of security before the STF arguing that the appointment had the sole goal of preventing ordinary federal courts from hearing and deciding those lawsuits against the former president in the wake of the so-called 'Car Wash Operation', a task force of the Federal Police against corruption schemes. Although the Constitution does not mention any exception to the full discretion of the President in appointing and dismissing her ministers, the STF issued a provisional decision that prevented former President Lula from taking office.[32]

[31] Art 12, § 3, VII. This requirement was added by EC 23/1999.

[32] See MS 34070 (2016) and MS 34071 (2016). The provisional decision was taken by the judge rapporteur alone, which used his agenda-setting power (see ch 4) to prevent

XI. IMPEACHMENT AND REMOVAL FROM OFFICE

Since 1988, two Brazilian presidents have been removed from office: Fernando Collor in 1992 and Dilma Rousseff in 2016.[33] Impeachment and removal from office[34] are thus an important part of the recent Brazilian constitutional experience, and therefore it is worthwhile to analyse them in detail here.

A. Offences and Procedure

Removal from office may occur due to the committing of either impeachable offences or ordinary crimes. Impeachable offences, which in Brazil are called crimes of responsibility (*crimes de responsabilidade*), are defined in Art 85. These are 'acts of the President of the Republic that breach the Federal Constitution' especially acts against: (a) the existence of the Union; (b) the free exercise of the powers of the Legislative, Judiciary, Public Ministry and the constitutional powers of the units of the federation; (c) the exercise of political, individual and social rights; (d) internal security; (e) probity in administration; (f) the budgetary law; or (g) compliance with the law and court decisions.

The single paragraph of Art 85 provides that impeachable offences, along with the rules of procedure and trial, shall be defined in a special law. This law already existed when the 1988 Constitution was promulgated; it is Federal Law 1079/1950. The trials against both President Fernando Collor and President Dilma Rousseff were based on the general provisions laid down by the Constitution and the special provisions of this latter federal law.

Articles 86, 51, 52 and 102 of the Constitution, combined with provisions of Federal Law 1079/1950 and the internal rules of the Chamber of Deputies (RICD) and the Federal Senate (RISF), set forth the rules for

the plenum of the Court of timely deciding the case. Since this decision, on at least one additional occasion the Court again interfered with the President's discretion to appoint ministers. See Rcl 29508 (2018).

[33] For an analysis of the removal from office of President Collor, see Argelina Cheibub Figueiredo, 'The Collor Impeachment and Presidential Government in Brazil' in Mariana Llanos and Leiv Marsteintredet (eds), *Presidential Breakdowns in Latin America* (New York, Palgrave Macmillan, 2010).

[34] Unlike the case of the United States, where impeachment is only the first step of the process of removal from office and takes place in the House of Representatives before trial in the Senate, in Brazil the term 'impeachment' (which is not employed by the Constitution itself) is used as a synonym for 'removal from office'.

the trial of the President of the Republic in the cases of both impeachable offences and ordinary crimes. The most important of these rules are as follows: (a) any citizen may request the impeachment of the President of the Republic before the Chamber of Deputies (RICD, Art 218); (b) the President of the Chamber of Deputies has a preliminary and largely discretionary power to reject petitions that he or she deems unjustified, but this decision may be overruled by the floor of the Chamber (RICD, Art 218, § 3);[35] (c) the President is only tried if two-thirds of the members of the Chamber of Deputies authorise it (Art 51, I, and Art 86);[36] (d) a trial for impeachable offences takes place before the Federal Senate and for ordinary crimes before the STF (Art 52, I, Art 102, I, *b*, and Art 86); (e) even if the Chamber of Deputies authorises the proceeding against the President of the Republic for impeachable offences, the Senate may, by the majority of its members, nevertheless decide not try him or her;[37] (f) the President of the STF presides over the proceeding within the Federal Senate (Art 52, single paragraph); (g) the President of the Republic is suspended from his or her functions for 180 days if the STF accepts the accusation or criminal complaint for ordinary crimes or the Federal Senate starts the proceedings against impeachable offences (Art 86, § 1, I and II, and § 2); (h) after this period of 180 days, if the trial has not yet been concluded the suspension shall cease, without prejudice to normal progress of the proceedings (Art 86, § 2); (i) the President shall not be arrested for ordinary crimes until a criminal conviction is not rendered by the STF (Art 86, § 3); (j) the decision of the Federal Senate concerning impeachable offences shall be rendered by a two-thirds majority (Art 52, single paragraph);[38] and (k) the decision of the Federal Senate shall be limited to removal from office, with disqualification to hold any public office for a period of eight years (Art 52, single paragraph).

Art 86 has also a fourth paragraph, which, unlike the rest of the article, is not related to the proceedings. Art 86, § 4, states that the President of

[35] But not by the STF. See MS 20941 (1990).

[36] According to Art 23 of Federal Law 1079/1950, voting in the Chamber of Deputies is nominal (open voting). President Fernando Collor challenged the constitutionality of this nominal voting before the STF, but the Court upheld the provision. See MS 21564 (1992).

[37] This power of the Senate is not clearly stated anywhere (not even in the internal rules of the Senate) and is highly controversial, because it mitigates the role of the Chamber of Deputies in the whole process. It was established by the STF during the proceedings against President Fernando Collor in 1992 and confirmed by the Court during the proceedings against President Dilma Rousseff in 2015 (see ADPF 378-MC (2015)).

[38] The vote in the Federal Senate is also nominal (Federal Law 1079/1950, Art 31).

the Republic may not be held liable for acts unrelated to the performance of his or her duties in the course of his or her term.

B. Removal from Office as a Political Decision

Convictions both for impeachable offences and for ordinary crimes are non-appealable. In the latter case, this is intuitive, since the decision is made by the STF and there is no higher judicial authority in the country. However, in the case of removal from office for impeachable offences the non-appealable character is far less clear. After all, one could argue that like many other decisions made by the legislative branch, the decision of the Federal Senate could also be reviewed by the STF. However, there is a consensus on the matter stating that even though it is legitimate for the STF to intervene to enforce compliance with formal procedural rules during impeachment trials – and it has done so on several occasions[39] – the Court cannot review the result of a trial in the Senate. An impeachment trial begins and ends in the political arena.

The STF has repeatedly stated that both the decision of the Chamber of Deputies that authorises the institution of the proceedings against the President and the final decision of the Federal Senate to remove him or her from office are political.[40] If this means merely that no judicial review is possible, then there seems to be no doubt about it. However, the characterisation of an impeachment trial and removal from office as 'political' cannot mean equating them with a vote of no confidence in a parliamentary system. If it is true that the likelihood of a successful impeachment trial has more to do with the cohesion and strength of the presidential coalition in the legislature than with whether or not the President of the Republic committed an impeachable offence,[41] impeachment and removal from office, unlike a vote of no confidence in a parliamentary system, are a punishment for wrongdoing. Further, while the consequence of a vote of no confidence in a parliamentary system is simply either the formation of a new government or a call for new elections (and in both cases, it is likely that the

[39] See, for instance, MS 21564 (1992), ADPF 378-MC (2015).

[40] See MS 20941 (1990), MS 21623 (1992), ADPF 378-MC (2015), MS 34441-MC (2016).

[41] See Virgílio Afonso da Silva, 'Making Brazil Work: Checking the President in a Multiparty System' (2017) 15 *International Journal of Constitutional Law* 519, 523.

former prime minister will continue to be a member of parliament), within the Brazilian presidential system, a president who is removed from office is punished with disqualification from holding any public office for a period of eight years, as mentioned above.

Thus, the reasons for removing a president from office must be (at least also) legal, not (only) political. The fact that to prematurely end a presidential term, one needs 55 out of 81 senators voting 'yes' and that this decision is final does not make the decision 'political' in the same sense as a vote of no confidence. No one would depict as 'political' a decision of the Supreme Court that convicts the President of the Republic for an ordinary crime simply because one only needs six out of 11 judges voting 'yes' and because the decision is final. Such a decision is a legal one because six judges were convinced that the President did something illegal. The fact that it is possible and makes sense to characterise both the decision of the Federal Senate (in cases of impeachable offences) and the decision of the STF (in cases of ordinary crimes) as 'right' or 'wrong' but that it would make less sense (or no sense at all) to characterise them as 'convenient' or 'inopportune' is evidence that a 'political decision', in the case of impeachment and removal from office, cannot mean a decision merely based on considerations of political opportunity.

In contrast, because a vote of no confidence in a parliamentary system is not a punishment for wrongdoing, its characterisation as 'political' fully applies. It is not a coincidence that in such cases, it makes sense to depict a given decision as 'inopportune', but it makes no sense to characterise it as 'wrong'.

C. Legal and Political Consequences

Both a conviction for impeachable offences and a conviction for ordinary crimes lead to the removal of the President of the Republic from office. However, there is an important difference between the two situations. In the case of impeachable offences, removal from office is the main penalty, while in the case of ordinary crimes, removal from office is a result (an ancillary penalty) of the criminal conviction, according to Art 15, III, of the Constitution, which sets forth one of the cases of suspension of political rights (in case of a 'final and non-appealable criminal conviction', for as long as its effects last).

This seemingly purely terminological divide has already given rise to intense political and judicial controversies. On 29 December 1992, when voting on the floor of the Federal Senate against President Fernando Collor for impeachable offences was about to begin, he resigned from office as President of the Republic. His aim was clear: since the penalty for a conviction for impeachable offences is the removal from office, his resignation would prevent the trial from continuing, because one cannot remove from office someone who is no longer an officeholder. Further, and more importantly, if the trial could not continue because the main penalty could not be enforced, the ancillary penalty set forth in Art 52, single paragraph ('disqualification to hold any public office for a period of eight years'), could not be enforced either. But the Senate decided differently and continued the trial. In the end, although President Fernando Collor could not be removed from office because he had already resigned, the Senate decided that he was unable to hold any public office for a period of eight years.[42]

In 2016, at the end of the trial of President Dilma Rousseff, the divide between the main and the ancillary penalties played an even more important role. The Federal Senate – with the blessing of the President of STF, acting as the president of the trial process – decided to split its vote on the penalties. First, it should be decided whether President Rousseff should be removed from office and if so, in a second vote, whether she should also be disqualified from holding other public offices. The senators answered 'yes' to the first question but 'no' to the second question.[43]

As I have argued elsewhere, by creating a sort of *impeachment-lite* – ie, impeachment with removal from office, but without the disqualification from holding public offices for eight years – the Federal Senate (and the President of the STF) may have weakened the constraints on resorting to this extreme measure in the future.[44]

[42] President Collor appealed to the STF against the decision of the Federal Senate to continue the trial even after his resignation, but the Court upheld the Senate's decision. See MS 21689 (1993). President Collor was also tried before the STF for ordinary crimes, but the Court acquitted him for lack of evidence. See AP 307 (1994).

[43] Splitting the vote was a strategy that served the interests both of the government party and of part of the opposition. The government party was convinced that the President would be removed from her office and splitting the vote could save her from being disqualified from holding other offices in the following eight years. Part of the opposition, although willing to vote for removing President Rousseff from office, deemed that ostracising her for eight years would be too harsh a punishment.

[44] See da Silva, 'Making Brazil Work' (n 41) 524.

XII. EMERGENCY POWERS

A. State of Defence

Art 136 of the Constitution provides that after hearing from the Council of the Republic and the National Defence Council, 'the President of the Republic may decree a state of defence in specific restricted locations to preserve or promptly re-establish public order or social peace threatened by grave and imminent institutional instability or affected by large scale natural calamities'.

The seven paragraphs of Art 136 regulate the procedure for the declaration of a state of defence. The decree that institutes the state of defence must determine the period of its duration, the areas affected and the coercive measures that will be in force. The period may not exceed 30 days and it may be extended once for an identical period 'if the reasons justifying the respective decree persist'. The possibility of restricting some fundamental rights (rights to assembly, secrecy of correspondence and telephone communication) is the most relevant measure that may be taken during the state of defence.

Art 136, § 3, has strict provisions concerning imprisonment during a state of defence. Imprisonment for a crime against the state must be immediately communicated to the judiciary; no person shall be imprisoned or detained for more than 10 days unless the judiciary so authorises; it is prohibited to keep a prisoner incommunicado.

The necessary interaction between the powers of the President of the Republic and the National Congress for the declaration of a state of defence is regulated by Art 136, §§ 4 to 7. As stated above, the President of the Republic must first hear from the Council of the Republic and the National Defence Council. The opinions of these councils are not binding. Binding is the decision of the National Congress only. If the Congress rejects the declaration of the state of defence, it ceases immediately.

B. State of Siege

Like the case of a state of defence, the power to declare a state of siege belongs to the President of the Republic, who must first hear from the Council of the Republic and the National Defence Council. Their opinions are also not binding in the case of a state of siege. However, unlike the case of a state of defence, the President of the Republic cannot first declare a state of siege and then submit the decree to the National Congress. The National Congress must have previously authorised it by an absolute majority.

Four situations may justify the declaration of a state of siege: (a) a serious disturbance with national effects; (b) the occurrence of events that show the ineffectiveness of a measure taken during the state of defence; (c) a declaration of a state of war; or (d) a response to foreign armed aggression. Although the procedure for declaring a state of siege is similar for all four of the contexts, they differ in some crucial aspects.

In context (b), the declaration of a state of siege is the continuation of a previous declaration of a state of defence (which has proven insufficient). In contexts (a), (c) and (d), the declaration of a state of siege is independent of a previous declaration of a state of defence.

Concerning the period of their duration, situations (a) and (b) are similar: it may not exceed 30 days and extensions may be requested several times, but each one requires the prior approval of the National Congress and cannot exceed 30 days. In contrast, the duration of a state of siege based on situations (c) and (d) is not established in advance and may be decreed 'for the entire period of war or foreign aggression'.[45]

The measures that may be taken during a state of siege are listed in the seven clauses of Art 139. An important – and highly problematic – peculiarity of Art 139 is the fact that it mentions only those measures that may be taken during a state of siege 'decreed under article 137, I', ie, a state of siege within contexts (a) and (b) mentioned above. Art 139 contains no provision whatsoever concerning the measures that may be taken during a state of siege decreed in wartime or in the case of foreign aggression. Many argue that from this omission, it follows that there is no restriction on which measures (especially restrictions of fundamental rights) may be taken during a state of siege in wartime. However, the incorporation of the International Covenant on Civil and Political Rights (ICCPR, 1966) into Brazilian domestic law in 1992[46] clearly precludes this interpretation. According to the Covenant, although in times of emergency state parties may take measures derogating from some of their obligations, these measures must be consistent with their other obligations under international law and cannot 'involve discrimination solely on the ground of race, colour, sex, language, religion or

[45] Art 138.

[46] See Decree 592/1992.

social origin'.[47] Moreover, Art 4, 2, of the Covenant establishes that 'no derogation from articles 6, 7, 8 (paragraphs 1 and 2), 11, 15, 16 and 18 may be made under this provision'. Those articles are related to the right to life, protection against torture or cruel, inhumane or degrading treatment or punishment, slavery and servitude, imprisonment on the ground of inability to fulfil a contractual obligation, *nullum crimen, nulla poena*, recognition as a person before the law and the right to freedom of thought, conscience and religion.

It is therefore impossible to argue that any constitutional right may be suspended during a state of siege in wartime, although many still make this argument. Even if the Constitution does not establish limits, the International Covenant on Civil and Political Rights does. Furthermore, the debate on the hierarchy of international treaties vis-à-vis the Constitution is not relevant in this realm because the Covenant is not incompatible with the Constitution, that is, there is no conflict between the two that must be solved by resorting to arguments based on such a normative hierarchy.[48] Therefore, the limitations established by the Covenant fully apply.

C. Political and Judicial Control of Emergency Powers

The declaration of a state of defence or siege is subject to previous, simultaneous and subsequent controls. Previous control has been mentioned above: the National Congress must approve or authorise a declaration of a state of defence or siege. Art 140 establishes simultaneous control when it provides that the directing board of the National Congress shall, after hearing from party leaders, 'designate a committee comprised of five of its members to monitor and supervise the implementation of the measures concerning the state of defence and the state of siege'. Furthermore, the fact that the National Congress shall remain in session as long as either a state of defence or a state of siege is in force (Art 136, § 6, and Art 138, § 3) is also evidence that the responsibility of the Congress does not end with approval or authorisation.

Finally, the single paragraph of Art 141 requests that as soon as the state of defence or state of siege ceases, 'the measures taken during the period it was in force shall be reported by the President of the Republic in a message to the National Congress, specifying and justifying the actions

[47] ICCPR, Art 4, 1.
[48] For details on this issue, see ch 5.

taken, listing the names of those affected and indicating the restrictions applied'.

The most relevant question in this realm is whether the National Congress may reject the report and, in an affirmative case, what the consequences may be. The Constitution is silent in this respect. However, Federal Law 1079/1950, which regulates the impeachable offences of the President of the Republic, provides that it is an impeachable offence 'to take or to authorise, during state of siege, coercive measures that exceed the limits established by the Constitution' (Federal Law 1079/1950, Art 7, 10).

In addition to the political control exercised by the National Congress, the head of Art 141 points to the possibility of judicial control when it provides that once the state of defence or state of siege ceases, its effects shall also cease, 'without prejudice to liability for unlawful acts committed by its executors or agents'. The most controversial issue is whether there may be judicial control not only after one of these states but also when one of these states is still in force. Since the Constitution establishes that 'the law shall not exclude any injury or threat to a right from review by the Judiciary' (Art 5, XXXV), the Brazilian constitutional literature seems to be unanimous in arguing that measures taken during a state of defence or state of siege may be reviewed by the judiciary even when those states are still in force. Although this stance seems unproblematic in most situations, one should not forget that the same literature tends to argue that in the case of a state of siege during wartime, any fundamental right may be suspended. If this is true, then the very guarantees established in Art 5, XXXV, and others – such as the guarantees of habeas corpus or the writ of security – could also be suspended. Admittedly, this does not prevent judicial control *a posteriori*, but it may clearly undermine judicial control during a state of defence or state of siege. The Brazilian constitutional literature does not sufficiently address this issue.

XIII. PUBLIC ADMINISTRATION AND REGULATORY AGENCIES

In addition to being the head of the state, government, and Armed Forces, the President of the Republic exercises 'the upper management of the federal administration'.[49] The Constitution dedicates an entire chapter

[49] Art 84, II.

to public administration (Chapter VII of Heading III). This is an unusually detailed chapter compared to the constitutions of other countries. It entails general principles for the public administration, detailed provisions concerning civil and military servants and rules concerning social security, retirement, and tenure.[50] Because the provisions of this chapter are so detailed, this is one of the most frequently amended parts of the Constitution,[51] and almost no provision (articles, paragraphs, clauses) has the wording it had when the Constitution was promulgated.

In the wake of the privatisation of public services in the 1990s, several independent regulatory agencies were created with broad powers that include rule making, enforcement and adjudication in the areas under their jurisdiction. The most important regulatory agencies are the National Telecommunications Agency (Anatel), the National Oil and Gas Agency (ANP), the National Energy Agency (ANEEL), the National Supplementary Health Agency (ANS), the National Health Regulatory Agency (ANVISA), and the National Water Agency (ANA).

From the point of view of constitutional law, it is important to mention that although these agencies were created in the 1990s, the limits of their powers, especially in the realm of rulemaking, remain highly controversial. The STF has decided many cases on the matter and has often upheld the rules issued by those agencies.[52]

XIV. ARMED FORCES

The President of the Republic exercises 'supreme command over the Armed Forces' and appoints the commanders of the Navy, the Army and the Air Force.[53] Until 1999, each member of the Armed Forces had a portfolio of its own in the presidential cabinet, that is, there was a minister of the Army, a minister of the Navy, and a minister of the Air Force. This had long been the tradition in Brazilian presidential system and meant that although the President of the Republic has always been free to appoint and dismiss his or her ministers, three of them must be officials chosen from among the highest-ranked generals of the Army, Navy and Air Force. Although there were proposals in the Constituent Assembly of 1987–88 to merge the three military portfolios into a ministry of

[50] Arts 37 to 42.
[51] See, for instance, EC 3/1993, 18/1998, 19/1998, 20/1998, 41/2003, 47/2005, 88/2015.
[52] See, for instance, ADI 4878 (2018).
[53] Art 84, XIII and Art 142.

defence, the Armed Forces strongly and successfully opposed it. Hence, a cabinet fully composed of civilians had been impossible until 1999, when the three military portfolios were finally extinguished and the ministry of defence was created.[54]

The Constitution dedicates an entire chapter to the Armed Forces (Chapter II of Heading V). The relationship between constitutional order and the Armed Forces in Brazil has definitely not been an easy one. On many occasions, the latter has not protected but instead overthrown the constitutional order. The 1988 Constitution was written after the end of 21 years of authoritarian rule in which the military played a central role[55] and unsurprisingly, provisions related to the organisation and especially the constitutional role of the Armed Forces were the subject of fierce disputes.

Everywhere else, the Armed Forces usually have one clear task: national defence. Still, Brazilian constitutions (at least since 1891) have always added a domestic role for the Armed Forces: the guarantee of law and order. This role, coupled with the provision that the Army, Navy and Air Force are obedient to the President of the Republic 'within the limits of the law', frequently justified military intervention into governmental matters in Brazil. It sufficed that the Armed Forces saw a danger to law and order and challenged the legality of the acts of the President of the Republic.

Although the 1988 Constitution maintained the controversial second role for the Armed Forces ('guarantee of law and order'), the 'obedience within the limits of the law' clause was abandoned. Art 142 of the Constitution now provides that the Armed Forces, which is composed of the Navy, Army and Air Force, 'are permanent and regular national institutions, organised on the basis of hierarchy and discipline, under the supreme authority of the President of the Republic, and intended to defend the country, guarantee the constitutional branches and, on the initiative of any of these, law and order'. Thus, according to Art 142 the Armed Forces also guarantee the functioning of the constitutional branches – legislative, executive and judiciary – and any of these three branches may request the intervention of the Armed Forces to preserve law and order.[56] This is a highly problematic provision, since protecting

[54] See Federal Complementary Law 97/1999.

[55] See ch 1.

[56] The task of protecting law and order is regulated by Federal Complementary Law 97/1999 and Decree 3897/2001.

law and order is also one of the aims of the states of defence and siege. However, unlike the case of these emergency powers, whose granting requires both the will of the President of the Republic and the absolute majority of the National Congress (in addition to being subject to political and judicial control), a request for the intervention of the Armed Forces could be made unilaterally.[57]

FURTHER READING

Amorim Neto O and Santos F, 'The Executive Connection: Presidentially Defined Factions and Party Discipline in Brazil' (2001) 7 *Party Politics* 213

Cheibub JA and Limongi F, 'Legislative-Executive Relations' in T Ginsburg and R Dixon (eds), *Comparative Constitutional Law* (Cheltenham, Edward Elgar, 2011)

Figueiredo AC and Limongi F, 'Political Institutions and Governmental Performance in Brazilian Democracy' in D de la Fontaine and T Stehnken (eds), *The Political System of Brazil* (Berlin, Springer, 2016)

Figueiredo AC and Limongi F, 'Presidential Power, Legislative Organization, and Party Behavior in Brazil' (2000) 32 *Comparative Politics* 151

Melo MA and Pereira C, *Making Brazil Work: Checking the President in a Multiparty System* (Basingstoke, Palgrave Macmillan, 2013)

Negretto GL, 'Government Capacities and Policy Making by Decree in Latin America: The Cases of Brazil and Argentina' (2004) 37 *Comparative Political Studies* 531

[57] In this sense, see Jorge Zaverucha, 'The 1988 Brazilian Constitution and Its Authoritarian Legacy: Formalizing Democracy While Gutting Its Essence.' (1998) 15 *Journal of Third World Studies* 105, 112.

4

The Judiciary: Independence, Activism, and Publicity

Brazilian Justice System – Brazilian Supreme Court (STF) – Proportionality – Concrete Judicial Review of Legislation – Abstract Judicial Review of Legislation – Activism – Functions Essential to Justice

THE BRAZILIAN SUPREME Court (STF) has never been as visible in everyday life as it is today. If one analyses the case law of the Court during the first 15 years after the promulgation of the 1988 Constitution, one will find only a few decisions that have captured the attention of people with no juridical background. Back then, the STF was composed of 11 persons with 'outstanding legal knowledge' (as laid down by Art 101) whom almost nobody knew by name (not even lawyers); today the court and its judges are in newspapers and on prime-time TV news programmes almost every day, and some of the judges are much better known than many politicians. It is possible to argue that no supreme or constitutional court in the world has experienced such a radical change in profile in such a short period of time.

To be sure, there are several reasons for this radical change. Some of these reasons include a growing awareness of rights within Brazilian society, leading to strategic litigation that brought several important moral debates to the court in recent years (such as abortion, affirmative action, stem-cell research, same-sex civil unions), along with a change in the personal profile of the members of the Court. But probably the main reasons for putting the STF in the spotlight are the self-presentation of the Court as a democratic institution (supposedly an alternative to legislative inertia) and the intense use of different kinds of media. In recent years, the Court has organised several public hearings that have allowed stakeholders that are not parties to a case to express their views directly to the court. Additionally, since 2002 all of the court's plenary sessions have been broadcast on live TV (and can be seen later on the Internet).

This central and activist role of the STF in political and constitutional life is strengthened by its solid independence vis-à-vis political power. The decision in the *Mensalão* trial, a corruption scandal involving several members of the Worker's Party and other political parties belonging to the presidential government coalition during President Lula's terms, is only one example, among many others, of this independence. Although eight of the 11 judges of the STF were nominated by a President belonging to the Worker's Party (either by Lula himself or by his successor, Dilma Rousseff), almost all the defendants were found guilty. Unlike supreme or constitutional courts in other countries, it is not possible to attach a label to the STF based on the party that nominated the majority of its judges.[1] The STF judges (like all other judges in Brazil) have life tenure (with compulsory retirement at age 75) and enjoy several other constitutional guarantees that ensure their autonomy and independence. STF decisions are also characterised by a high degree of compliance.

I. THE BRAZILIAN JUSTICE SYSTEM

The organisation of the Brazilian justice system may be best understood as falling along two axes. First, the horizontal assignment of powers is based on two dichotomies: (1) ordinary and specialised courts, and (2) federal and state courts. Secondly, the vertical organisation is based on the following scheme: within the ordinary justice system, there are first and second instance courts; within the specialised justice system, in addition to the first and second instance courts there are high courts. Furthermore, there is the Superior Court of Justice (*Superior Tribunal de Justiça*) and the Brazilian Supreme Court (*Supremo Tribunal Federal*). The first could be considered a surrogate of a high court for the ordinary (state and federal) justice system. The latter is the apex of the entire system, but its main function is 'safeguarding the Constitution'.[2]

[1] See Daniel M Brinks, '"Faithful Servants of the Regime": The Brazilian Constitutional Court's Role under the 1988 Constitution' in Gretchen Helmke and Julio Ríos-Figueroa (eds), *Courts in Latin America* (Cambridge, Cambridge University Press, 2014).

[2] Art 102.

A. Federal and State Courts

For historical reasons, state and federal court systems coexist in Brazil. Both have lower courts (first instance) and appellate courts (second instance). In the realm of the state court system, there are 27 appellate courts (*tribunais de justiça*): one for each state and one for the federal district.

The federal court system consists of five regional appellate courts (*tribunais regionais federais*), each one encompassing more than one state. The number of states included in each region varies considerably. The first region, for instance, encompasses 13 states and the federal district, whereas the second and third regions include only two states each. Lower federal courts (first instance), however, are organised following the limits of the states and the federal district.

The jurisdiction of the federal courts is exhaustively defined by Art 109 of the Constitution. Residual jurisdiction is thus held by the state courts. Federal courts judge and decide: (a) all cases in which the Union takes part, not only as plaintiff or defendant; (b) cases based on a treaty or a contract of the Union with a foreign state or international organisation; (c) political crimes; (d) crimes committed aboard ships or aircraft; (e) cases related to the irregular entry or stay of a foreigner, cases related to the enforcement of foreign court decisions, and cases related to nationality, among several others defined in the other clauses of Art 109.

Additionally, since the Judiciary Reform Act of 2004, federal courts have also had the power to judge cases of grave violations of human rights whenever the Federal Procurator-General requests before the Superior Court of Justice that the jurisdiction on the matter be taken to the federal justice system to assure compliance with obligations stemming from international human rights treaties.

State courts, in contrast, decide all cases that do not fall into the jurisdiction of the federal justice system (or into one of the specialised jurisdictions). The state justice system is the largest of the justice systems in Brazil both in the number of cases and in the number of subjects.

B. Ordinary and Specialised Jurisdictions

Brazil has three types of specialised jurisdictions: electoral, labour, and military courts. Cases within these subject areas are decided by these courts. For each of these areas, there are first instance courts, second instance courts and high courts. However, these three levels of jurisdictions are differently organised within each of these three areas.

i. Labour Courts

According to Art 111, the labour court system consists of: (a) the High Labour Court; (b) Regional Labour Courts; and (c) labour judges.

The High Labour Court is composed of 27 judges appointed by the President of the Republic after approval by the Federal Senate. However, unlike the appointment of judges to the STF, whenever the President appoints judges to the High Labour Court she or he does not have full discretion: one-fifth of the judges must be selected among members of the Labour Public Ministry (*Ministério Público do Trabalho*) and among lawyers;[3] the other four-fifths must be selected among judges from regional labour courts, from within a list prepared by the High Labour Court itself.

Since labour courts are federal, not state courts, the number of regional appellate courts does not necessarily coincide with the number of states. Some of these regional courts (currently there are 24) have jurisdiction over more than one state. In the state of São Paulo, there are two appellate courts: one for the capital of the state (the city of São Paulo) and one for the rest of the state. Those courts decide appeals of the decisions of first-instance labour judges.

Art 114 defines which cases are decided by labour judges and labour courts. The most important of them are controversies arising from labour relations, along with those involving the exercise of the right to strike and those concerning labour union representation.

ii. Electoral Courts

The electoral justice system consists of: (a) the Superior Electoral Court; (b) Regional Electoral Courts; (c) electoral judges; and (d) electoral boards (*juntas eleitorais*).

The Superior Electoral Court has an unusual composition: its seven judges do not exclusively serve the electoral court. Three of them are judges of the STF, two are judges of the Superior Court of Justice and

[3] The presence of lawyers and members of the Public Ministry serving as judges in courts is not a peculiarity of labour courts. According to Art 94, one-fifth of the seats on the federal regional courts and the state appellate courts shall be occupied by members of the Public Ministry and lawyers with more than 10 years of professional activity.

the other two are lawyers.[4] The jurisdiction of the regional electoral courts, unlike the labour courts, does coincide with the limits of each state and the federal district. This means that there are 27 regional electoral courts. Although these courts have original jurisdiction in some matters, they primarily decide appeals of the decisions of first-instance electoral judges.

Although the electoral justice system is, like all three specialised justice systems, a federal system, the case of the electoral courts and judges is peculiar because several of the judges are actually judges from the state justice system. The regional electoral courts, for instance, are composed of seven judges: two from among the judges of the state appellate court; two from among the judges of state trial courts; only one from the federal judges of a federal regional appellate court; and two lawyers (from a list of six lawyers created by the state appellate court).

Although part of the judiciary branch, the electoral justice system has powers that in other countries usually belong to other branches. The Constitution does not define these powers, stating only that they shall be provided for by complementary law (Art 121). These powers are defined by the Electoral Code. The electoral justice system performs all powers related to the electoral process: rule making, rule application and rule adjudication.[5] Thus, in addition to deciding electoral cases and controversies (rule adjudication), the electoral justice system organises all elections in Brazil (rule application) and has broad regulatory powers (rulemaking).[6] The Superior Electoral Court has used these regulatory powers quite often and on some occasions, creates rules that have a strong impact on electoral competition.

iii Military Courts

The third specialised justice system is the military justice system. The powers of military courts are not defined by the Constitution. Art 124

[4] These two lawyers are appointed by the President of the Republic from a list, created by the STF, of six lawyers 'of outsanding legal knowledge and good moral character' (Art 119, II).

[5] See Vitor Marchetti, 'Electoral Governance in Brazil' (2012) 6 *Brazilian Political Science Review* 113.

[6] Of course, the electoral rules are primarily made by the legislature (the most important of them being the Electoral Code and the Elections Act). Still, Article 23, IX, of the Electoral Code, explicitly provides that the Superior Electoral Court shall 'issue the regulations it deems necessary for the enforcement of this Code'.

simply provides that the military justice system tries and adjudicates 'military crimes, as defined by law'. These crimes are those defined by the Military Criminal Code (Decree-Law 1001/1969). The Superior Military Court is composed of 10 military and five civilian judges, all of them appointed by the President of the Republic and with life tenure (Art 123).

C. The Superior Court of Justice (STJ)

The Superior Court of Justice was created by the 1988 Constitution. One of its most important jurisdictions is to decide on *special appeal* (*recurso especial*) those cases decided by federal regional appellate courts or by state appellate courts 'when the appealed decision … is contrary to a treaty or federal law, or denies the effectiveness thereof'.[7] Until 1988, such cases had been decided by the STF, and the creation of the Superior Court of Justice aimed at reducing the workload of the STF.

As mentioned above, the Superior Court of Justice also functions as a high court for the ordinary justice system. Art 105, III, c, is an example of such jurisdiction. According to that article, the Superior Court of Justice decides appeals when the appealed decision 'interprets federal law differently from another court'.

In addition to the power to decide the special appeals described in Art 105, III, the Superior Court of Justice has both original and ordinary appellate jurisdictions. It has original jurisdiction to judge some criminal cases (for instance, when the defendant is the governor of the state or of the federal district), to decide writs of habeas corpus that involve these and other authorities established in Art 105, I, to resolve conflicts of jurisdiction between courts (except those conflicts involving the Superior Court of Justice itself and those that involve other high courts), and to homologate decisions of foreign courts, among others. Ordinary appellate jurisdiction encompasses, for instance, appeals against decisions of state or federal courts that denied a writ of habeas corpus or a writ of security.

D. The National Council of Justice (CNJ)

The question, 'Who controls the Judiciary?' was frequently asked after the promulgation of the 1988 Constitution. Many argued that unlike

[7] Art 105, III, *a*.

the Executive and Legislative branches, which are accountable to the people by means of periodically held elections, the Judiciary has never been accountable for its acts and decisions, at least not in the same form, because judges are not elected, have life tenure, may not be transferred from their current offices to different ones (except by reason of public interest) and cannot have their compensation reduced.[8] For this reason, the demands for some type of external control strengthened in the first decade after the promulgation of the Constitution.

In 2004, the Judiciary Reform Act (EC 45/2004) created the National Council of Justice (CNJ, *Conselho Nacional de Justiça*), which should perform this external control. Its creation was very controversial, especially among judges. A direct action of unconstitutionality was filed before the STF, arguing, among other things, that the creation of the National Council of Justice violated the separation of powers because many of its members are not from the Judiciary itself. The Court, however, declared the CNJ constitutional.[9]

According to Art 103-B, the National Council of Justice controls not only the administrative and financial operation of the Judiciary but also the proper discharge of the judges' duties. The Council has powers that include rule making, enforcement and adjudication in the areas under its jurisdiction. It cannot, however, review judicial decisions. The exact boundaries of these powers are still contested and the STF has frequently decided cases related to it.[10]

II. THE BRAZILIAN SUPREME COURT (STF)

The Brazilian Supreme Court (*Supremo Tribunal Federal*, STF) was created in 1890, shortly after the proclamation of the republic, by the so-called provisional constitution (Decree 510/1890), which also introduced the judicial review of legislation in Brazil. Both were confirmed by Decree 848/1890, which defined the organisation of the federal justice system, and by the 1891 Constitution.

Since its creation, the number of judges in the STF has varied considerably. The 1891 Constitution established 15 judges; the 1934, 1937 and 1946 Constitutions provided for a Supreme Court with 11 judges but granted to the Court the power to propose an increase in this number. In 1965 – that is, in the beginning of the authoritarian period – Institutional

[8] Art 95, I, II, III.
[9] See ADI 3367 (2005).
[10] See, above all, ADC 12 (2008).

Act 2 increased the number of judges to 16, which was maintained by the 1967 Constitution. In 1969, Institutional Act 6 reduced the number again to 11 judges. Since the authoritarian regime did not alter the composition of the STF at first, the decision to increase the number of judges from 11 to 16 was a strategy to increase the number of judges aligned with the rulers. The decision to decrease the number again in 1969 followed a similar rationale. In January 1969, three judges critical of the regime – Hermes Lima, Victor Nunes Leal and Evandro Lins e Silva – were expelled from the Court; two other judges – the then-President of the Court, Gonçalves de Oliveira, and Antônio Carlos Lafayette de Andrada – voluntarily retired in protest. With the dismissal of five judges not aligned with the regime, there was no longer any reason to keep the number at 16. The majority of pro-regime judges were already assured.

During the session of the National Constituent Assembly of 1987–88, many judges of the STF attempted to influence the members of the Assembly to keep the changes in the composition and powers of the Court to a minimum. Some of them were afraid to be removed from office or, alternatively, feared that the STF would be transformed into a Constitutional Court with more restricted powers whose judges would lack life tenure. In the end, important changes were made to the powers of the Court, but they were much less profound than many had expected and others had feared. The profile of the Court as 'Guardian of the Constitution' was strengthened, but it lost some of its powers as the highest court on matters concerning federal legislation, which were transferred to the newly created Superior Court of Justice. All 11 judges of the STF, each of them appointed by the rulers of the authoritarian regime, remained in their offices. Form of appointment and life tenure were also kept unaltered

A. Composition, Appointment, Term

The STF is composed of 11 judges.[11] The appointment procedure has been virtually the same since 1891. According to Art 101, single paragraph, Art 84, XIV, and Art 52, III, a, of the Constitution, the judges of the STF are appointed by the President of the Republic after confirmation by the Federal Senate. The confirmation process within the Senate has two steps. First, there is a confirmation hearing in the Senate's Committee

[11] In Brazil, judges of the supreme, superior and high courts are called *ministros* (ministers).

of Constitution, Justice and Citizenship, in which the nominated judge answers questions posed by the senators, who decide by secret ballot and absolute majority (RISF, Art 383, VI). This decision, however, is only final if the nomination is unanimously rejected. There may be an appeal of a non-unanimous rejection by the committee, provided that at least 10 per cent of the senators agree (RISF, Art 101, § 1). If the nomination is confirmed in the committee, the floor of the Federal Senate make the final decision, also by secret ballot and absolute majority (RISF, Art 383, VII). Until now, only five nominations have been rejected by the Senate, all of them in the late nineteenth century.[12]

According to Art 12, § 3, IV, and Art 101, the nominee must fulfil some formal and substantial requirements: (1) be a native-born Brazilian; (2) be over 35 and under 65 years old; and (3) have 'outstanding legal knowledge and impeccable reputation'. Unlike the case of many constitutional courts, the STF judges serve no fixed term. They are appointed 'for life'.[13] This does not mean, however, that judges stay in office until they die or voluntarily resign. As with every public servant, STF judges must compulsorily retire at age 75 (Art 40, II).[14]

According to the Court's rules of procedure (hereafter RISTF), the court has three organs – the plenum, panels and president – each with very specific powers, of which the most important will be presented in the following subsections.

B. The Plenum

The plenum (*plenário*) is composed of all 11 judges and decides *en banc*. Although the most important power of the plenum is to decide constitutional actions related to the abstract constitutional review of legislation, this power is not mentioned in the RISTF because those rules date from 1980 and constitutional actions were created by the 1988 Constitution. Although the rules of procedure have been amended

[12] For an analysis of the nominations to the STF since 1988, see Mariana Llanos and Leany Barreiro Lemos, 'Presidential Preferences? The Supreme Federal Tribunal Nominations in Democratic Brazil' (2013) 55 *Latin American Politics and Society* 77.

[13] Art 95, I.

[14] Until 2015, the age for compulsory retirement was 70, but this was altered by EC 88/2015. The background of this constitutional amendment was a political dispute between President Dilma Rousseff and the President of the Chamber of Deputies Eduardo Cunha. The latter strove to pass a constitutional amendment to prevent President Rousseff from nominating judges to replace the five judges who would have retired by the end of her term.

several times since 1988, constitutional actions are still not mentioned. The power of the plenum to decide these actions stems from the association of three factors: (a) the representation of unconstitutionality, which was the forerunner of the abstract actions of constitutional review introduced by the 1988 Constitution, had always been decided by the plenum (and although this representation of unconstitutionality no longer exists, it is still mentioned in Art 5 of the RISTF); (b) Art 97 of the Constitution establishes that legislation may only be declared unconstitutional by the vote of the absolute majority of the members of a court or its special body;[15] and (c) Art 22 of Federal Law 9868/1999, which regulates the procedure of direct actions of unconstitutionality, provides that decisions on the abstract constitutional review of legislation shall only be undertaken if at least eight judges attend the judgment session.

In addition to the power to decide actions on the abstract constitutional review of legislation, the plenum exercises judicial review of legislation in concrete cases and controversies as the court of last resort. However, such cases are sometimes decided in panels, notwithstanding Art 97 of the Constitution, according to which legislation may only be declared unconstitutional by a vote of the absolute majority of the members of a court or its special body.

Other cases to be decided by the plenum primarily include criminal trials involving the President and the Vice-President of the Republic, the presidents of the Chamber of Deputies and Federal Senate, the judges of the STF themselves and the Federal Procurator-General, and disputes between foreign states or international bodies and the Union, the states, and the federal district.

C. The Panels

The STF is divided into two panels (*turmas*) composed of five judges each. The President of the Court does not sit on any panel. When the president's term finishes, he or she will take the seat on the panel of the

[15] Special bodies (*órgãos especiais*) may be created within courts with more than 25 judges (Art 93, XI). For reasons of efficiency, these bodies may then decide those cases that as a general rule would require a decision by the vote of all the members of a given court. The State Court of São Paulo, for instance, is composed of more than 350 judges, and it would be impossible to demand that every constitutional issue be decided by the vote of all of them. Thus, this power is delegated to a special body composed of 25 judges.

newly elected president. Both panels have the same powers over the same matters (RISTF, Arts 9 to 11), that is, this division is not based on the subject matter of the cases to be decided. If a seat on one of the panels is vacant, a judge of the other panel may request to be transferred (RISTF, Art 19).

The allocation of powers between plenum and panels is complex and follows no clear rationale. Changes in this allocation are not rare and it is not unusual for actions that were once decided by the plenum to be decided by the panels, and vice versa. However, it is possible to establish two divides that although not perfectly overlapping the divide between plenum and panels, may nevertheless roughly explain their main tasks. These divides are: (1) between constitutional and non-constitutional cases, and (2) between original and appellate jurisdiction.

As mentioned above, the most important decisions – especially the abstract constitutional review of legislation – are made by the plenum. Since the STF does not decide constitutional cases only, one of the main powers of the two panels is to decide ordinary – ie, non-constitutional – cases. Additionally, the panels usually decide cases in which the STF functions as an appellate court.

It would not be remiss to re-emphasise that there are several exceptions to this criteria, that is, the plenum also decides non-constitutional and appellate cases, and the panels also decide original and (a few) constitutional cases (but never a constitutional case in which the court has original jurisdiction). As will be explained below, the only constitutional actions that are filed directly before the STF are those aiming at an abstract constitutional review of legislation. These claims are always decided by the plenum (*en banc*).

D. The President of the Court

According to the RISTF, the President of the STF is elected by his and her peers for a two-year term (RISTF, Art 12). Practice, however, is slightly different: there is an informal rotation system according to which the president to be elected is always the judge longest in office who has not yet served as president. This means that almost every judge will eventually be President of the Court, unless a judge reaches the age for compulsory retirement before his or her turn in this rotation system. However, this has very rarely occurred, almost always in cases in which, by the time of the appointment of the Court, the judge was almost 65 years old (age limit). Since the age for compulsory retirement is now 75, the odds of a judge serving for at least 10 years and not having the chance to become President of the Court are now even lower.

In addition to the typical powers and duties of the presidents of supreme or constitutional courts, such as representing the court before other institutions or branches of government and directing the plenary sessions, the President of the STF also has highly controversial powers, the most relevant of which is the power to decide alone in some circumstances. Although these individual decisions are always provisional, they may nevertheless have a considerable impact on the final decision of a case (to be made by the plenum or one of the panels), especially if there is a long delay between the two decisions.[16] According to the RISTF, the President of the Court may decide alone during the court's recess and in certain lawsuits. Additionally, the President of the Court votes in tied decisions, if the rules of procedure do not provide a different solution (RISTF, Art 13, IX). The President of the Court is also the fourth (and last) person in the line to succeed the President of the Republic.

E. Deliberation and Decision-Making Process

The sessions of the STF are always public. In judgments involving the abstract judicial review of legislation, the Court always decides *en banc*. This does not mean that all judges are present in all sessions, but at least eight judges must be. The President of the Court has the right to vote in these cases. Decisions that declare the unconstitutionality of legislation require the vote of the absolute majority of the Court.

Especially in the most controversial cases, decisions can be very lengthy, sometimes more than 500 pages long, because in those cases all judges tend to publish separate written opinions. The style of writing and deciding is very encyclopaedic, with long historical digressions and many citations of scholarly works (Brazilian and foreign) and decisions of other countries' supreme and constitutional courts. This material frequently carries more weight than the precedents of the Court themselves. Nothing in the published decision is written collectively, and there is no opinion of the court, only a summary decision (*ementa*) that summarises the result. This summary is written by the judge rapporteur and primarily reflects her or his arguments.

[16] The same problem occurs in urgent cases when the justice rapporteur decides alone (provisionally). See Diego Werneck Arguelhes and Leandro Molhano Ribeiro, '"The Court, it is I"? Individual Judicial Powers in the Brazilian Supreme Court and their Implications for Constitutional Theory' (2018) 7 *Global Constitutionalism* 236.

i. Judge Rapporteur

Every case filed before the STF is assigned to a judge rapporteur, who is chosen by lot. The judge rapporteur is responsible for writing both a report and his or her opinion. The report is a short description of the case. The written opinion is the decision the rapporteur proposes for the case. This written opinion is not distributed beforehand to the other judges, who learn its content only when the rapporteur reads it in the judgment session.[17] A case is submitted to the plenum (or to the panels) only when the judge rapporteur finishes his or her report and opinion, and there is no control whatsoever over how long this process takes. As a result, the judge rapporteur exercises an important agenda-setting power in relation to the cases under her or his responsibility.[18]

ii. Opinion Reading and Decision

In the STF, decisions are made based on the number of votes of each judge in favour of one or another position. Strictly speaking, there is nothing in the decisions of the Court that is collectively written. Especially in the most relevant cases, the judges read their previously written opinion in the reverse order of seniority, and a debate among them only rarely takes place.[19] The form of decision and publication is thus not *per curiam*, as is typical in civil law countries, but *seriatim*. As a result, the fact that a given decision has several written opinions does not mean that it was not unanimous. There are several unanimous decisions with 11 written opinions because the judges write them before the judgment session, that is, before knowing the opinion of the rapporteur and of the other judges.

iii. Vista

One important feature of the decision-making processes of every Brazilian court is the fact that any judge may interrupt the judgment

[17] For more details on the role of the judge rapporteur along with other features of the decision-making process and the deliberation praxis of the STF, see Virgílio Afonso da Silva, 'Deciding Without Deliberating' (2013) 11 *International Journal of Constitutional Law* 557.

[18] In this sense, and with further discussion, see Arguelhes and Ribeiro (n 16).

[19] For an account on how the judges themselves assess the deliberation praxis of the STF, see Virgílio Afonso da Silva, 'Do We Deliberate? If So, How?' (2017) 9 *European Journal of Legal Studies* 209.

session if he or she needs time to reflect upon the controversy being decided.[20] According to the RISTF, a judge who has interrupted a judgment session must return the case files no later than the second ordinary session after the interruption. This provision notwithstanding, judges of the STF usually keep files for much longer, sometimes for years. This practice has far-reaching consequences because if the judge does not return the files, the case is not decided. It goes without saying that the reason for keeping files for a long time frequently has nothing to do with time for careful consideration, but rather for timing control.[21]

iv. Publicity

'In the Brazilian Supreme Court, publicity has been pushed to the extreme'.[22] Plenary sessions are not only public, they are transmitted live on TV and may also be watched later on the official channel of the Court on YouTube. The live broadcast of judgment sessions is usually positively evaluated. As Judge Barroso argues, '[I]nstead of non-public hearings and deliberations behind closed doors, as in almost every court in the world, here the decisions are taken under the relentless gaze of TV cameras … The public visibility contributes to transparency, to social control and, ultimately, to democracy'.[23] But many judges of the Court do not share this view.[24] As I have argued elsewhere, 'Deliberating in public clearly lessens one's openness to counterarguments and above all the willingness to change one's opinions. Especially in the most polemical cases, after a justice has read her opinion in front of the cameras, it is less than plausible that she, also in front of the cameras, would be willing to recognize that her arguments were not the best and that, in fact, the best interpretation of the Constitution and the best solution for the case is exactly the opposite of what she has just proposed'.[25]

[20] Brazilian Code of Civil Procedure, Art 940.

[21] For in-depth analysis of the relationship between interrupting the judgment session and influencing the agenda of the Court, see Diego Werneck Arguelhes and Ivar A Hartmann, 'Timing Control without Docket Control: How Individual Justices Shape the Brazilian Supreme Court's Agenda' (2017) 5 *Journal of Law and Courts* 105.

[22] da Silva, 'Deciding Without Deliberating' (n 17) 580.

[23] Luís Roberto Barroso, 'Judicialização, ativismo judicial e legitimidade democrática' (2009) 13 *Revista de Direito do Estado* 71, 73.

[24] See Virgílio Afonso da Silva, 'Big Brother is Watching the Court: Effects of TV broadcasting on judicial deliberation' (2018) 51 *Verfassung in Recht und Übersee*.

[25] da Silva, 'Deciding Without Deliberating' (n 17) 581.

v. Reasonableness and Proportionality

It is frequently said that proportionality is one of the cornerstones of global constitutionalism. Here, I do not discuss the soundness of this claim, nor even whether there is something that may be called 'global constitutionalism'.[26] In any event, the spread of proportionality is undeniable and the STF is surely affected by it. Nevertheless, it would still be controversial to claim that proportionality plays a crucial role in the case law of the Court.

Until at least the mid-1990s, the STF barely mentioned the proportionality test in its decisions. From then on, it started to make increasing references to it, always alongside the reasonableness test. Those references, however, could hardly be considered evidence that either one or the other test or both were being performed. They were instead rhetorical devices for obfuscating a (sometimes very superficial) means-ends analysis. In most cases, the following general formulation was used: 'in light of the principle of proportionality or reasonableness, the provision is to be considered unconstitutional',[27] without any further details. At that time, the three stages of the proportionality test – suitability, necessity, and proportionality in the narrow sense (balancing) – were not part of the argumentative praxis of the Court.

In the early 2000s, however, this scenario began to change. Today, an analysis of the database of the STF will show that decisions referring to the proportionality test abound and in most cases even its three stages are mentioned (even though they are, if at all, usually rather superficially applied).[28]

The application of the proportionality test has had an impact and relevance that could be considered much more modest than one might expect, especially due to the deliberation and decision-making process of the STF. Since in the most important decisions of the Court each judge tends to present an opinion that was written before the judgment session, even if one or two judges resort to the proportionality test, ultimately this does not mean that the decision was based on it. It is

[26] On this matter, see, for instance, Virgílio Afonso da Silva, 'How Global is Global Constitutionalism?: Comments on Kai Moller's The Global Model of Constitutional Rights' (2014) 10 *Jerusalem Review of Legal Studies* 175.

[27] See ADI 1407-MC (1996), HC 76060 (1998), ADI 1813 (1998), RE 175161 (1998), ADI 855-MC (1993).

[28] See, for instance, ADI 4424 (2012), ADI 5468 (2016). In some decisions, however, the old empty formula 'in light of the principle of proportionality or reasonableness' has still been used. See, for instance, RE 573675 (2009).

possible to argue that proportionality often remains lost amidst several other arguments, many of which are incompatible with the very idea of proportionality. In general, the proportionality test is mentioned in the summary of the given decision (*ementa*) only in those cases in which the rapporteur himself refers to it in his written opinion.[29]

F. Jurisdiction

The list of matters in which the STF has jurisdiction is extremely long. It is not the goal of this section to analyse all of them. I will present a general classification of the types of cases decided by the court and analyse only the most relevant constitutional actions. As mentioned above, the court has both original and appellate jurisdictions. The Constitution further divides the appellate jurisdiction into two subcategories: ordinary and extraordinary.

Original jurisdiction encompasses all suits filed directly before the STF, such as actions aiming at the abstract judicial review of legislation; some criminal cases (for instance, when the defendant is the President of the Republic or other authorities defined by Art 102, I, *b* and *c* of the Constitution); writs of habeas corpus that involve these same authorities; conflicts between the Union and states, the Union and the federal district, or between states; extradition requests from foreign states; and conflicts of jurisdiction between the Superior Court of Justice and other courts, between the high courts, or between the high courts and the courts of appeal, among others.

Ordinary appellate jurisdiction encompasses those cases that do not begin in an ordinary trial court but directly in a high court. In these cases, defined by Art 102, II, the STF functions as a second instance appellate court. This jurisdiction is restricted to specific actions: habeas corpus, writs of security, habeas data and writs of injunction. Additionally, the STF functions as an appellate court for political crimes.

Extraordinary appellate jurisdiction is related to one type of action: the extraordinary appeal (*recurso extraordinário* – RE). In Brazil abstract/centralised and concrete/diffuse models of judicial review of legislation coexist. The extraordinary appeal is the last stage of the diffuse and concrete judicial review of legislation. According to

[29] See, for instance, ADI 1800 (2007), ADI 5136-MC (2014), ADC 41 (2017), ADI 907 (2017), RE 878694 (2017).

Art 102, III, the STF decides on extraordinary appeal those cases 'decided in sole or last instance, when the appealed decision: (a) is contrary to a constitutional provision; (b) declares a treaty or a federal law unconstitutional; (c) upholds a law or act of local government challenged as unconstitutional; or (d) upholds a local law challenged as contrary to federal law'.[30]

In addition to this division into original, ordinary appellate and extraordinary appellate jurisdictions, established by the Constitution itself, it is possible to establish a division between constitutional cases and ordinary or non-constitutional cases. This division is more relevant to the goals of this section. In the following sections, I will briefly present and analyse the Brazilian system of constitutional review of legislation.

III. THE BRAZILIAN SYSTEM OF JUDICIAL REVIEW OF LEGISLATION

The creation of the Brazilian Supreme Court and the introduction of judicial review legislation took place in 1890, shortly after the 1889 proclamation of the republic. Both were clearly inspired by the US constitutional experience, that is, every judge could refrain from enforcing a piece of legislation whenever she or he was convinced that the statute was unconstitutional. The STF was the apex of this system. During the twentieth century, this system has gradually evolved to a more concentrated model of judicial review.

The 1946 Constitution introduced the first seed of an abstract and centralised review of legislation.[31] According to its Art 8, single paragraph, the Federal Procurator-General could challenge before the STF the compatibility of acts and legislation of the member states with the

[30] To understand subclause *d* of Art 102, III, in the context of judicial review of legislation, an additional explanation is necessary: the extraordinary appeal cannot be used simply to resolve interpretive questions about local or federal law; it must be a question about the allocation of powers between the constituent units of the federation. Since this allocation of powers is defined by the Constitution (see ch 7), claims related to it become constitutional litigation and fall within the scope of the extraordinary appeal.

[31] Constitutional scholars in Brazil usually identify the first seed of a centralised review in the 1934 Constitution. However, according to the 1934 Constitution, the Supreme Court should examine a decision of the National Congress to intervene in a member state, not determine the unconstitutionality of the state law itself. Therefore, it is difficult to argue that this truly represents a case of judicial review of legislation.

constitutional principles laid down in Art 7, VII, of the 1946 Constitution. The STF could then declare the act or piece of legislation unconstitutional. In this case the National Congress could either simply suspend the enforcement of the act or legislation, if this measure sufficed to restore federal harmony, or declare federal intervention into the member state. Although limited to the realm of federalism and to the review of acts or legislation of the member states (ie, not federal legislation), for the first time power was granted to the STF to directly declare – that is, not as an appellate court – the unconstitutionality of legislation.

In 1965 – that is, under the authoritarian regime – a constitutional amendment (EC 16/1965) added a further clause to Art 101, I, of the 1946 Constitution. From then on, the STF could also decide, as matters of original jurisdiction, 'the representation against the unconstitutionality of federal or state law … filed by the Federal Procurator-General'. At that time, and until 1988 – that is, during the entire authoritarian regime – the Federal Procurator-General was appointed by the head of the executive branch and could be freely dismissed by him. Currently, although the Federal Procurator-General is still appointed by the President of the Republic, she or he has a fixed two-year term and can only be removed from office if an absolute majority of the Federal Senate agrees to do so.

The 1988 Constitution considerably expanded the abstract review of legislation in Brazil both by introducing other means of bringing a case before the STF and by enlarging the list of persons and institutions who may bring a constitutional claim before the Court. Over the years that followed, the centralised and abstract constitutional review of legislation gradually became more robust, and ordinary judges have been losing a considerable part of their autonomy for exercising the kind of diffuse judicial review of legislation created at the end of the nineteenth century. However, concrete and diffuse and abstract and centralised review continue to coexist in Brazil. In the next sections, I will present the most important features of the Brazilian model of judicial review of legislation.[32]

[32] Although hybrid or mixed model are terms usually employed to refer to models like the Brazilian model, I will not use them in this book because, among other things, these terms seem to imply that these models are simply a mixture of pure models, not models in their own right. For more details about this reasoning, see Virgílio Afonso da Silva, 'Beyond Europe and the United States: The Wide World of Judicial Review' in Erin F Delaney and Rosalind Dixon (eds), *Comparative Judicial Review* (Cheltenham, Edward Elgar, 2018).

IV. CONCRETE JUDICIAL REVIEW OF LEGISLATION

A. Extraordinary Appeal (RE)

Extraordinary appeal (*recurso extraordinário*) is the oldest constitutional action in the Brazilian system of judicial review. It was introduced by the provisional constitution of 1890 (Decree 510/1890). As its name indicates, extraordinary appeal was not a direct action, but an appeal against a decision of a lower court.[33] From the late nineteenth century until 2004, the characteristics of the extraordinary appeal remained virtually unchanged.

According to Art 102, III, of the Constitution, the STF decides, 'on extraordinary appeal, cases decided in sole or last instance, when the appealed decision: (a) is contrary to a provision of the Constitution; (b) declares a treaty or a federal law unconstitutional; (c) upholds a law or act of local government challenged as contrary to the Constitution; (d) upholds a local law challenged as contrary to federal law'.

In a nutshell, extraordinary appeal is the main path through which a constitutional controversy that began in any lower court reaches the STF.[34] The massive workload of the STF is largely explained by the number of extraordinary appeals filed every year. In 2003, 106,997 extraordinary appeals or related actions[35] were filed before the STF. Back then, these appeals added up to 97.3 per cent of all actions brought before the court. Until that year, the court had to review all appeals that were filed. There were no formal mechanisms allowing the court to review only the most relevant. One of the most important aims of the Judiciary Reform Act of 2004 (EC 45) was to create such a mechanism, which exists for many supreme and constitutional courts.

The Judiciary Reform Act added a third paragraph to Art 102, providing that when filing an extraordinary appeal, 'the appellant must demonstrate the general repercussion of the constitutional issues argued in the case … in order for the court to examine the admissibility of the appeal, which may be rejected only by decision of two-thirds of its

[33] The 1891 Constitution did not name this an extraordinary appeal. This designation was introduced only in 1908 by decree 1939/1908 (Art 3).

[34] Constitutional controversies may also arise within other types of action, such as habeas corpus and the writ of security, among others.

[35] What is primarily meant by 'related actions' is the *agravo de instrumento* (AI), which is generally used as an appeal against the denial of a lower court to submit an extraordinary appeal to the STF.

members'. On the one hand, the so-called 'general repercussion' (*repercussão geral*) is similar to other mechanisms adopted in other countries: only appeals that involve constitutional controversies that are relevant to people in addition to the parties involved will be reviewed.[36] On the other hand, the necessary majority for rejecting an appeal without reviewing it is extremely high: two-thirds of the STF judges.

Still, 10 years later, in 2013, only 21,896 extraordinary appeals (and related actions) were brought before the STF. They added up to 79.54 per cent of all filed actions. The numbers are still very high compared to similar courts in many countries, but nevertheless are more than four times lower than in 2003. One could therefore suppose that despite the necessary two-thirds majority for rejecting an extraordinary appeal without reviewing it, the mechanism is working. However, these numbers may be deceptive. A brief look at the statistics and a more precise understanding of how the requirement of general repercussion works may explain what has actually happened.

Strictly speaking, extraordinary appeals are not filed before the STF, but before the court that judged the appealed decision. It is this court that submits the appeal to the STF. Since 2004, whenever there is a multiplicity of extraordinary appeals based on the same constitutional controversy, the president or vice-president of the appealed court selects a few appeals that are representative of the controversy to submit to the STF; all similar pending cases in the state or region under the jurisdiction of the appealed court are retained until the STF decides the representative case.[37]

It is this procedure, not an allegedly 'filtering-out effect' of the general repercussion mechanism, that is responsible for reducing the number of appeals brought before the STF. Through 2017, only 32.54 per cent of appeals were rejected. This means that the STF is still reviewing almost 70 per cent of all filed extraordinary appeals. Moreover, among the rejected appeals, almost all were rejected because the Court argued that no constitutional issue whatsoever was present. From 2007 to 2017, a mere 42 appeals were rejected because the Court did not recognise their general repercussions, notwithstanding the fact that constitutional issues were identified.

[36] Art 1035, § 1, of the Code of Civil Procedure establishes that cases have general repercussions when they involve 'issues that are relevant from the economic, political, social or legal point of view and that go beyond the subjective interests of the case'.

[37] Art 1036, § 1, of the Code of Civil Procedure.

In other words, the workload of the STF has not been significantly reduced. Before the introduction of the general repercussion requirement, the Court would issue the same decision in all identical appeals; since the introduction of the general repercussion, the STF decides a few representative appeals and the lower courts replicate those decisions in the identical appeals that were retained. Admittedly, the STF has decreased its administrative work, but its judges may still be deciding almost as many singular (non-identical) appeals as they did before. Additionally, the judges now have an additional preliminary decisional round to decide whether or not an appeal has a general repercussion.

In a nutshell, it seems that the introduction of the general repercussion requirement has not been used to filter out relevant cases that deserve to be decided by the STF. It has been used only to rationalise the workflow of the Court.[38] But there is more: since the decisions on those extraordinary appeals whose general repercussion had been recognised are binding, the Court may have been accepting almost all appeals in order to grant binding effects to decisions that otherwise would not have them. In other words, the decision to recognise general repercussion for almost all extraordinary appeals has clearly paid off: lower courts must automatically follow the STF decision. The final decision is made by the STF, not by the lower courts.

B. The Role of the Federal Senate in the Judicial Review of Legislation

In the first decades after the introduction of judicial review of legislation in Brazil, the effects of a decision on an extraordinary appeal were limited to the parties, even after a final decision by the STF. There was nothing similar to a binding precedent or to the *stare decisis* doctrine in Brazil. It was only in 1934 that a surrogate for binding precedents was introduced by the Constitution promulgated that year. According to Art 91, IV of the 1934 Constitution, the Federal Senate might 'suspend the enforcement, in whole or in part, of laws … declared unconstitutional by the judiciary'. Since the 1946 Constitution, a similar provision has been replicated in every Brazilian constitution. The Federal Senate, however, has very rarely used this power, meaning that at least until recently,

[38] I am indebted to Luiza Andrade Correa for pointing out that the STF has not been using the general repercussion mechanism to filter out appeals but rather for rationalising its workflow and managing a large number of similar cases.

decisions involving the diffuse judicial review of legislation almost always had only *inter partes* effects.

C. Expanding the Binding Effects: Binding Guidelines

One of the most controversial innovations introduced by the Judiciary Reform Act of 2004 (EC 45/2004) are the binding guidelines (*súmulas vinculantes*). Since the 1960s, the STF has published a summary of its settled case law (*súmula da jurisprudência predominante*). It consists of numbered guidelines (*enunciados*), which very concisely summarise the opinion of the STF on given subjects that are settled steadily over the time.

Within a jurisdiction in which judicial precedents traditionally have not played a decisive role,[39] these guidelines have never been much more than an argumentative tool (at least outside the STF). The introduction of the binding guidelines in 2004 radically changed this scenario. Art 103-A, introduced by EC 45, provides that the STF may 'by decision of two-thirds of its members, after reiterated decisions on constitutional matters, … approve guidelines that … shall have binding effects on the other organs of the judiciary and the federal, state and municipal public administration, both direct and indirect'.

The aim of these guidelines is to grant binding effects to decisions that generally do not have such effects. Several types of decisions do not usually have binding or *erga omnes* effects. As a rule, the effects of such decisions are limited to the parties to the case and need not be followed by other courts. Since 2004, however, whenever a binding guideline is issued, decisions in actions such as these will have a binding effect that they never had before.

Until 2004, to extend the effects of a decision in a concrete case to all similar cases it would have been necessary that either: (i) someone filed a direct action of unconstitutionality (abstract control) to challenge the same article of the same law, or (ii) the Federal Senate suspended the enforcement of that article. If neither of these happened, lower courts could continue to enforce the statute as if it had never been declared unconstitutional by the STF.

[39] For an analysis of the role of judicial precedents in Brazil, see Thomas Bustamante, 'Precedent in Brazil' in Ewoud Hondius (ed), *Precedent and the Law* (Bruxelles, Bruylant, 2007).

Since the introduction of the binding guidelines, the STF has had a power that it never had before: the power to decide whether or not to grant binding and *erga omnes* effects to decisions made within concrete cases and controversies. Now it suffices to issue a binding guideline.[40]

V. ABSTRACT CONSTITUTIONAL REVIEW OF LEGISLATION

Abstract judicial review of legislation had become part of the Brazilian system of judicial review in a piecemeal fashion. It was not until the 1988 Constitution that a comprehensive abstract constitutional jurisdiction was created through the introduction of several actions aimed at triggering this kind of review directly before the STF and by enlarging the list of persons and institutions who have standing to bring a constitutional claim before it.

Currently, there are four constitutional actions in Brazil that have this aim: the direct action of unconstitutionality (ADI), the direct action of unconstitutionality for omission (ADO), the declaratory action of constitutionality (ADC), and the allegation of disobedience of fundamental precept (ADPF). The procedures for these four actions are regulated by two federal statutes: Federal Law 9868/1999 regulates the procedures for the ADI, ADO and ADC, whereas Federal Law 9882/1999 regulates the procedure for the ADPF.

A. Direct Action of Unconstitutionality (ADI)

The main and most often-filed action aiming at an abstract review of legislation is the direct action of unconstitutionality (ADI). It was introduced by the 1988 Constitution as the successor of the 'representation of unconstitutionality', which between 1965 and 1988 could be filed before the Court only by the Federal Procurator-General.

The 1988 Constitution not only changed the name of this constitutional action but also enlarged the list of persons and institutions enfranchised to bring such an action before the STF. According to Art 103, these persons and institutions include the following: the President of the Republic, the directing boards of the Federal Senate and Chamber of Deputies, the directing board of any state legislature

[40] In Rcl 4335 (2014), some judges of the STF attempted to push the boundaries of this power even further, arguing that declarations of unconstitutionality made in concrete cases automatically have binding and *erga omnes* effects, ie, without the need to issue a binding guideline. But this thesis was not accepted by the plenum of the Court.

(including the legislative chamber of the federal district), state governors and the governor of the federal district, the Federal Procurator-General, the federal council of the Brazilian Bar Association, political parties with representatives in the National Congress, and nationwide confederations of trade unions or professional associations.[41]

According to Art 102, I, *a*, the STF has the power 'to try and to decide, as matters of original jurisdiction … direct actions of unconstitutionality of federal or state laws or normative acts'. On the one hand, this provision is clear when it limits the scope of an ADI to federal and state laws, thus excluding the constitutional review of municipal laws. Until 1999, the review of municipal laws could only take place within a concrete case in the diffuse judicial review. Since 1999, however, it has been possible to trigger the abstract and centralised review of municipal laws directly before the STF by means of an ADPF, which will be presented below.

On the other hand, Art 102, I, *a*, is not especially clear when it established that an ADI may be filed against other 'normative acts' that are neither federal nor state legislation. The case law of the STF on this subject, although sometimes difficult to grasp, may be summarised as follows: if a federal or state normative act is not a formally enacted law but nevertheless is abstract and general, it may be challenged before the STF by an ADI. This criterion allows the Court to review acts that are hierarchically below ordinary legislation, such as decrees, directives, resolutions, regulations. Provided that these acts are abstract and general and that they (supposedly) violate the Constitution directly, the Court may admit an ADI against them.[42] The other side of this criterion is that if a normative act is not general and abstract (at least in the eyes of the STF), an ADI that challenges its constitutionality will be rejected, even if this normative act is federal ordinary legislation;[43] this other side of the criterion developed by the Court is completely at odds with the wording of Art 102, I, *a*.

There are two further relevant issues regarding the admissibility of ADIs, which are not clearly regulated by the Constitution itself and the responses to which, provided by the STF during the early years of the 1988 Constitution, were of paramount importance for configuring the system of abstract judicial review of legislation in Brazil.

[41] The STF does not accept constitutional actions filed by confederations of trade unions or professional associations that do not fall within their professional scope. These entities must demonstrate what the Court calls 'thematic pertinence' (*pertinência temática*). See, for instance, ADI 1157 (1994), ADI 1873 (1998).

[42] See, for instance, ADI 482-MC (1991), ADI 8 (1996), ADI 3731-MC (2007), ADI 3664 (2011).

[43] See, for instance, ADI 643 (1991), ADI 842-MC (1993), ADI 1673-QO (1997).

One week after the promulgation of the Constitution, the ADI 2 was filed. In it, the National Federation of Private Schools argued for the unconstitutionality of two decrees that regulated tuition prices in private schools. Both decrees had been issued before the promulgation of the 1988 Constitution. The majority of the judges argued that there is a difference between the unconstitutionality of a piece of legislation and its non-reception by a new constitutional order. They argued that an act can only be unconstitutional in relation to the Constitution that was in force at the time the act was issued. In the words of the Court: 'Past law cannot be unconstitutional in relation to a supervening Constitution; nor could the legislature have violated a future Constitution. The ensuing Constitution does not make unconstitutional earlier laws that conflict with it: it revokes them'.[44] Since the aim of an ADI is to declare the unconstitutionality of a piece of legislation, the consequence of the divide established by the Court is that an ADI cannot be filed against any act (laws, decrees, among others) that was enacted before 5 October 1988.

A second relevant feature of the ADI that cannot be directly inferred from the wording of the Constitution is the possibility of using it to challenge the constitutionality of constitutional amendments.[45] The possibility of challenging the constitutionality of a constitutional amendment may seem odd at first sight. After all, if the aim of a constitutional amendment is to change the Constitution, asking if the two are compatible seems to be nonsense. However, since the Constitution protects some of its provisions against amendments (so-called bedrock clauses),[46] it may be argued that the idea of an unconstitutional constitutional amendment ceases to be odd, since a constitutional amendment that changes the provisions protected against changes could be considered unconstitutional. Still, the fact that there may be constitutional amendments that violate the eternal core of the Constitution says nothing about the question of 'who should protect this core?'.

For the STF, the answer to this question was very easy: the Court itself. In the first decision on this matter under the 1988 Constitution, the judge rapporteur opened his written opinion as follows: '*There is no doubt* that, in our constitutional system, this Court has the power

[44] ADI 2 (1992).

[45] In more precise terms, the issue is rather the power of the STF – irrespective of the type of action – to exercise judicial review of constitutional amendments, but since the ADI is the most important vehicle for triggering this review, it can be argued that it is also an important feature of this type of constitutional action.

[46] See ch 8.

to review the constitutionality … of a constitutional amendment challenged as violating explicit or implicit bedrock clauses'.[47] Although the decision on the merits – the anticipation of a plebiscite on the form and the system of government – was not unanimous, the power of the Court to review the constitutionality of a constitutional amendment was unanimously recognised and has been since then frequently exercised.[48]

An even more controversial power – which few or no other courts in the world likely enjoy – is the power that the STF granted to itself to block deliberation and voting on constitutional amendments in the houses of the National Congress, that is, the power to review the constitutionality of amendments before they are discussed and voted on. Although it is true that supreme or constitutional courts in many countries may exercise preventive judicial review, that is, examine the constitutionality of a piece of legislation before it is enacted, the aforementioned power of the STF to block deliberation and voting goes much further. It combines three highly charged features: (a) it is not judicial review of ordinary legislation but of constitutional amendments; (b) it does not aim at striking down an approved bill (promulgated or not) but at blocking free deliberation within the National Congress; and (c) it is not clearly provided for by the Constitution.

The STF justifies its self-attributed power to block deliberation and voting based on a very narrow textual interpretation of the wording of Art 60, § 4, which states that 'No proposal of [constitutional] amendment shall be admitted to consideration if it tends to abolish …'. According to the STF, the wording of this provision justifies stricter control, because the *approval* of a constitutional amendment that conflicts with the eternal clauses of the Constitution is not the only action that is forbidden: the National Congress could not *even consider and deliberate on* such a proposal.

It is true, however, that although the STF grants to itself this unique power, there seems to be no decision that has ever blocked deliberations

[47] ADI 833 (1993) [emphasis added]. Two years earlier, the STF decided ADI 466 (1991). This ADI was filed against a constitutional amendment proposal that had not been voted upon by the National Congress. The Court rejected the possibility of an abstract review against mere proposals of constitutional amendments (although it accepts it within the concrete judicial review; see below). Still, in his written opinion, the judge rapporteur stated that constitutional amendments may be reviewed by the STF.

[48] See ADI 939 (1994), ADI 1946 (2003), ADI 2356-MC (2011), ADI 4425 (2013), ADI 4357 (2013), ADI 4372 (2013), ADI 4400 (2013), ADI 4425 (2013), and ADI 5316-MC (2015). See Oscar Vilhena Vieira, 'Ambitious Constitutions: Prominent Courts' in Rosalind Dixon and Tom Ginsburg (eds), *Comparative Constitutional Law in Latin America* (Cheltenham, Edward Elgar, 2017) 263–65.

in Congress based on the argument presented above. Since the first case to address this issue,[49] every decision seems to follow the same pattern:[50] the Court first admits, in a provisional decision, the case for review and affirms its power to decide this type of issue; thereafter, it decides that a decision on the merits has become moot on formal grounds (for example, because the proposal of a constitutional amendment has already been rejected or approved by the National Congress).

Nevertheless, in 2013 certain judges of the Court attempted to push the boundaries of the power of the Court even further to stop deliberations in the National Congress. A writ of security was filed before the STF aiming to stop deliberation on an ordinary bill (ie, not a constitutional amendment proposal). According to the plaintiffs, the proposed bill conflicted with the eternal clauses of the Constitution. In a provisional, individual, and unparalleled decision, Judge Gilmar Mendes ordered the National Congress to stop deliberating on the bill and stated that the STF has the power to stop deliberations not only on proposals of constitutional amendments but also on ordinary bills that violate the eternal clauses of the Constitution.[51] Two months later, however, the plenum of the Court emphatically rejected the decision of Judge Mendes on the ground that his arguments were absolutely incompatible with both the Brazilian model of judicial review and the Court's own case law.[52]

B. Direct Action of Unconstitutionality for Omission (ADO)

Although constitutional claims usually aim to challenge the constitutionality of an existing piece of legislation, the Brazilian Constitution also provides for a specific action to challenge state inertia. The Constitution defines state inertia very broadly as the 'lack of a measure to make a constitutional provision effective'.[53] In this provision, 'measure' can mean at least two different things: a piece of legislation or a public policy. Even though public policies are based on enacted law, it is still possible to distinguish situations that require only the enactment of a piece of legislation from situations that demand the implementation of a more complex public policy.

[49] See MS 20575 (1980). This case was decided still under the 1969 Constitution.
[50] MS 21311 (1999), MS 24645 (2003), MS 23047 (2003), and MS 24609 (2003).
[51] See MS 32033-MC (2013).
[52] See MS 32033 (2013).
[53] Art 103, § 2.

The Constitution contains several provisions that explicitly mention future ordinary legislation as a condition for the exercise of fundamental rights. Art 37, VII, for instance, provides that public servants' right to strike 'shall be exercised in the manner and within the limits defined by specific law'; Art 7, XXI, establishes that workers have the right to 'advance notice of dismissal proportional to the length of service, of at least thirty days, as provided for by law'. If the National Congress does not pass the laws mentioned in these provisions, those rights cannot be fully exercised.

In contrast, several provisions do not mention any future legislation, but strongly depend on state actions to be effective nonetheless. Provisions granting socioeconomic rights are probably the best example. Art 6 of the Constitution simply states that 'education, health, food, work, housing, transportation, leisure, security, social welfare, protection of motherhood and childhood and assistance to the destitute, are social rights, as set forth by this Constitution'. Unlike Arts 7 and 37 mentioned above, Art 6 does not mention any future legislation whatsoever. However, the realisation of all those socioeconomic rights strongly depends on public policies in the fields of education, health, etc.

Even after three decades of the 1988 Constitution, several constitutional provisions still depend either on the enactment of a piece of legislation or on more effective public policies (or on both) to produce their sought-after effects. Against this background, one could expect the STF to be flooded with direct actions of unconstitutionality for omission. But this is not the case, and ADOs are rarely filed before the STF.[54]

One possible reason for this unexpectedly low number of filed ADOs may be the limited effects of decisions acknowledging legislative omissions. According to Art 103, § 2, whenever the STF declares that the 'lack of a measure' is unconstitutional, 'the appropriate branch shall be notified to adopt the necessary measures'. This means that a decision within an ADO has only one effect: the court ascertains an omission and notifies the appropriate branch (legislative or executive). The Court understands that it cannot compel the National Congress to legislate, for example, by stipulating deadlines. Moreover, a lack of compliance on the part of the Congress does not have any concrete consequences.[55]

[54] Between 2008 and 2017, 1810 ADI and only 44 ADO have been filed.

[55] It should be mentioned that at times the Court does stipulate deadlines. Still, a lack of compliance on the part of the Congress does not trigger any consequences. See, for instance, ADI 3682 (2007).

C. Declaratory Action of Constitutionality (ADC)

The declaratory action of constitutionality (ADC) was created in 1993 after a constitutional amendment (EC 3/1993). Its goal is exactly the opposite of that of the ADI, that is, instead of demanding a declaration of the unconstitutionality of a statute the plaintiff demands a declaration of its constitutionality.

Though this may seem to be a strange goal, since every enacted law is deemed constitutional unless a court decides otherwise, demanding a declaration of constitutionality may nonetheless make sense if one bears in mind that the Brazilian system of constitutional review of legislation has not only abstract and centralised but also concrete and diffuse elements. In this context, the ADC can be considered a tool for centralising the constitutional review of legislation. Since every judge in the country may refrain from enforcing a statute whenever she or he considers it incompatible with the Constitution, it may happen – and it frequently does – that a statute is enforced by some and not enforced by other judges throughout the country.

The introduction of the ADC into the Brazilian model of abstract constitutional review of legislation – the first constitutional claim with explicit binding effects – aimed at preventing the coexistence of contradictory decisions on the same constitutional controversy. Whenever decisions concerning the constitutionality of a given statute vary considerably throughout the country, an ADC aiming at the harmonisation and centralisation of this interpretation may be filed directly before the STF.

D. Allegation of Disobedience of Fundamental Precept (ADPF)

The allegation of disobedience of fundamental precept (ADPF) is the most recent constitutional claim in the Brazilian system of abstract constitutional review. It was created in 1999 by Federal Law 9882. The original wording of Art 102, single paragraph, of the Constitution established that an 'allegation of disobedience of a fundamental precept stemming from this Constitution shall be heard by the Supreme Court, as provided by law'.[56] Until 1999, it was not completely clear what this provision meant, let alone that it should be about an autonomous constitutional action. Since there was already a constitutional action aimed at

[56] This single paragraph was renumbered in 1993 and is now § 1 of Art 102.

challenging the compatibility of a piece of legislation with any provision of the Constitution (the ADI), it did not seem plausible to think of that provision as demanding the creation of further constitutional action for challenging the compatibility of a piece of legislation with only some provisions of the Constitution (the 'fundamental precepts').

The few scholars who did attempt to interpret that provision argued that something similar to the German *Verfassungsbeschwerde* could be created, that is, a constitutional complaint aimed at protecting individuals against the violation of one of their fundamental rights or other explicitly enumerated rights.[57] But this did not happen. The new constitutional action, called ADPF, was essentially a copy of the existing ADI. Even the persons and institutions who have standing to bring an ADPF before the STF are the same as those who have standing to bring an ADI.[58]

It is not an easy task to distinguish the scope of the ADPF from that of the ADI. According to Art 1 of Federal Law 9882, the aim of the ADPF is to avoid or redress harm to fundamental precepts of the Constitution. However, neither the Constitution nor Federal Law 9882 provides any definition of 'fundamental precept'. The STF itself does not have a clear-cut definition of 'fundamental precept' either. The minimum core of this concept surely encompasses the provisions of Heading II of the Constitution, called 'fundamental rights and guarantees'. The provisions of Heading I (Fundamental Principles) and provisions that are protected against constitutional amendments[59] are also considered by the court (though not unanimously) as fundamental precepts. Usually, the court defines fundamental precepts in terms that are as broad and vague as the expression 'fundamental precepts' itself, for instance, when it defines it as 'the basic norms of the constitution'.[60]

Notwithstanding the vagueness of the expression 'fundamental precept', the decision about whether to file an ADI or an ADPF frequently flows from a relatively concrete and pragmatic criterion, based on the few differences between both actions. As a general rule, the ADI is the action par excellence for triggering the abstract constitutional review

[57] See, for instance, José Afonso da Silva, *Curso de direito constitucional positive*, 8th edn (São Paulo, Malheiros, 1992) 487–88.

[58] It is necessary to stress, however, that the bill approved by the National Congress in 1999 did provide that every person should have standing to file an ADPF before the STF (Art 2, II of the approved bill), but the President of the Republic vetoed it, arguing that the Court would be flooded with complaints.

[59] See ch 8.

[60] ADPF 33 (2003).

of legislation before the STF, primarily because there is no substantial limitation of its scope. In other words, a law's incompatibility with even the least fundamental provision of the Constitution (irrespective of how fundamentality is defined) can be a reason to file an ADI (but not an ADPF). However, in some situations an ADPF is the only possibility for triggering the abstract control of legislation before the STF: if the law at stake is either municipal law or older than the Constitution.

In the first case, the Constitution does not include municipal laws in the scope of ADIs. In the second case, as mentioned above, although the Constitution does not have any provision on the matter, the STF decided shortly after the promulgation of the 1988 Constitution that it cannot review the constitutionality of laws that were enacted before the Constitution came into force.[61]

The statute that regulates the ADPF procedure explicitly allows for the use of this action to challenge both municipal law and laws that were enacted before the promulgation of the Constitution (Federal Law 9882, Art 1, single paragraph, I). In a nutshell, since 1999 municipal laws and statutes enacted before the promulgation of the Constitution may be challenged before the STF, but only if they violate a fundamental precept of the Constitution.

E. Effects of the STF Decisions

In 1988 the binding effects of the decisions of the STF in cases involving constitutional review of legislation were rather weak; in the following decades these binding effects were gradually and considerably strengthened. The first move in this direction was the creation of the ADC by the EC 3/1993. Six years later, the previously mentioned statutes defining the procedure of abstract constitutional review of legislation before the STF made the binding effects even more explicit. Art 28 of Federal Law 9868 states that 'the declaration of constitutionality or unconstitutionality, including the interpretation according to the Constitution and the partial declaration of unconstitutionality without wording change, shall have *erga omnes* effects that shall be binding with respect to the organs of the judiciary and to the federal, state and local public administration'.[62] In 2004, the Constitution was amended and a similar

[61] See ADI 2 (1992).

[62] Art 10, § 3, of Federal Law 9882 is similar, though more concise: 'The decision shall have erga omnes effects and shall be binding with respect to the other organs of the Public Power'.

paragraph was added to Art 102 (§ 2): 'Final decisions on the merits pronounced by the Supreme Court within direct actions of unconstitutionality and declaratory actions of constitutionality shall have *erga omnes* effects that shall be binding with respect to the rest of the judiciary and the federal, state and municipal public administration, both direct and indirect'.[63] These provisions introduce the concepts of *erga omnes* and binding effects. Although they are similar, their scope is different.

i. Erga Omnes Effects

Erga omnes effects are the opposite of *inter partes* effects. Judicial decisions usually have *inter partes* effects, that is, they affect only the parties to the case. Different judicial systems have different ways of extending the effects of a judicial decision to future decisions. Binding precedents and *stare decisis* are two of the most common strategies, especially in common law countries. In civil law countries, however, the existence of binding precedents, if not rejected, is frequently a controversial issue. Until 1965, the judicial review of legislation in Brazil had been diffuse and occurred within concrete cases and controversies; for that reason, declarations of unconstitutionality affected only the parties to the case. Even after the introduction of the abstract review in 1965, the extension of the effects of an STF decision declaring a statute unconstitutional in the abstract was not a settled matter, and the Court continued to send its decisions to the Federal Senate to suspend its enforcement, as it had always done before in the context of concrete review of legislation. In other words, even after the introduction of the abstract review of legislation the STF was unsure whether its decision had *erga omnes* or only *inter partes* effects. Even though this self-doubt was mitigated over the years, a clear provision stating that (at least some of the) court's decisions have *erga omnes* effects came only in 1993, with the creation of the ADC (declaratory action of constitutionality). And – interestingly – the introduction of *erga omnes* effects, although unambiguous, concerned only decisions within an ADC but not within an ADI, the most important constitutional action. As already mentioned, only in 1999 and 2004, by means of two federal laws and a constitutional amendment, were the *erga omnes* effects extended to all actions involving abstract review.

[63] A similar provision had already been added to the Constitution by the EC 3/1993, but its scope was limited to the ADC.

ii. Binding Effects

The idea of binding effects does not directly relate to the contrast between *inter partes* and *erga omnes* effects, but to the question of which authorities are bound by the STF decisions. Art 102, § 2, states that STF decisions within the constitutional review of legislation bind 'the rest of the judiciary and the federal, state and municipal public administration, both direct and indirect'. Therefore, two authorities are not bound by the STF decisions within the constitutional review of legislation: the STF itself and the legislature. The reason for this is straightforward: if they were bound by those decisions, it would be impossible to change the status quo whenever the STF strikes down a piece of legislation. If the legislature could not pass a piece of legislation with the same or similar content as a statute that had already been declared unconstitutional by the Court in the past, this past decision would necessarily hold forever, even if the context (political, social, cultural and economic) completely changes. Suppose that in the distant past the STF declared unconstitutional a law granting equal rights to women and men. If the legislature could not pass a law with the same content, this unequal status quo would be maintained forever (since the STF itself could not change it, because, once the statute is declared unconstitutional, it is expelled from the legal system, and not even the Court could resurrect it).

iii. Complaints

As much as the STF decisions are binding, it is not possible to prevent other authorities from disobeying them. A lower court may *de facto* refrain from enforcing a statute it deems unconstitutional, even if the STF had already declared it constitutional; the public administration may also attempt to do the same. Against this type of non-compliance, Art 102, I, *l*, of the Constitution (along with the Code of Civil Procedure and the RISTF) provides for an action called 'complaint' (*reclamação*) 'to preserve its jurisdiction and to guarantee the authority of its decisions'.

Complaints are not decided by the plenum, but by one of the panels. In general terms, a complaint is a fast track aiming to suspend an administrative act or judicial decision that does not comply with an STF decision. However, in view of what has been explained above, if the legislature passes a statute that is identical (or similar) to a statute already declared unconstitutional by the Court, it is not possible to challenge it by means of a complaint. In this case, no fast track is available and it is necessary to file an action of unconstitutionality (and the reasoning underlying it cannot be 'the legislature disobeyed the court' but rather 'the statute – like the previous one – is unconstitutional').[64]

iv. Modulation of Effects

As a general rule, whenever the STF strikes down a piece of legislation within the abstract judicial review, this decision is retroactive to the moment the law was enacted (so-called *ex tunc* effects). Until 1999, the case law of the STF was settled concerning these retroactive effects: an unconstitutional piece of legislation had always been considered null and void. But the Court itself had already realised that in many situations it is impossible to completely annul the effects that a law had produced before it was declared unconstitutional. Furthermore, in many situations it may not even be convenient to do so.[65]

Based on this assumption, Federal Law 9868/1999 introduced the possibility of what is known in Brazil as the 'modulation of effects' (*modulação de efeitos*). According to its Art 27, whenever the STF declares the unconstitutionality of a piece of legislation, if there are reasons related to legal certainty or exceptional social interest, it may, by the vote of two-thirds of the judges, rule that the effects of its decision shall not be retroactive and will be effective only from the moment of the decision (*ex nunc*) or even from a different moment that the Court may establish. The constitutional literature usually calls this last possibility *pro futuro* effects. This is not quite accurate, however. Although it seems plausible to suppose that if the decision will not be retroactive to the moment of the enactment of the law nor it will be effective at the moment of the decision itself, this means that the decision will have prospective effects (hence, *pro futuro*). However, at least theoretically, the Court may define any moment whatsoever, that is, not necessarily in the future, but also in the past.

v. Reinstatement

As a general rule, a piece of legislation that is repealed by an ensuing statute is not reinstated if the latter is eventually also repealed.[66] However, if

[64] See ADI 864 (1993) and ADI 907-MC (1993).

[65] See, for instance, RE 78549 (1974), 78209 (1974), 78533 (1981).

[66] See Art 2, § 3, of the Decree-Law 4657/1942, also called the Introductory Act to Brazilian Law (*Lei de Introdução às Normas do Direito Brasileiro*).

the STF declares a statute null and void, and if this statute had repealed a previous statute on the same matter, then the previous statute is automatically reinstated.[67]

However, because the Court may establish a different moment from which the declaration of unconstitutionality should be considered effective, it may be argued that if this happens, there cannot be a reinstatement of the former statute. Since the reinstatement had always been based on the assumption that the declaration of a statute's unconstitutionality is retroactive to the date of its enactment (as if the unconstitutional statute had never had any effect at all), if the Court set a different moment for its decision to be effective, this assumption collapses, as does the reinstatement effect.

vi. Partial Unconstitutionality without Text Changing

Declaring a legal provision incompatible with the Constitution usually implies that this provision is null and void, even though sometimes the STF may decide that the effects of the declaration of unconstitutionality will not be retroactive, being effective only from the moment of the decision or from a different moment that the Court may establish. A further exception to the 'null and void' rule is the so-called declaration of partial unconstitutionality without text changing. In some circumstances, the Court may decide that although a legal provision is not facially incompatible with the Constitution, its enforcement in some contexts may be unconstitutional. Based on this rationale, the Court declares that the provision is only partially unconstitutional. This declaration does not affect the wording or the validity of the provision, which remained unaltered, but it blocks future enforcement of the provisions in those cases that fall within the scope of the decision. In other words, even if those cases could be subsumed into the wording of the legal provision, this subsumption shall not occur because of the blocking effect of the Court's decision.[68]

F. Participants in the Process of Abstract Review of Legislation

The process of abstract review of legislation involves participants other than the STF itself and those persons and institutions who have brought

[67] See ADI 2215-MC (2001), ADI 2867 (2003), ADI 3148 (2006).

[68] In the case law of the STF, see, for instance, ADI 491-MC (1991), ADI 4426 (2011), RE 580963 (2013), ADI 4425 (2013), ADI 4650 (2015), ADI 3278 (2016).

a constitutional action before the Court. Some of these additional participants necessarily take part in every action, whereas others do not. In the next subsections, both groups will be presented.

i. The Advocate-General of the Union and the Federal Procurator-General

After a file is lodged, the rapporteur first demands information from the authority that issued the act whose constitutionality is being challenged (most frequently the National Congress). Subsequently, she or he hears both the Advocate-General of the Union and the Federal Procurator-General. The Constitution is quite clear about each one's role: 'the Advocate-General of the Union … shall defend the impugned act or text' and 'the Federal Procurator-General shall be previously heard'.[69]

According to the wording of these provisions, while the first *shall defend* the piece of legislation challenged before the Court, the latter shall only *be heard*, that is, give his or her opinion on the constitutionality or unconstitutionality of the act challenged before the Court. Nevertheless, there is some controversy about the role of the Advocate-General of the Union. This controversy stems from the fact that the Advocate-General may be convinced that the piece of legislation is unconstitutional and in this case, it would be odd to be compelled to defend its constitutionality.

On the one hand, the STF frequently stresses that the Advocate-General must defend the constitutionality of every act challenged before the Court irrespective of her or his opinion;[70] on the other hand, the Court also understands that the Advocate-General of the Union is not compelled to defend the constitutionality of a claim if the 'Court has already established an understanding on its unconstitutionality'.[71]

Moreover, since the duty of defending the constitutionality of acts challenged before the Court includes legislation enacted by the states,[72] it may be that the Advocate-General of the Union must defend the constitutionality of state law even if it is contrary to the interests of the Union itself. The STF, however, seems insensitive to these issues.

[69] See, respectively, Art 103, § 3 and § 1.

[70] See, for instance, ADI 72-QO (1990), ADI 242 (1994), ADI 1254-AgR (1996), ADI 3413 (2011) and ADI 4983 (2016).

[71] See ADI 1616 (2001) and ADI 3916 (2010).

[72] See ADI 1254-AgR (1996).

ii. Amicus Curiae and Public Hearings

The settled case law of the STF has always opposed the intervention of third parties[73] and the following rule was eventually laid down by Art 7 of Federal Law 9868/1999: 'No intervention of third parties will be admitted in the direct action of unconstitutionality'. The same law, however, admits some important exceptions and opens the abstract judicial review of legislation for stakeholders in civil society that are not formally considered parties to the process.

Art 7, § 2, of this statute provides that the judge rapporteur, 'taking into account the relevance of the case and the representativeness of the applicants', may permit the participation of other stakeholders. Although Federal Law 9868/1999 does not explicitly mention *amici curiae*, this provision was the basis for allowing for their participation in constitutional actions in Brazil. Furthermore, although it only refers to the ADI (and, indirectly, to the ADO),[74] the STF has frequently accepted the intervention of *amici curiae* in other types of constitutional actions as well.[75] Currently, the 2015 Code of Civil Procedure has a section explicitly dedicated to the participation of *amici curiae* in all types of actions.[76]

A second innovation introduced by Federal Law 9868/1999 is the possibility of summoning so-called public hearings. Art 9, § 1, establishes that if there is a need to clarify matters or facts, the judge rapporteur 'may request additional information, appoint an expert or expert commission to issue an advisory opinion on the matter, or set a date for public hearings of persons with experience and authority in the matter'.[77]

The first public hearing in the STF took place in 2007. It related to the ADI 3510, in which the constitutionality of the Biosafety Act – and more specifically, the constitutionality of research on embryonic stem cells – was being challenged. Since that time, several public hearings have been held on such varied topics as the right to health, the abortion of an anencephalic foetus, religious education in public schools, affirmative action in universities, a ban on asbestos, campaign financing, the use of end-to-end encryption in messaging applications and criminal investigations, among many others.

[73] See, for instance, ADI 1286-AgR (1995) and ADI 1434-MC (1996).

[74] Because Art 12-E of the same Federal Law 9868/1999 stipulates that whenever possible the procedure of the ADO follows the rules that are applicable for the ADI.

[75] See ADC 18 (2007), ADC 14 (2008) and ADC 24 (2010); ADPF 187 (2011); RE 595964 (2010) and RE 597165 (2011).

[76] See Code of Civil Procedure, Art 138.

[77] See also Federal Law 9882/1999, Art 6, § 1.

It is not an easy task to assess the impact of both *amici curiae* and public hearings on the decision-making process of the STF. Opening this process to the participation of stakeholders whose opinion would otherwise not be heard is undoubtedly a positive step. Still, some objections are worth mentioning. In its decisions, the Court only rarely explicitly mentions documents submitted by *amici curiae* or testimony given during public hearings. This does not mean, of course, that neither these documents nor this testimony has an impact on the decision-making process of the Court, nor does it mean that the simple participation of these stakeholders cannot have a positive impact outside the Court. Still, at least in the case of public hearings, it can be argued that the manner in which they are organised considerably limits its potential impact, because: (a) specialists are chosen by the judge rapporteur alone (although sometimes there is a call for applications); (b) hearings are usually a simple sequence of brief individual statements (usually 15 minutes), with no room for discussion either among the experts or among the experts and the judges; and most importantly, (c) with the exception of the judge rapporteur who summoned the public hearing, the other judges of the Court rarely participate.

Even though the effects of both the participation of *amici curiae* and the realisation of public hearings are still not clear, one thing is beyond doubt: the STF is well aware that irrespective of measurable effects, its legitimacy vis-à-vis the civil society can be boosted by the simple fact that *amici curiae* are allowed and public hearings are summoned. The Court frequently stresses the importance of the participation of *amici curiae* because it 'makes the constitutional debate more plural and … settles … the undesirable "deficit" of legitimacy of the decisions of the Supreme Court in the exercise of constitutional review of legislation'.[78] The Court's self-praise concerning the public hearings is even more explicit. In ADI 3510 (research on embryonic stem cells), the emphasis on the importance of the public hearing was much more frequent than the reference to concrete arguments presented by the participants.[79] The Court's web page does this with pomp and circumstance: 'April 20, 2007. The date entered the history of the Supreme Federal Court for on this day the Brazilian people got an active voice in the most controversial decisions of the Supreme Court, through the

[78] ADI 5022-MC (2013).

[79] For similar findings concerning other public hearings, see Thiago Luis Sombra, 'Why Should Public Hearings in the Brazilian Supreme Court Be Understood as an Innovative Democratic Tool in Constitutional Adjudication?' (2016) 17 *German Law Journal* 657.

realisation of public hearings'.[80] In a nutshell, at least for the STF, public hearings and *amici curiae* 'turn the Court into a *democratic space* ... with wide repercussion on the civil society and on the democratic institutions'.[81]

VI. AN ACTIVIST COURT?

The STF has been frequently portrayed as a very activist court. Yet, as is typical whenever expressions such as 'activist court' or 'judicial activism' are employed, neither the meaning nor the consequences of these terms are always clear. A precise diagnosis is frequently blurred by the fact that there is no consensus on what these expressions mean, let alone if this or that court should be classified as activist or not.

There are at least two widely used concepts of activism. The problem is not only that they are based on completely different premises but also that they demand different approaches to assess whether or not a court should be considered activist.

The first concept is based on an interpretive issue and is used above all by legal scholars. According to that concept, judicial activism denotes a divergence between the content of judicial decisions and the meaning of the constitutional text. In this sense, a court is activist when its decisions are (at least to a certain extent) not fully ascribable to a sound interpretation of the Constitution. The reasons for this divergence may be manifold. An example of this approach is Benvindo's assessment of the praxis of the STF. According to him, the Court 'moved ... from stagnation to activism, understood as the replacement of law by the judge's subjective judgments'.[82]

It is easy to realise that this understanding of activism is based on several open-ended concepts, the most important being the assumption that it is always possible to differentiate between a sound and an unsound interpretation of the Constitution or between 'the law' and 'the judge's subjective judgments'. It is interesting to note that political scientists frequently assume a similar divide – without reference to 'judicial activism' – when they contrast the legal model on the one hand to strategic and attitudinal models on the other hand.

[80] See http://www.stf.jus.br/portal/cms/verNoticiaDetalhe.asp?idConteudo=124643.
[81] ADI 3510 (2008), emphasis in original.
[82] Juliano Zaiden Benvindo, *On the Limits of Constitutional Adjudication: Deconstructing Balancing and Judicial Activism* (Heidelberg, Springer, 2010) 94.

The second concept of judicial activism is based on institutional, not interpretive considerations. It has a clear link to the idea of separation of powers. In this sense, a court is activist when it frequently contests the decisions of the political powers. One example of this approach is Oliveira's assumption that 'when the Supreme Court declares a law or act unconstitutional, it is acting in an activist direction. This is because the court is taking an active role in the exercise of constitutional control of the legislation'.[83]

Assessing a court's profile based on this latter concept of activism is an empirical, not an interpretive matter. Although the precise boundary between activism and non-activism may be controversial in a quantitative sense (ie, how many single activist decisions are necessary to define a court as activist), the classification of single decisions as activist or non-activist (or restrained) is uncontroversial.

In Brazil (and elsewhere), whenever the Court is depicted as activist, the issue of which of these concepts of activism provide the basis for this assessment is seldom clear. This sloppy use of the concept of activism has led some authors to avoid it altogether. As Mendes puts it, 'The diagnosis of activism itself, rather than being based on a comprehensive analysis, remains conceptually hasty and empirically impressionistic, if not myopic'.[84] Mendes argues further that the diagnosis of activism of the STF is 'inspired by an outdated conception of the separation of powers and by a vulgar text-based approach to constitutional interpretation'.[85] His assessment also identifies the quantitative issue mentioned above that is common to both concepts of activism irrespective of how well or poorly defined they are: how many single activist decisions are necessary to classify a court as activist? According to him, the diagnosis of activism is 'based on a handful of intrusive decisions that the court has indeed taken', and 'is still far from taking full account of the immense docket of the court'.[86] This leads Mendes to argue that the STF may be much more passive than generally assumed because the Court frequently procrastinates to avoid controversial decisions, that is, it often decides not to decide: 'Underneath the vocal activism, there seems to lie a deliberately

[83] Fabiana Luci Oliveira, 'Justice, Professionalism, and Politics in the Exercise of Judicial Review by Brazil's Supreme Court' (2008) 2 *Brazilian Political Science Review* 93, 99.

[84] Conrado Hübner Mendes, 'The Supreme Federal Tribunal of Brazil' in András Jakab and others (eds), *Comparative Constitutional Reasoning* (Cambridge, Cambridge University Press, 2017) 116.

[85] ibid 117.

[86] ibid.

disguised and selective passivism, yet to be duly acknowledged, quantified and appraised'.[87]

Although Mendes' diagnosis is largely accurate, rejecting the activist label for the STF may not be an inevitable consequence. A third concept of activism, coupled with a more detailed definition of some terms used in both concepts presented above, may offer a more accurate picture of the STF.

The third concept uses elements of the two concepts presented above. However, it is neither a mixture nor a middle ground or compromise between them. On the one hand, it is based on an interpretive matter; on the other hand, it has strong institutional implications. According to this concept, activism implies exercising powers that are not clearly granted to the judiciary. The interpretive dimension stems from the fact that attribution of powers is a matter of interpretation. The institutional dimension is related to the assumption that if power is a limited resource, the more it is assigned to one institution, the less its rivals get. The implications for the separation of powers are evident.

The advantages of this concept are clear. First, it avoids the quantitative issue, since what is at stake is not how often a given court uses this or that power, but rather that the court has them at its disposal. Secondly, it also avoids the unsound assumption that judicial decisions should count as activists whenever they strike down legislation. The power to strike down legislation is clearly granted to the STF by the Constitution. Exercising it therefore cannot be considered activism, at least not without further arguments. Thus, a court whose decisions are 30 per cent against the government's interests is not necessarily more activist than a court that decides only 10 per cent against the government's interests.

The STF has assigned to itself, without any constitutional provision that could clearly justify doing so, at least the following powers: (a) to exercise judicial review of constitutional amendments;[88] (b) to block deliberations in Congress in the cases of constitutional amendment proposals; (c) to have a final say in the appointment of political positions such as state ministers; (d) to keep individual and provisional decisions of its judges in force for long periods of time – sometimes reaching a point of no return – even in those cases in which a decision *en banc* would have been necessary; (e) to restrict the standing for filing

[87] ibid 118.

[88] It is interesting to note that this self-attributed power led Mendes to argue in an older text that the STF has gone perhaps too far in its activism. See Conrado Hübner Mendes, 'Judicial Review of Constitutional Amendments in the Brazilian Supreme Court' (2005) 17 *Fla J Int'l L* 449.

constitutional actions; (f) to disregard parliamentary immunities whenever the public opinion seems to demand it; and even (g) to decide not to decide whenever it prefers not to decide.

A passive or restrained court could never have granted these (and possibly other) powers to itself. Furthermore, it would not be amiss to re-emphasise that this is not a quantitative issue. It does not really matter whether the case law of the Court is wholly or substantially marked by the use of these powers (it should even be stressed that the STF used some of them only once or twice). What is important is that the Court has them at its disposal, uses them at least from time to time, especially in pivotal moments,[89] and, also very importantly, may expect a high degree of compliance with decisions based on them. Hence, contrary to what Mendes argues, it is not necessary to take a full account of the immense docket of the Court to call it an activist court. Nor is this label simply based on a handful of intrusive decisions. The (maybe much more than a) handful of intrusive decisions – many of which are referred to throughout this book – only reinforce this label, but are not essential for justifying it.

VII. FUNCTIONS ESSENTIAL TO JUSTICE

In the heading dedicated to the separation of powers (Heading IV, *Organização dos Poderes*), there are not only three, but four chapters. In addition to the chapters dedicated to the legislative, executive and judiciary branches, there is a fourth chapter titled 'Functions Essential to Justice'. This chapter is divided into four sections dedicated to the Public Ministry, public advocacy, the legal profession, and the Public Defender's Office.

In this book, the analysis of these functions in the chapter dedicated to the judiciary follows merely pragmatic considerations: these functions are often related to judicial activity. But none of them is part of the judiciary. If a formal classification were necessary, it should be argued they are in many aspects linked to the executive branch, with the exception of the legal profession, which is not involved in a state activity.

[89] As Judge Roberto Barroso puts it, with not too modest words: 'supreme courts occasionally play the role of an enlightened vanguard, in charge of pushing History forward when it stalls' (Luís Roberto Barroso, 'Reason Without Vote: The Representative and Majoritarian Function of Constitutional Courts' in Thomas Bustamante and Bernardo Gonçalves Fernandes (eds), *Democratizing Constitutional Law* (Cham, Springer, 2016)).

A. Public Ministry

The Public Ministry (*Ministério Público*) is one of the most powerful state agencies in Brazil.[90] Its name has frequently been translated as 'Public Prosecutor's Office', but this term is not quite accurate because it is usually associated with criminal prosecution and criminal justice. Although criminal prosecution is an important task of the members of the Public Ministry, it is not the only one and, in some contexts, it is not even the most important one.

According to Art 127, the Public Ministry is 'a permanent institution, essential to the jurisdictional function, with responsibility for defending the legal order, the democratic regime and the inalienable social and individual interests'. Similar to the organisation of the justice system, there are also federal and state public ministries (one in each state); additionally, and also similar to the organisation of the justice system, there are specialised divisions: the Constitution mentions the labour and military public ministries. Furthermore, there is an electoral division of the federal and the state public ministries, although these are not autonomous institutions such as the labour and military public ministries.

Art 129 defines a wide array of powers and duties of the Public Ministry, such as the power to present constitutional actions aiming at initiating judicial control of legislation before the STF, to defend the rights and interests of indigenous populations in courts and to bring public criminal prosecutions before the judiciary. In addition to the clear-cut duties and powers established by the Constitution, the Public Ministry has frequently taken advantage of some very general provisions to enlarge its powers even more. Art 129, II, for instance, states that it is the duty of the Public Ministry 'to ensure effective respect … for the rights guaranteed by this Constitution, taking the necessary action to protect them', while Art 129, IX, allows that other functions may be granted to the Public Ministry whenever they are compatible with its institutional purposes.

The Public Ministry enjoys a functional and budgetary autonomy that is similar to that of the judiciary branch. Additionally, its independence is further strengthened by personal guarantees that are also similar to those enjoyed by judges. Members of the Public Ministry have life

[90] See Maria Tereza Sadek and Rosângela Batista Cavalcanti, 'The New Brazilian Public Prosecution: an agent of accountability' in Scott Mainwaring and Christopher Welna (eds), *Democratic Accountability in Latin America* (Oxford, Oxford University Press, 2003).

tenure (with compulsory retirement at age 75), cannot be transferred to other functions, positions or places without their consent, and cannot have their compensation reduced.

B. Advocacy-General of the Union

The section called 'Public Advocacy' is mainly dedicated to defining the organisation, duties and powers of the Advocacy-General of the Union (AGU, *Advocacia Geral da União*). The head of the Advocacy-General of the Union is the Advocate-General of the Union, who is freely appointed and may be freely dismissed by the President of the Republic. According to Art 131, the Advocacy-General of the Union has two main functions: to legally represent the Union judicially or extra-judicially and to assist and advise the federal executive branch.

Within the scope of this book, one of the most important tasks of the Advocacy-General of the Union was presented above: whenever the constitutionality of a normative act is challenged before the STF, the Advocate-General of the Union shall defend its constitutionality.

C. Public Defender's Office

The Public Defender's Office (*Defensoria Pública*) was created by the 1988 Constitution with the duty to provide judicial and extrajudicial legal assistance to those who cannot afford legal representation. The Constitution emphasises the close link between the legal assistance that shall be provided by the Public Defender's Office and both democracy and the promotion of individual and collective fundamental rights. Indeed, the Public Defender's Offices – at the levels of both the Union and the states – have proven to be of central importance for widening access to justice in Brazil. The persistent inequality in access to justice and problems in the enforcement of the rules of due process,[91] which among other things have led to mass incarceration of the socially disadvantaged (and especially of the poor and blacks) and to a prison system in which almost 40 per cent of the prisoners are pre-trial detainees (many without concrete reasons to remain in prison) would probably be even worse had it not been for the efforts of the Public Defender's Offices to make access to justice more equal.

[91] See ch 5.

Although Art 134 grants to the Public Defender's Offices 'functional and administrative autonomy and the power to initiate their budget proposal', their autonomy and budget are still not comparable to those of other institutions such as the Public Ministry or the Advocacy-General of the Union. The mission of the Public Defender's Offices is still not considered as essential as that of these institutions. Unsurprisingly, although the Constitution provides for the creation of Public Defender's Offices in the states, in some of them – such as Santa Catarina – this took almost 25 years to happen.[92]

D. Legal Profession

As one of the most powerful professional associations in Brazil, the Brazilian Bar Association (OAB, *Ordem dos Advogados do Brasil*) was an important and influential player during the Constituent Assembly of 1987–88. Moreover, many members of the Assembly were lawyers. As a result, the Constitution grants powers both to the Bar and to lawyers that are seldom (if ever) found in other constitutions. Some of them have already been mentioned: the Brazilian Bar Association has unrestricted standing to bring constitutional actions before the STF, two lawyers appointed by the Bar have seats on the National Council of Justice, and 10 per cent of the seats of federal regional courts and state appellate courts shall be occupied by lawyers.[93] Additionally, two lawyers, also appointed by the Bar, sit on the National Council of Public Ministry, and the Brazilian Bar Association participates in all public examinations for the selection of judges in every court in Brazil, along with the selection of new members of the Public Ministry and public advocacy institutions in all states.[94]

The fact that the Constitution has an article dedicated to the legal profession is a further example of the power of the Brazilian Bar Association. According to Art 133, 'lawyers are indispensable to the administration of justice and they are immune for their acts and manifestations in the practice of their profession, within the limits of the law'. It is not the aim of this section to provide a detailed analysis of

[92] For an analysis of the institutionalisation of the Public Defender's Offices in the states, see Lígia Mori Madeira, 'Institutionalisation, Reform and Independence of the Public Defender's Office in Brazil' (2014) 8 *Brazilian Political Science Review* 48.

[93] See, respectively, Art 103, VII, Art 103-B, XII, and Art 94.

[94] See, respectively, Art 130-A, V, Art 93, I, Art 129, § 3, and Art 132.

the implications of this provision, particularly the idea that 'lawyers are indispensable to the administration of justice', which has been the source of several controversies since 1988. The law that regulates the legal profession in Brazil is largely based on a very expansive interpretation of this idea, and several of its provisions have been declared unconstitutional by the STF.[95]

FURTHER READING

Arguelhes DW and Ribeiro LM, '"The Court, it is I"? Individual Judicial Powers in the Brazilian Supreme Court and their Implications for Constitutional Theory' (2018) 7 *Global Constitutionalism* 236

Brinks DM, '"Faithful Servants of the Regime": The Brazilian Constitutional Court's Role under the 1988 Constitution' in G Helmke and J Ríos-Figueroa (eds), *Courts in Latin America* (Cambridge, Cambridge University Press, 2014)

Kapiszewski D, 'How Courts Work: Institutions, Culture, and the Brazilian Supremo Tribunal Federal' in JA Couso, A Huneeus, and R Sieder (eds), *Cultures of Legality* (Cambridge, Cambridge University Press, 2010)

Mendes CH, 'The Supreme Federal Tribunal of Brazil' in A Jakab, A Dyevre, and G Itzcovich (eds), *Comparative Constitutional Reasoning* (Cambridge, Cambridge University Press, 2017)

da Silva VA, 'Deciding Without Deliberating' (2013) 11 *International Journal of Constitutional Law* 557

Taylor MM, *Judging Policy: Courts and Policy Reform in Democratic Brazil* (Stanford, Stanford University Press, 2008)

[95] See Federal Law 8906/1994. See also ADI 1105 (2006) and ADI 1127 (2006).

5

Rights: Enforcing Civil Liberties in an Unequal Society

Bill of Rights – Horizontal Effects – Right to Life – Equality – Freedom of Expression – Right to Privacy – Freedom of Religion – Due Process – Nationality – Political Rights – Political Parties – The Inter-American Human Rights System – Constitutional Remedies

BRAZIL ADOPTED A constitution with a Bill of Rights quite early. The 1824 Constitution had a comprehensive list of fundamental rights in the 35 clauses of its Art 179. As is widely known, however, declaration of rights does not necessarily imply realisation of rights. It has been argued before, and it will be argued several times in this chapter, that constitutional text and constitutional reality have diverged considerably in Brazil's history.

The Bill of Rights of Brazil's 1988 Constitution is quite lengthy. The list of topics it covers includes civil liberties (such as freedom of expression, freedom of association, freedom of the press, equality before the law, right to life), political rights (right to vote, freedom of party affiliation), and social rights (right to health, education, housing, food, social assistance), among others.

The main challenge in this realm is to decrease the gap between constitutional text and constitutional practice. In recent decades, much has been done. The promulgation of the 1988 Constitution was without any doubt a moment of inflexion. Still, provisions that protect the right to life, the right to security, freedom of the press, and equality before the law coexist with high rates of criminality and homicides, violence against journalists in some regions of the country, racism, violence against women, a regressive tax system, and a persistent difference in treatment between rich and poor in their access to public services and institutions.

I. THE BILL OF RIGHTS OF THE 1988 CONSTITUTION

Unlike the constitutions of many countries, whose Bill of Rights encompasses many articles, from a strictly formal point of view, the Brazilian constitutional tradition is that provisions concerning fundamental rights are part of only one article.[1] In the 1988 Constitution, this article is Art 5. All freedom rights (and even others) are provided for in the various (and numerous) clauses of this article. However, since the Bill of Rights of the 1988 Constitution also includes other categories of rights, such as socioeconomic rights, workers' rights, and political rights, among others, the Bill of Rights is slightly longer than in past Brazilian constitutions. If we consider that all the rights guaranteed in Heading II (Fundamental Rights and Guarantees) are fundamental rights and therefore are part of the Bill of Rights, then the Constitution entails a Bill of Rights which is structured into five chapters, all belonging to Heading II: Chapter I, individual and collective rights and duties; Chapter II, social rights; Chapter III, nationality; Chapter IV, political rights; and Chapter V, political parties.

II. HOLDERS OF FUNDAMENTAL RIGHTS

Fundamental rights are generally seen as universal rights. Not necessarily in a geographical sense, that is, valid and enforceable regardless of national borders – which is a debate that will not be addressed here – but in a personal sense, that is, fundamental rights are rights that everyone has. They are 'everyone's rights'. Nevertheless, there are fundamental rights that only individuals belonging to a particular group can exercise. In the Brazilian context, the rights in Arts 7 to 11 are rights that only workers can exercise. The case of political rights is similar: only Brazilian (in some cases, only Brazilian-born) citizens may exercise them.

However, the rights guaranteed by Art 5, especially those provided in the head of this article, are usually considered universal, 'everyone rights': life, liberty, equality, security and property are not the rights of one group, but of everyone. Still, the head of Art 5 employs an ambiguous

[1] See 1824 Constitution, Art 179; 1891 Constitution, Art 72; 1934 Constitution, Art 113; 1937 Constitution, Art 122; 1946 Constitution, Art 141; 1967 Constitution, Art 150; 1969 Constitution, Art 153.

expression, which if interpreted strictly makes fundamental rights less universal. Art 5 guarantees the inviolability of the rights to life, liberty, equality, security and property to Brazilians and foreigners *residing in Brazil*. This expression clearly excludes foreigners who do not reside in Brazil from the scope of Art 5. The Brazilian constitutional literature and the case law of the STF, however, tend to mitigate this distinction and to understand that most of the rights set forth in Art 5 are to be exercised by everyone, including foreigners who do not reside in Brazil (ie, tourists and other foreigners without a permanent visa).[2]

III. HORIZONTAL EFFECTS OF FUNDAMENTAL RIGHTS

Although the so-called horizontal (or third-party) effects of fundamental rights have been discussed by the constitutional literature in Brazil, there are only a few STF decisions on this issue. The tendency of the Court is to assume a direct application model,[3] in which fundamental rights are directly binding to the parties in private relations, that is, to relations in which the state does not participate. However, the Court has never developed a fully articulated account of this model. Indeed, with few exceptions, the Court does not even acknowledge that its decisions involve the horizontal effect of fundamental rights. Since one of the most controversial features of the direct application model is the risk of not taking personal autonomy seriously enough, the lack of a robust case law on the matter is particularly problematic.

IV. RIGHT TO LIFE

As mentioned above, the right to life is mentioned in the head of Art 5 together with another four rights: liberty, equality, security, and property. Unlike these four rights, which are rendered more precisely throughout the several clauses of Art 5, the right to life is only mentioned in the head of the article and indirectly, in clause XLVII, *a*, which is related to the prohibition on capital punishment. The protection of the right to life is thus very general. As is the case in many countries, defining the constitutional protection of the right to life is of paramount importance,

[2] See, for instance, HC 72391-QO (1995) and RE 215267 (2001).
[3] See, for instance, RE 161243 (1996), RE 158215 (1996), RE 201819 (2005).

especially for discussing issues such as abortion, euthanasia, and the death penalty.

A. Abortion

Abortion is a felony in Brazil and is punishable by one to three years of incarceration for a mother who performs or merely consents to it and by one to four years' arrest for a third party who performs it. The Criminal Code provides for only two exceptions: if there is no other way to save the mother's life or if the pregnancy is the result of rape.[4]

In 2012, the STF allowed for a third situation in which abortion shall not be punished: in the case of an anencephalic foetus, that is, when a significant part of the brain of the foetus is absent. In such cases, if the foetus develops at all, the newborn usually does not survive more than a few hours. Although this is clearly a third exception to the prohibition on abortion, the Court – following the reasoning of the plaintiffs – took great pains to avoid presenting its decision as such. The judges in the majority frequently avoid using the term 'abortion' and preferred to use the expression 'therapeutic termination of pregnancy'. The summary of the decision (*ementa*) does not even refer to a third exception to the prohibition on abortion and employs a relatively indirect formulation: the Court declared 'the unconstitutionality of the interpretation according to which the interruption of the pregnancy of an anencephalic foetus is a criminal offence as defined in articles 124, 126 and 128, I and II, of the Criminal Code'.[5] In more direct terms, the Court decided that interrupting the pregnancy in the case of an anencephalic foetus cannot be considered an exception to the prohibition on abortion because it is no abortion at all. In a country such as Brazil, where abortion remains a highly sensitive subject still opposed by the majority of the population, the Court adopted a strategic stance to avoid the possibility that its decision would be perceived as allowing any kind of abortion.[6]

[4] See Criminal Code, Art 124, 126, and Art 128. Additionally, the Misdemeanours Act of 1941 imposes monetary fines for the 'advertising of a process, substance or object aiming at bringing about an abortion' (Art 20).

[5] ADPF 54 (2012).

[6] For more details on the case, see Luís Roberto Barroso, 'Bringing Abortion into the Brazilian Public Debate: Legal Strategies for Anencephalic Pregnancy' in Rebecca J Cook and others (eds), *Abortion Law in Transnational Perspective: Cases and Controversies* (Philadelphia, University of Pennsylvania Press, 2014); Keith S Rosenn, 'Recent Important Decisions by the Brazilian Supreme Court' (2013) 45 *U Miami Inter-Am L Rev* 297.

Four years later, however, when the spotlights were not on the Court (at least not as they were when it decided the anencephaly case), the first panel of the STF went further and in very clear terms decided that abortion shall not be punished at all when performed within the first 12 weeks of pregnancy.[7] Since the decision was not made in a constitutional action but in a concrete case (a habeas corpus case), it has no binding effects on future decisions.[8] In 2017, an ADPF was filed before the Court challenging the articles of the Criminal Code that make abortion a felony, arguing for the unconstitutionality of their enforcement in the case of abortions performed in the first 12 weeks of pregnancy.[9]

The goal of this section is not to develop a normative argument either for or against abortion. The arguments for or against abortion are widely known and are similar across different countries. However, the inequalities that are pervasive in Brazilian society render the debate on abortion even more complex than it usually is from a purely theoretical point of view or within the context of more egalitarian societies. In unequal societies, an abortion ban has a much stronger impact on poor women. Middle and upper middle-class women have access to and can afford private clinics that perform illegal abortions with all the necessary medical care; poor women usually perform their abortions at home, employing the most hazardous means. As a result, a ban on abortion leads to more deaths or serious injuries among poor women. In Brazil, this scenario is aggravated by the fact that social and racial inequalities are frequently linked, and the odds that a poor woman is also a non-white woman are high. Thus, a ban on abortion has an impact not only on the life of the foetus and the freedom of the mother but also on the life of the mother and on equal protection.

B. Embryonic Stem Cell Research

In 2008, the STF decided ADI 3510. This case had been brought before the Court by the Federal Procurator-General, who challenged the constitutionality of Art 5 of the so-called Biosafety Act (Federal Law 11105/2005). Art 5 of the Biosafety Act allows for the use of

[7] HC 124306 (2016).

[8] See ch 4 for more details on the binding effects of decisions of the STF.

[9] ADPF 442 (pending). For an analysis of the shift from Congress to the STF as the main arena in which the debate over abortion takes place, see Marta Rodriguez de Assis Machado and Débora Alves Maciel, 'The Battle Over Abortion Rights in Brazil's State Arenas, 1995–2006' (2017) 19 *Health and Human Rights Journal* 119.

embryonic stem cells from human embryos that were generated by (but not used in) *in vitro* fertilisation, provided that either the embryos are not viable or that they have been frozen for three years or longer and were already frozen on the date of publication of the Biosafety Act.

The Federal Procurator-General argued that the use of embryonic stem cells is a violation of the right to life because the embryos are destroyed in the process. The Court did not accept this argument and upheld the constitutionality of Art 5 of the Biosafety Act.

C. Euthanasia

The debate on euthanasia in Brazil is incipient. The STF has rendered no judicial decision on the matter. Neither is there specific legislation. The Brazilian Criminal Code defines both homicide and instigation or abetment to commit suicide as felonies (Criminal Code, Art 121 and 122). However, Art 121, § 1, of the Criminal Code, which provides for extenuating circumstances in the case of homicide 'if the perpetrator commits the crime impelled by reason of significant social or moral value', is frequently applied to the case of euthanasia. In this case, the penalty may be reduced by one-sixth to one-third.

In 2006, the Federal Council of Medicine issued an ordinance (Ordinance 1805/2006) allowing what is usually called orthothanasia. Although the term orthothanasia means 'natural death', in the medical context it also refers to the act of stopping artificial means of maintaining someone's life. Art 1 of the aforementioned ordinance provides that 'the physician is allowed to limit or suspend procedures and treatments that prolong the life of the terminally ill patient of a serious and incurable disease, respecting the wishes of the person or his or her legal representative'.[10]

In 2012, another ordinance of the Federal Council of Medicine (Ordinance 1995/2012) introduced the 'advance healthcare directive', also known as a 'living will', that is, a document in which any person may specify in advance which treatments or procedures she wants if she 'is incapacitated to freely and autonomously express her will'

[10] A similar provision can be found in the Brazilian Medical Code of Ethics. Its fundamental principle, XXII, forbids dysthanasia, providing that 'in irreversible and terminal clinical situations, the physician shall avoid unnecessary diagnostic and therapeutic procedures'.

(Ordinance 1995/2012, Art 1). Advance directives must be considered by the physician (Art 2) unless they are incompatible with the Medical Code of Ethics (Art 2, § 2). This means that a 'living will' demanding orthothanasia will be valid, but one demanding euthanasia will not, since Art 41 of the Brazilian Medical Code of Ethics (2009) established that physicians are forbidden 'to shorten the life of the patient, albeit at his or his legal representative's request'. Advance directives also prevail over the wishes of family members (Art 2, § 3).

D. Death Penalty

Among the 78 clauses of Art 5, only one is related to the right to life. Art 5, XLVII, *a*, provides that 'there shall be no penalties ... of death'. However, this ban on the death penalty is only partial. The same provision states, 'except in case of declared war'. Hence, even though it is true that the last time Brazil entered a war in South America was more than 150 years ago,[11] Brazil is one of the few constitutional democracies worldwide that has not completely abolished the death penalty.[12]

V. EQUALITY

Throughout this book, the gap between constitutional text and social reality has been emphasised several times. Although this is not a Brazilian peculiarity, it is nevertheless possible to state that in Brazil, the gap could in many cases be much narrower than it is. Equality is one such case. There is perhaps no other realm in which the gap is more evident.[13]

[11] The so-called Paraguayan War (*Guerra do Paraguai*) was fought from 1864 to 1870 between the Triple Alliance (Argentina, Brazil, and Uruguay) and Paraguay. This war cost hundreds of thousands of lives and is usually known in Argentina and Uruguay as the War of the Triple Alliance (*Guerra de la Triple Alianza*) and in Paraguay as the Great War (*Guerra Grande* in Spanish and *Ñorairõ Guazú* in Guarani).

[12] The Military Criminal Code (Decree-Law 1001/1940) defines more than 30 acts that are punished by death in wartime, from betrayal and conspiracy to disobedience, abandonment of post, abandonment of convoy, and damage to equipment or devices of military use, even if still under construction. In all cases, the death penalty involves execution by firing squad (Military Criminal Code, Art 56).

[13] In the realm of social rights, the gap between constitutional text and practice is also wide. This is no coincidence, since social rights are directly linked to the idea of equality.

Brazil is not a poor country, but it is an extremely unequal one. Depending on the ranking[14] and the criterion adopted,[15] Brazil is the seventh-, eighth- or ninth-largest world economy. However, in rankings based on human development or inequality, Brazil's performance slumps. For instance, in the ranking based on the Human Development Index, developed by the United Nations Development Program (UNDP), Brazil ranks 79th.[16] In the UNDP Gender Inequality Index, the performance is even worse: 92nd.[17] When the ranking is based on income inequality, the extent of Brazilian inequality becomes even clearer. In the ranking developed by the World Bank, based on the GINI Index, Brazil ranks the 9th worst in the world and the worst in Latin America.[18]

Still, it is possible to argue that the situation has been worse in the past. The first mention in this book of the gap between constitutional provisions and social reality refers to the context of the 1824 Constitution. Although this constitution had an equal protection clause, a considerable share of the Brazilian population was enslaved. Even after the abolition of slavery – that is, even under the ensuing constitutions – a considerable share of the Brazilian population has always lived with marginal access to basic rights, goods and services, especially due to their social class, race or gender.

In this context, the 1988 Constitution can be considered a watershed. While it is true that a constitutional text alone does not change the reality of a country, it is also true that legislation and public policies proposed after the promulgation of (and based on) the Constitution have created the conditions for decreasing inequality in Brazil. In other words, whereas it is an often-overlooked fact that changes within this realm are largely the result of protracted struggles from below and the outcome of the prolonged engagements of social movements and civil society, and therefore are not gifts bestowed from above, it is undeniable that the Constitution has encouraged and promoted such mobilisation.

The most important constitutional provisions in this realm are Art 5, *caput* and I, and Art 3, IV. The head of Art 5 employs the paradigmatic formula 'everyone is equal before the law'; and Art 5, I, applies this formula expressly to the relation between women and men: 'men

[14] United Nations, International Monetary Fund, or World Bank.

[15] Nominal or PPP (purchasing power parity) GDP (gross domestic product).

[16] See United Nations Development Programme (ed), *Human Development Report 2016: Human development for everyone* (New York, UNDP, 2016) 199.

[17] See ibid 215.

[18] See http://databank.worldbank.org/data/reports.aspx?source=2&series=SI.POV.GINI&country=.

and women have equal rights and duties'. In the Brazilian constitutional tradition, this equality has always been called 'formal equality'. Although this provision may be sensitive to some types of inequalities, based on its supposed corollary 'treat like cases alike and different cases differently', formal equality is still not primarily intended to reduce inequalities. It does not, therefore, have a necessary connection to another form of equality: equality of opportunities. Thus, until 1988, equal protection had always been considered reconcilable with upholding an extremely unequal status quo.

The 1988 Constitution attempts to alter this state of affairs. Alongside formal provisions on equal protection, it assigns goals to be promoted by the state, with the reduction of inequalities being one of them. Before the equal protection clause of Art 5, Art 3 defines the 'fundamental objectives of the Federative Republic of Brazil', which include the following: to reduce social and regional inequalities and to promote the well-being of all without prejudice as to origin, race, sex, colour, age and any other forms of discrimination. Although not explicit, it is possible to read in these and other provisions[19] a duty to promote equality of opportunities, which in Brazil is often called 'substantial equality'.

Based on the assumption presented above, according to which a constitutional text alone cannot alter reality, especially reality that has existed for centuries, as is the case of inequality in Brazil, the following sections are dedicated to presenting not only the main advances but also the main bottlenecks and challenges in this realm. It will become clear that the 1988 Constitution has nevertheless helped ensure the enactment of laws and the development of public policies with the aim of reducing inequalities and increasing equality of opportunities.

A. Gender

Notwithstanding the explicit constitutional provision according to which 'men and women have equal rights and duties',[20] equality between them is still far from reality. This is not, of course, a Brazilian peculiarity. Inequality between women and men is an inconvenient worldwide truth that cannot be ignored. Nevertheless, it is a fact that in Brazil, the road to this equality remains very long.

[19] See, for instance, Art 170, VII, and Art 206, I.
[20] Art 5, I.

Inequalities between women and men are noticeable in all areas, including political positions, corporate boards of directors, and pay gaps. Violence against women is also common in Brazil; it can be physical or psychological and it can happen at home, in the workplace, on the streets.

Nevertheless, following the premise stated above, one must acknowledge the 1988 Constitution as a moment of inflection in the realm of gender equality. Although women were seriously under-represented in the Constituent Assembly (fewer than 5 per cent of its members were women), the participation of civil society in the drafting of the Constitution led to more advances than would be expected from an assembly composed almost entirely of men and with a rather conservative profile.[21]

An important document demanding special attention to women's rights in the Constituent Assembly was the 'Letter of the Brazilian Women to the Constituent Assembly', written during the National Meeting of the National Council for Women's Rights in 1986. In this letter, advances in the rights of women were demanded, especially in areas such as family, work, health, education, culture, and in the fight against violence. Many of these proposals were incorporated by the Constitution.[22]

In addition to Art 3, IV, and Art 5, I, which were presented above, the most important provisions in this realm are several clauses of Art 7, which grant the right to maternity leave without loss of job or wages for a period of 120 days,[23] paternity leave,[24] and protection of the job market for women through specific incentives.[25] Additionally, Art 5, L, provides

[21] See ch 1.

[22] For a short description of these demands and the challenges in implementing them after the enactment of the 1988 Constitution, see Florisa Verucci, 'Women and the New Brazilian Constitution' (1991) 17 *Feminist Studies* 557.

[23] Federal Law 11770/2008 grants tax deductions for companies that extend maternity leave to 180 days. Additionally, Federal Law 12873/2013 introduced a new article into the Code of Labour Laws (Art 392-A, Decree-Law 5452/1943) extending maternity leave to adoption cases.

[24] The law mentioned in this clause still has not been enacted. Art 10, § 1, of the ADCT establishes that until the law regulates the provisions of Art 7, XIX, 'the period of paternity leave … shall be five days'. Federal Law 11770/2008, mentioned in the previous note, also grants tax deductions to companies that extend paternity leave to 20 days.

[25] Although the bill of workers' rights tends to foster equality between women and men, it nevertheless contained an infamous clause (Art 7, single paragraph) that excluded domestic workers from the exercise of many of those rights that it explicitly granted to everyone. Since virtually all domestic workers in Brazil are women – and a great majority of them are black women – this provision clearly reinforced a historical inequality. This clause was amended only in 2013.

that 'female prisoners shall be assured conditions that allow them to remain with their children during the nursing period'. Finally, Art 226, §§ 5 and 8, provides for equality within the family, by establishing that the 'rights and duties of the conjugal society shall be exercised equally by the man and the woman' and that the State 'shall … create mechanisms to suppress violence within the family'.

This latter constitutional provision was effectively regulated by ordinary law only in 2006, when the so-called *Maria da Penha Act* (Federal Law 11340/2006) was enacted. Among other things, this Act created specialised courts for trying cases of violence against women and amended the Criminal Code to establish several aggravating circumstances when crimes are committed against women, especially at home.[26]

B. Race

On 13 May 1888, Brazil became the last country in the Western Hemisphere to abolish slavery. It did so without any concern about the past, the present, and the future of those who had been enslaved. No indemnities were granted and there was no public policy to provide for the social, economic and political inclusion of former slaves. The consequences not only of centuries of slavery but also of a defective abolition process are felt to this day.

For a long time, many assumed that Brazil was a perfect case of racial democracy. In the 1950s, UNESCO sponsored research to better understand the Brazilian experience. The results of some of these studies, however, showed a rather different reality. Indeed, it is possible to argue that racial democracy in Brazil is and always has been a myth. This myth and the racial inequalities in Brazil are the background of recent policies that will be presented below. Thus, understanding the

[26] The name of the Act is a reference to the case of Maria da Penha, whose husband made several attempts to kill her several times; as the result of one of these attempts, she was left paraplegic. She brought her case before the Inter-American Commission of Human Rights (IACHR), which declared that the Brazilian government was not taking effective measures to fight domestic violence and issued several recommendations on the matter. See IACHR, Report on the Merits 54/01, Case 12,051, *Maria da Penha Fernandes* (Brazil) 2001. For more about this subject, see Paula Spieler, 'The Maria da Penha Case and the Inter-American Commission on Human Rights: Contributions to the Debate on Domestic Violence Against Women in Brazil' (2011) 18 *Indiana Journal of Global Legal Studies* 121; Jodie G Roure, 'Domestic Violence in Brazil: Examining Obstacles and Approaches to Promote Legislative Reform' (2009) 41 *Colum Hum Rts L Rev* 67.

constitutional debate on the right to equality in this realm depends on understanding a broader debate on racism in Brazil.[27]

The Brazilian Institute of Geography and Statistics (IBGE) uses five racial categories in its censuses. The results of the most recent comprehensive census (2010) were as follows:[28] white (47.51 per cent), *pardo*[29] (43.42 per cent), black (7.52 per cent), *amarelo*[30] (1.10 per cent), and indigenous (0.43 per cent).

The non-white population was seriously under-represented in the Constituent Assembly of 1987–88. Since the IBGE classification is based on self-declaration and there is no information available regarding the members of that assembly, it is difficult to define precisely how many black representatives there were. The available information on this matter, however, usually points to a representation of blacks of less than 3 per cent.[31]

Since 2014, the Superior Electoral Court has required a racial self-declaration from all candidates. The result of the 2014 elections shows that even though the participation of non-whites has increased, it still deviates considerably from the general racial composition of Brazil, as can be seen in the table below.

	Brazilian population	**Chamber of Deputies**
White	47.51%	79.9%
Pardo	43.42%	16%
Black	7.52%	4.1%

[27] There is a good body of literature in English on this subject. See, for instance, Gilberto Freyre, *The Masters and the Slaves* (New York, Samuel Putnam tr, Knopf, 1946). Gilberto Freyre was one of the most influential Brazilian sociologists and the most important advocate of the idea of racial democracy in Brazil. For a good account of the process of revising this idea (including details on the UNESCO Project), see Emilia Viotti da Costa, 'The Myth of Racial Democracy in Brazil' in *The Brazilian Empire: Myths & Histories*, 2nd edn (Chapel Hill, University of North Carolina Press, 2000).

[28] Source: IBGE https://sidra.ibge.gov.br/Tabela/136.

[29] *Pardo* is a category that encompasses several mixed ethnic categories. It is a very contested category and there is a vast literature on the subject. See, for instance, Mara Loveman and others, 'Brazil in Black and White? Race Categories, the Census, and the Study of Inequality' (2012) 35 *Ethnic and Racial Studies* 1466, especially 1468–70 (and the literature cited there). For an in-depth analysis of this subject (among many others related to race and colour in Brazil), see also Edward E Telles, *Race in Another America: The Significance of Skin Color in Brazil* (Princeton, Princeton University Press, 2004).

[30] The IBGE uses the term *amarelo*, which literally means 'yellow' to define people of East Asian descent.

[31] See Ollie A Johnson III, 'Racial Representation and Brazilian Politics: Black Members of the National Congress, 1983–1999' (1998) 40 *Journal of Interamerican Studies and World Affairs* 97.

Given the deviation between the ethnic composition of the population and the composition of the legislature, the approval of federal laws aimed at increasing the equality of opportunities between non-whites and whites is not to be taken for granted. Although the approval of these laws is the result of many variables, it is important to emphasise the existence of well-organised and active social movements which have been able to take advantage of the egalitarian profile of the Constitution to provide an even more solid legal basis for their historical struggle to reduce inequality in Brazil.

i. Affirmative Action

The most important body of legislation and public policies were in the realm of education.[32] A very brief, but not inaccurate, way of depicting how inequality works within the Brazilian educational system is as follows. Generally, the best schools (especially secondary schools) are private and the best universities are public (tuition free). Children of the wealthier classes attend private schools, where they receive an education that facilitates their success in the entrance examination of public universities, where they will study without paying anything. In contrast, children from the less-affluent classes attend poorly performing public schools and are often unable to overcome the barrier of the entrance exams at public universities; consequently, they have to pay to study in middle- to low-quality private universities. Although there are exceptions to this narrative, it offers a good general picture of the Brazilian education system. This pattern is valid not only for public/private schools but also for the non-white/white divide.

One of the first pieces of legislation intended to change this situation was Federal Law 11096/2005 (ProUni Act). The main goal of the ProUni program was to grant scholarships (full or partial) to low-income students who had studied in public schools, with a pool of scholarships for blacks, pardos, indigenous persons and persons with disabilities. This law was challenged before the STF, which in 2012 upheld its compatibility with the Constitution.[33]

A few months later, Federal Law 12711/2012 was passed; the law created a comprehensive system of affirmative action in federal

[32] For a detailed account on recent developments in the realm of education and racial equality, see Ollie A Johnson III and Rosana Heringer (eds), *Race, Politics, and Education in Brazil* (New York, Palgrave Macmillan, 2015).

[33] See ADI 3330 (2012).

universities and professional schools.[34] According to this law, 50 per cent of the vacancies in federal universities should be reserved for students who are graduates of public schools. These vacancies must be filled by 'blacks, pardos, and indigenous persons and persons with disabilities … at a proportion at least equal to black, pardos, and indigenous persons and persons with disabilities in the federation unit [states or federal district] where the institution [university or professional school] is located'. This law was not challenged before the STF, particularly because shortly before its approval, the Court decided that another affirmative action programme – that of the University of Brasília (a federal university) – with rules that were similar to those established by Law Federal law 12711/2012, was constitutional.[35]

In both cases decided by the STF, the main issue at stake was the clash between formal and substantial equality, mentioned above. The Court has made it clear in both decisions that equality of opportunities is a goal of the Constitution and that formal equality must be interpreted against this background.

The same argument was pivotal to a further decision on an affirmative action policy establishing that 20 per cent of the vacancies offered in public examinations for positions in the federal public administration are reserved for blacks and *pardos*.[36] The Court ruled that this affirmative action was consistent with the Constitution.[37]

Lastly, Federal Law 12288/2010 – known as the Racial Equality Act – aims at establishing standards and objectives to 'ensure to the black population the realisation of equality of opportunities, the defence of individual, collective and diffuse ethnic rights and the fight against discrimination and other forms of ethnic intolerance'. This law has provisions related to, *inter alia*, health, education, culture, sports, leisure, religious freedom, and the right to housing and land.

[34] According to Rosenn, it is 'one of the most far-reaching affirmative action statutes in the world' (Rosenn (n 6) 328). See also Erich Dietrich, 'Ambition with Resistance: Affirmative Action in Brazil's Public Universities' in Ollie A Johnson III and Rosana Heringer (eds), *Race, Politics, and Education in Brazil* (Palgrave Macmillan, 2015) 155: 'the most ambitious affirmative action policies of any country in the world'.

[35] See ADPF 186 (2012). For more details in English on both decisions, see Rosenn (n 6) 323–29. Individual extraordinary appeals that challenge the constitutionality of affirmative action policies of other universities have also been consistently rejected by the Court. See, for instance, RE 597285 (2012).

[36] See Federal Law 12990/2014, Art 1. The law employs the Portuguese term *negro*, which, according to the official terminology of the Brazilian Institute of Geography and Statistics, encompasses blacks and *pardos*. The law itself makes this clear in Art 2.

[37] See ADC 41 (2017).

ii. Racism and Racial Slander

The 1988 Constitution was promulgated exactly 100 years after the abolition of slavery in Brazil. As presented above, the passing of time alone was not (and could not be) sufficient to mitigate the effects of slavery. Racial inequality remains a central feature of the Brazilian social structure and racism is still ubiquitous in Brazil. At the National Constituent Assembly of 1987–88, several proposals aimed at dealing with such problems. Art 5, XLII, is a direct outcome of these efforts. It states, 'the practice of racism is a non-bailable crime not subject to the statute of limitations and is punishable by imprisonment, as provided by law'. Shortly after the promulgation of the Constitution, Federal Law 7716/1989 was enacted with the goal of defining crimes of prejudice based on race and skin colour.[38] This law defines several crimes – including denying a job, a public position, or access to the Armed Forces; denying access to shops, hotels, restaurants, hairdressers and barber shops, or public transportation; prohibiting the use of the main social entrance and elevators in public and private buildings;[39] and impeding marriage – when these actions are based on racial grounds.

The most important controversies are associated with Art 20 of Federal Law 7716/1989, which punishes, by one to three years of incarceration, 'perpetrating, instigating or inciting discrimination or prejudice based on race, colour, ethnicity, religion or national origin'. This is clearly a speech crime. In this sense, it resembles other speech crimes such as libel and slander. In addition to ordinary and general slander, the Brazilian Criminal Code has an additional, more specific form of slander. Art 140, § 3, provides that 'if the slander entails elements referring to race, colour, ethnicity, religion, origin, or personal condition of old age or disability', the act is punishable by one to three years imprisonment and a fine (instead of one to six months or a fine, which is the punishment for ordinary slander).

[38] In 1997, this law was amended to widen its scope and explicitly include discrimination and prejudice based on ethnicity, religion and national origin.

[39] In Brazil, apartment buildings frequently have both a social and a service elevator. Although this divide may make sense if one thinks of a service elevator for the purposes of transporting goods or machines, in reality it has always been used as a way to segregate the rich from the poor, the whites from the blacks. Service elevators are usually located in a different part of the building so that flat owners do not have to share their elevators with housemaids and other (usually non-white) workers. This practice remains common in Brazil.

This duplicity of speech crimes related to race and colour (along with the other grounds mentioned above) has been the subject of fierce debates. The central question is as follows: what is the difference between racism perpetrated by speech and racial slander? The fact is that lawsuits for racism are often reclassified in courts as racial slander. Courts in Brazil have frequently based their decisions on the following distinction: a speech should be qualified as racism only if the racial offence targets an entire group, whereas it should be qualified as racial slander whenever the offence is aimed at an individual.[40] It is not the goal of this section to analyse whether this distinction is sound. However, it may be argued that it potentially mitigates the enforcement of Art 5, XLII, of the Constitution.[41]

C. Persons with Disabilities

Although the debate on the rights of persons with disabilities was virtually non-existent in the legal realm in Brazil during the 1980s, the 1988 Constitution contains advanced provisions on the matter. These provisions fall within the scope of labour rights, education, accessibility, social assistance, children and youths, along with preferential rules both for retirement and for receiving payments owed by the state treasury after court decisions.[42]

Additionally, Brazil incorporated the Convention on the Rights of Persons with Disabilities into domestic law in 2009.[43] This was the first international treaty approved following the rules set forth in Art 5, § 3, which had been added to the Constitution through the Judiciary Reform Act. This means that although formally this provision is a legislative decree, not a constitutional amendment, it has the same

[40] See, for instance, Brazilian Superior Court of Justice, RHC 19166 (2006).

[41] See Antonio Sérgio Alfredo Guimarães, 'Measures to Combat Discrimination and Racial Inequality in Brazil' in Rebecca Reichmann (ed), *Race in Contemporary Brazil: From Indifference to Inequality* (University Park, Pennsylvania State University Press, 1999). See also Marta Rodriguez de Assis Machado and others, 'The Juridification of Social Demands and the Application of Statutes: An Analysis of the Legal Treatment of Antiracism Social Demands in Brazil' (2009) 77 *Fordham Law Review* 1535.

[42] See Art 7, XXXI; Art 37, VIII; Art 208, III; Art 227, § 2, and Art 244; Art 203, IV and V; Art 227, § 1, II; Art 40, § 4, Art 201, § 1; and Art 100, § 2. The original wording of this latter provision did not include persons with disabilities. The reference to them was included via EC 94/2016.

[43] See Decree 6949/2009.

status as a constitutional amendment and ordinary legislation must therefore comply with it. Hence, judicial review of legislation may also have the Convention, not merely the Constitution, as a parameter.

However, it was not until 2015 that a comprehensive piece of legislation to enforce the rights of persons of disabilities was passed: the Persons with Disabilities Act (Federal Law 13146/2015). This does not mean that there were no laws related to the rights of persons with disabilities before 2015: there were. One of the most important of those laws is Federal Law 10436/2002, which defined Brazilian Sign Language (*LIBRAS – Língua Brasileira de Sinais*) as an official form of expression in Brazil. Furthermore, Federal Law 12711/2012 provides that a portion of the vacancies in federal universities should be reserved for students with disabilities.[44]

That said, the Persons with Disabilities Act is the most comprehensive piece of legislation on the matter. It has detailed provisions related to the rights mentioned above (health, education, labour, and accessibility, among others). Its enforcement has not been easy. In Brazil, the barriers that obstruct persons with disabilities are ubiquitous. These barriers include accessibility obstacles everywhere (buildings, sidewalks, public transportation), a lack of public policies in several areas, and the unwillingness of corporations and even schools to integrate persons with disabilities. Shortly after the enactment of the Persons with Disabilities Act, the Brazilian Confederation of Private Schools challenged the constitutionality of several of its provisions related to the integration of children with disabilities. According to the plaintiff, private schools have no duty to accept children with disabilities because the promotion of this type of equality and integration is exclusively a duty of the state. In other words, the plaintiff argued that only public schools, not private schools, have a duty to accept the enrolment of children with disabilities. Art 28, § 1 of the Persons with Disabilities Act not only establishes the duty of private schools to accept children with disabilities but also forbids these schools to charge them higher tuition. In 2016, the STF decided that the Act is constitutional and that private schools must therefore comply with its Art 28, § 1.[45]

[44] Another important piece of legislation prior to the enactment of the Persons with Disabilities Act was Federal Law 10098/2000, whose provisions are primarily related to accessibility, especially in the public space, public transportation and communication.

[45] See ADI 5357 (2016).

D. LGBT Rights

i. Same-Sex Marriage and Civil Union

All over the world, equal access to marriage and civil unions has been steadily growing and for some time has been an important fight for LGBT activists. Compared to the constitutions of other countries, the Brazilian Constitution poses some additional hurdles in this struggle. Even if those hurdles are not insurmountable, they create an argumentative burden against changing traditional views on marriage and other types of family partnerships. Constitutions very rarely have provisions on marriage. Even more rare are constitutions with provisions concerning civil unions or similar partnerships. The Brazilian Constitution not only has provisions on both matters, these provisions also explicitly state that marriage and civil unions are unions between a man and a woman. Art 226, § 5, provides that the rights and duties of the conjugal society 'shall be exercised equally by the man and the woman', while Art 226, § 3, provides that 'the stable union between a man and a woman is recognised as a family unit, and the law shall facilitate conversion of such unions into marriage'.

No other country that allows for same-sex marriage or civil union has a constitution with provisions that are similarly detailed and gender specific. Almost everywhere, the pattern of reasoning for allowing same-sex marriage or union has been quite straightforward: (a) the Constitution guarantees equal protection before the law; (b) ordinary legislation (civil code, marriage act or similar acts) limited this equal protection by denying to same-sex couples the possibility of getting married or establishing a civil union; and (c) therefore, ordinary legislation is unconstitutional. This rationale is inapplicable to the Brazilian case due to the specific constitutional provisions mentioned above.

Still, in 2011, the STF simultaneously decided two actions related to this issue and authorised same-sex civil unions in Brazil.[46] Although the decision is a milestone in the struggle for greater equality in Brazil,[47] it remains necessary to stress that it was very poorly argued, since the Court has never acknowledged the argumentative burden mentioned above. Some judges did not even mention Art 226, § 3, in their written opinions.

[46] See ADI 4277 (2011) and ADPF 132 (2011).

[47] See Adilson José Moreira, 'We Are Family! Legal Recognition of Same-Sex Unions in Brazil' (2012) 60 *Am J Comp Law* 1003.

Another problematic aspect of the decision is the fact that the Court completely bypassed the legislature throughout the process. The STF repeatedly states that the separation of powers prevents it from compelling Congress to legislate or to establish deadlines for the legislature to issue a given piece of legislation, even in clear cases in which the Constitution explicitly demands that an ordinary law with a given content should be enacted. This (apparently rhetorical) adherence to a doctrine of separation of powers seems to be completely at odds with the choice to bypass the National Congress. As I have argued elsewhere, 'it is very hard to grasp an interpretation of deference and of the separation of powers doctrine according to which the Court can neither impose on the Congress a duty to legislate nor establish a deadline for a legislative action, but may nevertheless autonomously do everything that, *according to its own understanding of the separation of powers doctrine*, actually falls within the powers of the Congress'.[48]

ii. Transgender Rights

In no other country in the world are there more homicides of transgender people than in Brazil. According to the Trans Murder Monitoring Project, in a ranking of almost 70 countries Brazil ranks number one in the absolute number of homicides and fourth in the relative number of homicides (reported homicides per million inhabitants).[49]

The STF has given signs of an awareness and sensitivity to transgender rights, which until recently could have been considered an almost invisible agenda in Brazil. In 2018, the Court decided a case related to the possibility of and the procedure for changing both one's name and one's gender in the civil registry.[50] Although there was no legislation on the matter in Brazil, many courts had frequently required judicial authorisation for changing one's name and the realisation of gender reassignment surgery as a condition for altering the civil registry of transgender persons. The STF ruled that transgender persons may change their names without the

[48] Virgílio Afonso da Silva, 'La unión entre personas del mismo género: ¿Cuán importantes son los textos y las instituciones?' (2014) 15 *Discusiones* 171, 191. On this subject, see also Diego Werneck Arguelhes and Leandro Molhano Ribeiro, 'Courts as the First and Only Legislative Chambers? The Brazilian Supreme Court and the Legalization of Same-Sex Marriage' (2017) 50 *Verfassung in Recht und Übersee* 281.

[49] For up-to-date data, see https://transrespect.org/en/trans-murder-monitoring/tmm-resources/.

[50] ADI 4275 (2018).

need for judicial authorisation and that such an invasive surgery cannot be a condition for changing a person's gender in the public registry.

Two weeks earlier, another important decision involving transgender rights was made by the Court. In a case involving two transgender women who were serving their sentences in a male-only prison, the STF decided that transgender detainees should serve their sentences in an establishment compatible with their gender identity.[51] The Court primarily based its decision on a joint resolution of two agencies of the Ministry of Justice, although it could have based it on Art 5, XLVIII, of the Constitution, which provides that 'sentences shall be served in separate establishments, according to the nature of the offence, and age and sex of the convict'.

E. Migrants

Throughout this section on equality, one thing has been constantly emphasised: although equality is a goal that still seems far away, the promulgation of the 1988 Constitution nevertheless marked the opening of an avenue of possibilities for fostering equality more effectively. However, this strain of thought does not apply in the case of migrants. In the realm of nationality and citizenship, the Constitution establishes a clear hierarchy for the full access to rights. The full exercise of all fundamental rights is granted only to native-born Brazilians, since some rights (access to certain political, judicial, diplomatic and military positions) are denied even to naturalised Brazilians. Migrants are subject to even more restrictions, and some rights – such as political rights – are completely denied to them. Finally, at least according to a strict interpretation of the constitutional text, a distinction between resident and non-resident foreigners could also be established, as explained above.

Admittedly, Art 3, IV, sets forth the goal of promoting 'the well-being of all, without prejudice as to origin … and any other forms of discrimination'. This surely includes fighting prejudice and discrimination against foreigners. However, in contrast to the case of inequalities based on gender, race, or disability, in the case of migrants the 1988 Constitution largely followed the Brazilian constitutional tradition. Although it is true that part of this tradition is favourable to migrants, such as

[51] HC 152491 (2018).

the fact that all those who are born in Brazil are considered native-born Brazilians regardless of the national origin of their parents, one may still argue that Brazil lags far behind when equality between nationals and migrants is at stake.

Nevertheless, there is a very widespread belief that Brazil is a hospitable country, which always has an open door to immigrants. Similar to the allegedly racial democracy mentioned above, it has long been assumed that Brazil and Brazilians are receptive to migrants. Starting in the middle of the nineteenth century, Brazil received millions of immigrants in several migratory waves, particularly involving the arrival of the Portuguese, Italians, Germans, Spaniards, Japanese, Poles, Syrians and Lebanese. In the beginning of the twentieth century, almost one-quarter of the population in some Brazilian states was made up of migrants. The fact that the subsequent generations of these immigrants have been fully integrated and that tens of millions of native-born Brazilians now have Brazilian given names alongside Japanese, Lebanese, German and (especially) Italian surnames created an image of harmony and hospitality that has been increasingly challenged.[52]

Recent studies have shown that the integration of migrants was usually much more conflicted than supposed when one sees the mosaic of nationalities that make up Brazil's current population. Additionally, it is now widely acknowledged that the promotion of immigration in the nineteenth century not only aimed at supplying the necessary labour force for a growing country – especially after the prohibition of the slave trade in 1850 – but also aimed at 'whitening' the Brazilian population. Less than a year after the proclamation of the republic, Decree 528/1890 was issued; that law's Art 1 established that the entrance of immigrants into Brazil was free, with the exception of natives of Africa and Asia, who would require authorisation from the National Congress. In the first half of the twentieth century, for example, the debates in the Constituent Assembly of 1933–34 were permeated by xenophobic and nationalist discourses and the 1934 Constitution had provisions that clearly allowed for discrimination against immigrants from certain countries, such as the possibility of prohibiting immigration 'totally … or by reason of national origin'.[53] Decree-Law 406/1938 established further that the

[52] See, for instance, Szilvia Simai and Rosana Baeninger, 'The National Myth of Receptivity in Brazil' (2011) 8 *AmeriQuests*. See also Jeffrey Lesser, *Negotiating National Identity: Immigrants, Minorities, and the Struggle for Ethnicity in Brazil* (Durham, Duke University Press, 1999).

[53] 1934 Constitution, Art 5, XIX, g.

government could 'limit or suspend … the entrance of individuals of certain races or origins'.

Admittedly, these last two provisions must be understood in light of a historical context in which nationalism was a dominant ideology, not only in Brazil. Especially with regard to the Decree-Law of 1938, one should keep in mind that Brazil was under an authoritarian and nationalist regime. Nevertheless, the aforementioned xenophobic debates of 1933–34 reappear after re-democratisation in the Constituent Assembly of 1946. One of the fiercest debates on the matter involved the inclusion of a constitutional provision that explicitly prohibited the entrance of Japanese immigrants into Brazil.[54]

Shortly beforehand, Decree-Law 7967/1945 established that the admission of immigrants in Brazil should consider 'the need to preserve and develop, in the ethnic composition of the population, the most convenient characteristics of the European ancestry …'. It is important to emphasise that this decree was revoked only in 1980 by Federal Law 6815/1980. Although it is difficult to accurately assess whether and how often this provision was applied as a criterion for the admission of immigrants in Brazil, mentioning it is relevant for at least two reasons: (1) because the simple fact that a piece of legislation that gives preference to European immigration vis-à-vis others had been valid law in Brazil until 1980 is a relevant sign that at least from the legal perspective, Brazilian receptivity to migrants must be reassessed; and (2) because this provision, irrespective of how effective it may have been from the legal perspective, does reflect a widespread position in the Brazilian population to measure out its hospitality depending on foreigners' origin. While it is true that there is great receptivity towards Europeans, this receptivity is considerably reduced when it comes to immigrants from Africa, the Caribbean and Latin America. To the extent that recent migratory waves to Brazil are formed especially by immigrants from these regions, selective receptivity may be an indication that integration and equality will be difficult to achieve.

Finally, and still from a legal point of view, it is important to note that Brazilian legislation has always been and continues to be rather unfriendly to migrants. The meagre number of permanent visa

[54] See Brasil, *Anais da Assembléia Constituinte* (Rio de Janeiro, Departamento de Imprensa Nacional, 1950) vol XXIII, 71–76. The voting on this proposal ended in a tie (99 to 99 votes) and the proposal was only rejected when the president of the Constituent Assembly cast the final vote.

concessions, the number of refugees received and the number of political asylums granted is an indication of this.

F. Tax System and Equality

The construction of an egalitarian society is heavily dependent on a just tax system. However, despite the clear constitutional option for a distributive, progressive and egalitarian tax system, the Brazilian tax system falls far short of fulfilling these requirements and functioning as a tool for fostering the goals defined by Art 3.

The most important tax to distributive goals – income tax – is only marginally progressive. Even though there are four tax rates, the highest tax rate is only 27.5 per cent, which means that middle-class workers pay the same percentage of their income as multi-millionaires.[55] The most striking fact is that this weakly progressive income tax model has been implemented under a constitution that strives for more equality and solidarity, while in the past, under much less egalitarian constitutions, the income tax was much more progressive. Although there has been an identifiable trend to decrease the highest income tax rate in many countries, the impact of this trend is surely much deeper in countries where inequality is very high, such as Brazil. In no other country in the world does the wealthiest 1 per cent possess a larger share of pre-tax national income – 27.8 per cent – than in Brazil.[56]

VI. FREEDOM OF EXPRESSION

The Constitution protects freedom of expression in three clauses of Art 5. These clauses not only define and protect freedom of expression but also explicitly establish limits on its exercise. Art 5, IV, for instance, contains both a general formulation of freedom of expression ('manifestation of thought is free') and a limitation ('anonymity is forbidden'). Art 5, V, regulates the remedies for those cases in which the exercise of the freedom of expression results in damages. It guarantees a 'right of

[55] Although effective tax rates vary within the same nominal tax rate, this variation is marginal and insufficient to compensate for the lack of progressiveness created by a highest rate that is as low as 27.5%.

[56] Source: World Wealth and Income Database (http://wid.world/country/brazil).

reply … in proportion to the offence'[57] and provides for 'compensation for pecuniary or moral damages or damages to reputation'. Art 5, IX, protects specific aspects of freedom of expression in certain realms and bans both censorship and licence requirements. It states, 'expression of intellectual, artistic, scientific, and communication activity is free, independent of censorship or license'.

It is possible to identify the following divide in the protection of freedom of expression in Brazil: legislatures and lower courts tend to impose or accept restrictions on freedom of expression much more frequently than does the STF. While, in many situations, the former tends to favour other rights such as honour, privacy, image and property, the case law of the STF is clearly favourable to a stronger protection of freedom of expression. This does not mean, of course, that freedom of expression is never restricted by decisions of the STF, only that this happens less frequently. Nevertheless, its most well-known decision in this realm did not follow this trend.

In 2003, the Court decided the so-called Ellwanger case.[58] Siegfried Ellwanger was an editor and writer who published books (written by himself and by other authors) with allegedly anti-Semitic content. The books were banned and Ellwanger was arrested. The STF decided that anti-Semitism is a form of racism and that freedom of expression is clearly restricted by the criminalisation of racism. In other words, racist speech is not protected by Art 5, IV.

In the realm of freedom of intellectual, artistic, and scientific expression, one of the most important decisions of the Court relates to Art 20 of the Brazilian Civil Code, according to which '[u]nless authorised, or necessary for the administration of justice or for maintaining the public order, the publication of written texts, the transmission of speeches, or the publication, display or use of a person's image may be forbidden at his or her request and without prejudice to payments for damages if they negatively affect their honour, good name, or respectability, or if they are intended for commercial purposes'. Especially in relation to biographies – and in any work in which those acts, rights and goods play a role – this provision was frequently interpreted as demanding the authorisation of anyone portrayed or depicted therein.

[57] The right to reply is regulated by Federal Law 13188 (2015). At least two actions have been filed before the STF challenging the constitutionality of some of its provisions. See ADI 5415 (pending) and ADI 5436 (pending).

[58] HC 82424 (2003). For a detailed summary of this decision in English, see Juliano Zaiden Benvindo, *On the Limits of Constitutional Adjudication: Deconstructing Balancing and Judicial Activism* (Heidelberg, Springer, 2010) 19–29.

In a unanimous decision, the Court decided not to strike down Art 20, but to declare the unconstitutionality of any interpretation of it that implies the need for prior authorisation by the portrayed and depicted persons.[59] However, unlike similar approaches that can be found in the case law of the constitutional and supreme courts of other countries, the STF did not explicitly differentiate between public persons – that is, persons who are part of history or current events – and those persons whose life is not a matter of public interest.[60]

A further peculiarity related to protection of freedom of expression in Brazil is the criminalisation of offensive expressions directed at public officials (*desacato*). Art 331 of the Criminal Code provides that insulting a civil servant on duty is punishable by six months to two years imprisonment or fine. In contrast, the *Declaration of Principles on Freedom of Expression*, approved in 2000 by the Inter-American Commission on Human Rights, clearly states that the criminalisation of *desacato* is incompatible with Art 13 of the American Convention on Human Rights. Only recently have some Brazilian courts begun to enforce Art 13 of the American Convention against Art 331 of the Criminal Code. Although the STF has already ruled that the Convention ranks above domestic ordinary legislation,[61] it has still has not decided any case concerning offensive expression directed at public officials.[62] Hence, such expression remains a criminal offence in Brazil.

Art 5, IV, protects the general freedom of 'manifestation of thought' while providing for an important limitation: 'anonymity is forbidden'. The mainstream (and almost unanimous) interpretation of this provision assumes that anonymity as such is forbidden – that is, the manifestation of thought is protected if and only if the author is either identified or identifiable. According to this interpretation, unidentified or unidentifiable publications could be forbidden, irrespective of their content. There are strong arguments for this mainstream interpretation. Freedom of expression can (and in many cases does) harm. Thus, identifiable authorship is necessary, for instance, for the enforcement of Art 5, V, which provides for 'compensation for pecuniary or

[59] ADI 4815 (2015).

[60] It should be emphasised, however, that the Court takes a different position in other decisions. See, for instance, Rcl 18638 (2014): 'Persons who hold positions in government enjoy a less intense level of protection of their right to privacy'.

[61] See below in this chapter.

[62] There is, however, a case pending of decision: ADPF 496 (pending), along with a decision of the Superior Court of Justice (STJ): REsp 1640084 (2016).

moral damages or damages to reputation' resulting from the exercise of freedom of expression.

Beyond the legal and moral arguments for or against an absolute ban on anonymity, it should be stressed that technology may on the one hand increase the importance of anonymity (as a defence against comprehensive network surveillance and massive collection of personal data) and on the other hand render the debate on the protection of anonymous speech irrelevant in some circumstances, since it has been increasingly easy to act with anonymity in cyberspace. Tools for ensuring anonymity on the Internet have posed important challenges to the full enforcement of the ban on anonymity. The Brazilian constitutional literature seems to remain unaware of this new reality. Either now or in the near future, the main issue will probably not be whether anonymous speech should be acceptable, but how to interpret the Constitution in a context in which anonymity is inevitable.

VII. FREEDOM OF THE PRESS

In addition to the general provisions on freedom of expression, presented in the previous section, the Constitution has a chapter dedicated to 'social communication' (Chapter V of Heading VIII). The articles in this chapter lay down general principles concerning freedom of the press, the production and programming of radio and TV stations, ownership of media corporations, and the concession of open TV and radio broadcasting services.

The central provision of the chapter is undoubtedly Art 220, which establishes that freedom of the press 'shall not be subject to any restrictions, observing the provisions of this Constitution' and that 'no law shall contain any provision that may constitute an impediment to full freedom of the press, in any medium of social communication, observing the provisions of Art 5, IV, V, X, XIII and XIV'. Hence, the Constitution itself provides possible justifications for limiting freedom of the press, namely, the protection of the rights and enforcement of the duties set forth in clauses IV, V, X, XIII and XIV of Art 5. These are freedom of expression and the ban on anonymity, the right of reply and the right to compensation for damages, the right to privacy, freedom of profession and freedom of information, respectively.

Just like freedom of expression, the STF conferred great importance upon freedom of the press. In one of the most important decisions in this realm, the Court declared the unconstitutionality – or, in the terminology of the Court for laws enacted before the promulgation of the Constitution, the non-reception – of Federal Law 5250/1967, also known as the Press Act (*Lei de Imprensa*), a piece of legislation enacted at the beginning of the authoritarian regime (1964–85).[63] The Press Act of 1967 contained several provisions that restricted the freedom of the press.

One year later, the Court declared the unconstitutionality of Art 45, II and III, of Federal Law 9504/1997 (Elections Act), which forbade radio and TV stations from broadcasting programmes that ridicule candidates or parties or expressing opinions that were either favourable or unfavourable to them.[64]

Even when the rights of children and adolescents are at stake, the Court has not deviated much from its almost unconditional defence of freedom of the press. Some provisions of the Children and Adolescents Act (Federal Law 8069/1990), which restricted the freedom of the press to protect the rights of children and adolescents, have already been struck down by the Court.[65] In one of the most important cases in this arena, although Art 21, XVI, of the Constitution grants to the Union the power to 'define an advisory rating system for public entertainment and radio and television programs', which encompasses the possibility to advise broadcasting times that are more suitable for each rating, the Court decided that ordinary legislation cannot make advisory broadcasting times binding, as did Federal Law 8069/1990. According to the Court, TV broadcasters are free to decide whether to follow the advisory rating system.[66]

It is an acknowledged fact that a free and robust press has played a central role in the consolidation of Brazilian democracy since 1988. The press has effectively checked the discretion of public officials, revealed several corruption schemes, and contributed to transparency in government.[67] Nevertheless, according to the World Press Freedom Index, published by the Reporters Without Borders, Brazil occupies the 103rd position, fairly far behind other South American countries such as

[63] See ADPF 130 (2009).
[64] See ADI 4451 (2018).
[65] For instance, Art 247, § 2, last sentence. See ADI 869 (1999).
[66] See ADI 2404 (2016).
[67] As Pereira and Melo argue, the Brazilian media has been a 'key independent player in the web of accountability institutions'. See Marcus Andre Melo and Carlos Pereira, *Making Brazil Work: Checking the President in a Multiparty System* (Basingstoke, Palgrave Macmillan, 2013) 17.

Uruguay (25th), Chile (33rd), and Argentina (50th).[68] The situation is not different in the Freedom House Freedom of the Press Ranking 2017: the press in Brazil is classified as only 'partly free'.[69]

There are several reasons for this bad performance. Among the most important of them is surely the fact that the press in Brazil is still less plural than it could and should be. The biggest newspapers, TV broadcasters and weekly magazines belong to a handful of corporations, which have been run by the same families for decades. Additionally, state-owned broadcasters play only a marginal role in providing more perspectives. Unsurprisingly, every attempt to regulate the media market in Brazil has failed due to, *inter alia*, the powerful opposition of those private corporations. Additionally, many newspapers, magazines and TV broadcasters are heavily dependent on resources from advertising by state governments, which potentially undermines their independence.

However, the economic and political interests of media corporations are only one side of the problem. Freedom of the press is further undermined by violence against journalists. In some circumstances, investigative journalism in Brazil can be a dangerous endeavour. According to Reporters Without Borders, 'Brazil continues to be one of Latin America's most violent countries for journalists'.[70] According to the Inter-American Commission on Human Rights, in 2015 alone, 11 journalists were killed in Brazil and many others were victims of physical aggression because of their journalist activity.[71]

VIII. FREEDOM OF INFORMATION

In addition to freedom of expression and freedom of the press, the Constitution provides for a right to freedom of information. Art 5, XIV, provides that 'access to information is assured to everyone and the confidentiality of source shall be safeguarded whenever necessary for professional activity'. This article thus guarantees two different

[68] See rsf.org/en/ranking/2017.

[69] See freedomhouse.org/report/freedom-press/freedom-press-2017.

[70] See rsf.org/en/brazil.

[71] See Inter-American Commission on Human Rights. Office of the Special Rapporteur for Freedom of Expression, *Liberdade de expressão no Brasil: Relatórios anuais da Relatoria Especial para a Liberdade de Expressão da CIDH 2005–2015* (Washington, DC, Organization of American States 2016) 25–28 www.oas.org/pt/cidh/expressao/docs/publicaciones/BrasilLibertadExpresion2016.pdf (the report is available in Portuguese only).

rights. The first is a right assured to everyone: freedom of information. The second is a right that only certain persons have, namely, the right not to disclose the source of a given piece of information whenever doing so can be considered necessary for professional activity.

The case law of the STF on access to information is mainly composed of decisions related to freedom of the press. The Court rightly assumes that restrictions on freedom of the press tend to negatively affect everyone's freedom to have access to information. However, there are also other areas in which freedom of information plays a central role, such as transparency in administration, access to public databases, and the right to petition, among others.

In addition to clause XIV, which is mentioned above, Art 5 has two further clauses related to access to information, especially when information is in the hands of the government. Art 5, XXXIII, guarantees that 'all persons have the right to receive from public agencies information in their private interest or of collective or general interest … except for information whose secrecy is essential to the security of society and of the state', while Art 5, XXXIV, *a*, provides that 'all persons are guaranteed, without the payment of fees, the right to petition public authorities in defence of rights or against illegality or abuse of power'.

The access to information provided for in Art 5, XXXIII, is regulated by Federal Law 12527/2011, also known as the Access to Information Act (LAI, *Lei de Acesso à Informação*). Although several governmental agencies still resist transparency, the Access to Information Act has clearly resulted in an important transformation in how information is treated by them and most importantly, in people's awareness of their right to receive information that is (or should be) public. Several of its provisions require that the Internet be used to increase access to information.

IX. RIGHT TO PRIVACY

Probably no other right that has undergone such a rapid transformation in its core meaning in recent decades as the right to privacy. If some decades ago privacy still meant the right to be left alone, recent technological developments have clearly shifted the focus to issues related to the mass collection of personal data.

Art 5 has three clauses directly related to several aspects of privacy. Art 5, X, is the most general and important of these clauses. It provides that 'personal intimacy, private life, honour and image of persons are inviolable, being assured the right to compensation for property or moral damages resulting from the violation thereof'. Art 5, XI, provides for the inviolability of the home, in which 'no one may enter … without the consent of the dweller, except in the event of flagrante delicto, disaster, or rescue, or, during the day, with a court order'. Art 5, XII, regulates the secrecy of communications, providing that 'the secrecy of correspondence and of telegraphic, data and telephone communications is inviolable, except, in the latter case, by court order, in the cases and in the manner established by law for the purposes of criminal investigation or the fact-finding phase of a criminal prosecution'.

A. Data Protection

Until August 2018, Brazil did not have a general, comprehensive data protection law. Until that date, data protection was partially regulated by various statutes. This fragmented regulation, however, did not cope with the type of data collection that currently poses the most serious threats to the right to privacy. Even the Brazilian Civil Framework for the Internet (Federal Law 12965/2014), even though it guarantees several rights directly related to the private sphere, did not provide for effective mechanisms for their enforcement. Moreover, the Civil Framework for the Internet has provisions on data retention, which have been the subject of criticism.[72]

Brazilian General Data Protection Law (Federal Law 13709/2018) was passed on August 2018 and was to a great extent inspired by the EU General Data Protection Regulation. It will come into effect in 2020 (18 months after its enactment). Even though it is still not possible to assess how the General Data Protection Law will be enforced and what will be the degree of compliance with its requirements, and even though two important of its provisions were vetoed by the President of the Republic (the creation of the National Data Protection Authority and of the National Council for the Protection of Personal Data and Privacy), it is nevertheless possible to argue that its enactment was a very important step for strengthening the protection of privacy in Brazil.

[72] See, for instance, Francis Augusto Medeiros and Lee A Bygrave, 'Brazil's Marco Civil da Internet: Does It Live up to the Hype?' (2015) 31 *Computer Law & Security Review* 120. For a detailed analysis of the process of creating the Brazilian Civil Framework for the Internet, see Carlos Affonso Souza and others, 'Notes on the Creation and Impacts of Brazil's Internet Bill of Rights' (2017) 5 *The Theory and Practice of Legislation* 73.

B. Privacy and Criminal Investigation

The protection of the right to privacy is an especially sensitive issue in the realm of criminal investigation. The Constitution guarantees the inviolability of the home and a right to the secrecy of communications. Since both rights clearly place limits on criminal investigation, police authorities, public prosecutors and even judges constantly attempt to undermine their enforcement.

i. Inviolability of the Home

The inviolability of the home, which is guaranteed by Art 5, XI, is a right with well-defined boundaries: no one may enter it 'without the consent of the dweller, except in the event of flagrante delicto, disaster, or rescue, or, during the day, with a court order'.[73] Still, police authorities, often with the support of public prosecutors and the approval of judges, frequently perform searches and seizures without search warrants, even at night. The STF has already upheld the constitutionality and the legality of such searches in some circumstances. According to the Court, in the case of permanent crimes, flagrante delicto is also a permanent state. Therefore, the Court decided that the police may enter one's home, without a search warrant, at night, simply because there are indications that the dweller possesses illegal drugs not for his or her own consumption at home.[74]

More recently, an additional method of circumventing the inviolability of the home has been receiving increasing attention. The issuance of a search warrant not only presupposes a probable cause, it must also be specific, that is, it must identify the person or the property to be searched.[75] Police authorities have been increasingly requesting, and several judges have been granting, unspecific search warrants, aiming to allow for searches and seizures in entire neighbourhoods. In a habeas corpus in the STF, whose decision is still pending, the Federal Public Ministry argued in favour of the issuance of unspecific search warrants.[76]

[73] The concept of 'home' encompasses not only where an individual lives. Hotel rooms also fall within the scope of this concept. See RHC 90376 (2007).

[74] See RE 603616 (2015).

[75] Code of Criminal Procedure, Art 243.

[76] See HC 154118 (pending).

ii. Eavesdropping

Art 5, XII, provides that interception and monitoring of telephone lines may be allowed 'by court order, in cases and in the manner established by law for the purposes of criminal investigation or the fact-finding phase of a criminal prosecution'. Telephone interception and monitoring is regulated by Federal Law 9296/1996. The maximum duration of telephone interception is 30 days.[77] Art 8 of the same law provides that the confidentiality of any recordings and transcripts obtained should be guaranteed. These provisions are often not strictly enforced by Brazilian judges, at the request of the Public Ministry or of police authorities. In a case in which Brazil is a party before the Inter-American Court of Human Rights, the Court decided that Brazil violated the plaintiffs' right to privacy and right to honour and reputation due to its interception, recording and dissemination of their telephone conversations.[78]

In the realm of the secrecy of communication, there is also an ongoing controversy as to whether Art 5, XII, allows or forbids the interception of other types of communication. Art 1, single paragraph, of Federal Law 9296/1996 states that the provisions of this law are also applicable to 'the interception of the communication in IT systems'. This provision has allowed the interception of several forms of digital communication, such as emails, SMS, and other types of messages transmitted by messaging applications, especially in smartphones.

Changes in the technological landscape have also brought about new tensions between the right to privacy and criminal investigation. As the examples above show, police authorities and public prosecutors have frequently attempted to undermine the protection of the former in favour of the effectiveness of the latter. Currently, one of the most important controversies in this realm is related to the use of encryption in messaging services. Almost all messaging applications currently employ end-to-end encryption, which makes the interception of messages a virtually useless procedure. In the course of criminal investigations, several judges in Brazil have required that the operator of one these messaging services (WhatsApp) either give the encryption keys to the authorities or disable encryption altogether. Due to the refusal of

[77] Federal Law 9296/1996, Art 5: 'The decision … shall also indicate the means of executing the procedure, which may not exceed 15 days, renewable for the same duration …'.

[78] See *Escher et al v Brazil* (2009), Inter-American Court of Human Rights. The STF has already recognised the general repercussion of an extraordinary appeal that involves the same issue, but a decision on the merits is still pending. See RE 625263 (pending).

the operator, judges have decided to temporarily suspend the services, a decision affecting millions of users in Brazil. At least two constitutional actions have been filed before the STF challenging such blockages, which are based on a possible interpretation of Art 10 and 12, III-IV, of the Civil Framework for the Internet.[79] In June 2017, the Court held a public hearing on the matter.[80]

X. FREEDOM OF ASSEMBLY

In June 2013, a wave of protests broke out across Brazil. One of the most important catalysts of these protests was the disproportionate use force by the São Paulo police to disperse a peaceful demonstration against an increase in bus, underground, and train fares. Neither the federal, state nor local governments were prepared to deal with the situation. Several constitutional questions arose. Can the government forbid a demonstration? What is the role of the police forces? If a demonstration includes walking from a meeting to an endpoint, is there a duty to inform authorities of the route in advance? What may the authorities do if the protest turns violent? Are the protesters allowed to wear masks?

Although the constitutional provision on freedom of assembly is one of the most detailed in Art 5,[81] the answer to these (and several other) questions involves more than an interpretive task. The questions raised by the exercise of freedom of assembly are complex and indicate the need for detailed regulation of this freedom by ordinary legislation. In Brazil, however, there is no such regulation. Many still fear that the regulation of the freedom of assembly necessarily implies an undue limitation of this right. However, the experience in Brazil shows that the absence of regulation may grant unchecked power to the authorities (and to the police) to arbitrarily decide what to do in each situation.

It is not infrequent that violent acts erupt within a peaceful demonstration. Since there is no regulation of the matter in Brazil, the decision on how to react to violence is made by the police, who frequently are unable – especially in the heat of the moment – to distinguish small and

[79] ADPF 403 (pending) and ADI 5527 (pending).

[80] See ch 4 for a brief description of public hearings in the STF.

[81] Art 5, XVI, provides that 'all persons may hold peaceful meetings, without weapons, in places open to the public, regardless of authorisation, provided that they do not interfere with another meeting previously called for the same place, subject only to prior notice to the proper authority'.

isolated acts of violence against private property (cars, shop windows) from generalised violence that threatens public security. This has led to all-too-frequent use of devices and strategies that could often be considered disproportionate, such as rubber bullets, tear gas, stun grenades, and pepper spray, among others.

Another issue related to the peaceful character of demonstrations is the use of masks by demonstrators. Especially during the demonstrations in June 2013, but also in others before and after that time, the police have not allowed masks to be worn, even when people were peacefully protesting. This lack of regulation leaves the final decision to the police, not to the legislature or to the courts.

The duty to give prior notice to the authorities also gives rise to questions such as the following: If the demonstration involves marching from one point to another, is it necessary to communicate the entire route in advance? Can the responsible authority reject one route and propose another one for safety reasons? What happens if a prior notice is not submitted? Can the assembly be dissolved or banned from marching?

These and several other questions cannot be definitively answered here due to the lack of legislation aimed at regulating freedom of assembly in Brazil. Given the existence of so many unanswered questions and the lack of legislation on the matter, it is surprising that the STF has not been called upon to establish rules for the exercise of freedom of assembly and the limits of police action in this realm. There are only a few cases decided by the Court, and none of them have implicated any of the controversial issues mentioned above. Indeed, the STF has shown a tendency to avoid such questions.

In 2007, the Court declared the unconstitutionality of several provisions of a decree of the governor of the federal district that banned the use of loudspeakers and amplifiers in demonstrations near the seats of the legislative, executive and judiciary branches in Brasília.[82] The reasoning of the Court is rather superficial and did not go any further than arguing that freedom of assembly is of paramount importance for democracy. The Court clearly missed the opportunity to discuss several relevant issues concerning the freedom of assembly, the most salient in this case being the possibility of banning demonstrations near the seats of the three branches. The Court did not even bother to justify why the decree of the federal district should be considered unconstitutional if the

[82] See ADI 1969 (2007).

Elections Act has a very similar provision prohibiting the use of loudspeakers and amplifiers in political rallies within less than 200 metres from the seat of the legislative, executive, and judiciary branches, along with any court or military barracks.

XI. SECULARISM AND FREEDOM OF RELIGION

A. Secularism

The republican movement, which culminated in the proclamation of the republic in 1889, was highly secular and largely anticlerical. This secular character is noticeable throughout the 1891 Constitution, the most secular in Brazilian history. From 1891 to 1988, although the Brazilian constitutions maintained a secular character, they gradually accepted more exceptions to it.

Of the almost 200 million inhabitants of Brazil (2010), 87.9 per cent are Christians and 64.6 per cent are Catholics.[83] Brazil is the country with the largest number of Catholics in the world,[84] and secularism cannot be understood detached from these numbers. Although the Constitution establishes that 'the Union, States, Federal District and Municipalities are forbidden to … establish religions or churches, subsidise them, hinder their functioning, or maintain dependent relations or alliances with them or their representatives',[85] elements of non-secularism are ubiquitous in Brazil, with the Catholic religion in many contexts being naturalised as almost official. The understanding of what the separation of state and church demands is rather peculiar in some situations and there is frequently an unclear mixture between what is a purposeful self-affirmation of certain religious groups and what is simply the reproduction of religious customs that permeate the history of Brazil.

Crucifixes hang on the walls of many government buildings, state legislatures and almost every court.[86] A crucifix even hangs on the wall

[83] Source: IBGE https://sidra.ibge.gov.br/tabela/2094.

[84] Still, the percentage of Catholics in the Brazilian population is clearly decreasing. In 2000, they were 73.6% of the population, whereas in 1970, they were still 91.77% of the population.

[85] Art 19, I.

[86] There have already been some attempts in the National Council of Justice to remove crucifixes from the walls of buildings of the judicial branch. All these requests were denied based on the argument that the crucifix is part of Brazilian history and culture. See PP 1344, 1345, 1346 and 1362 (2007).

of the plenary room of the STF, bigger and more prominent than the coat of arms of the republic. Crucifixes also hang in the plenary rooms of both the Chamber of Deputies and the Federal Senate. Floor sessions in both the Chamber of Deputies and the Federal Senate begin with the exhortation 'under the protection of God'. Even more controversial is the provision that requires that during the floor sessions 'the Holy Bible should … remain on the table of the directing board, at the disposal of those who wish to make use of it'.[87] The fact that the Constitution itself mentions God in its preamble is often used to justify similar references to God in other contexts.[88]

In 2017, the STF delivered its interpretation of Art 210, § 1, according to which 'religious education shall be an optional course during normal school hours in public elementary schools'.[89] The controversial issue in the case was whether secularism requires non-confessional religious education in the public schools. By a slight majority, and contrary to the written opinion of the judge rapporteur, the Court has ruled that religious education in public schools may be confessional.

B. Freedom of Religion

Art 5, VI, protects freedom of religion as follows: 'freedom of conscience and belief is inviolable, the free exercise of religious beliefs is protected and, as provided by law, the places of worship and their rites are guaranteed'. This 'freedom of conscience and belief' is complemented by other constitutional provisions such as the possibility of conscientious objection to compulsory military service.[90]

Art 5, VIII, has a broader scope than protecting conscientious objection. It aims to protect individuals against any form of disenfranchisement based on religious beliefs and practices. Conscientious objection is a stance against duties that are incompatible with personal beliefs, but this provision also aims to prevent these beliefs from being the reason – albeit indirect – that one is prevented from having access

[87] RICD, Art 79, § 1. In some state legislatures, an excerpt of the Bible is read at the beginning of every floor session (see, for instance, the internal rules of the legislature of the state of Goiás, Art 73, § 2).

[88] The preamble of the Constitution reads: 'We the representatives of the Brazilian People, convened in the National Constituent Assembly, … promulgate, under the protection of God, the following Constitution of the Federative Republic of Brazil'.

[89] See ADI 4439 (2017).

[90] Art 5, VII, and Art 143, § 1.

to rights, goods and services that are accessible to all. An example may illustrate this point.

In 2009, the Brazilian National High School Exam (*ENEM – Exame Nacional do Ensino Médio*) took place on a Saturday and a Sunday. A Jewish educational institute in São Paulo filed a lawsuit requesting an alternative date for the exam, because otherwise, the Jewish students who were represented by the institute would be deprived of the possibility of taking the exam on religious ground (the duty to observe the Sabbath). The rules of the National High School Exam already provided for an accommodation for such cases: those who could not take the exam during regular hours (from 14:00 to 18:00) for religious reasons could take the exam after 18:00. However, they must arrive at the exam location before 14:00 and wait until 18:00 in a closed room to prevent them from having access to the content of the exam in advance. The STF denied the request for an alternate date,[91] arguing that the solution offered by the government (the possibility of taking the exam after 18:00) was the best way to accommodate the right to equality before the law and freedom of religion. As a corollary, this means that the solution offered by the government does not entail disenfranchisement based on religious grounds in the sense of Art 5, VIII.

XII. PROPERTY RIGHTS

Property rights are regulated by Art 5, XXII to XXXI. These clauses refer to different types of properties: land, intellectual and artistic properties, copyrights, patents, industrial designs, and inheritances, among others. Some of these types of property do not raise constitutional controversies. The most important debate on the right to property in Brazil stems from the association of clauses XXII and XXIII of Art 5. The first concisely states that 'the right of property is guaranteed', while the second introduces an important limitation on this right, providing that 'property shall comply with its social function'.

The Constitution does not define 'social function', but it does deliver criteria for assessing whether or not urban and rural properties comply with their social function.[92] The establishment of criteria for assessing

[91] See STA 389-AgR (2009).

[92] Art 182, § 2, and Art 186, I-IV, respectively. For an analysis of the introduction of the concept of 'social function' into Brazilian legal culture, see Alexandre dos Santos Cunha, 'The Social Function of Property in Brazilian Law' (2011) 80 *Fordham L Rev* 1171. For an

compliance with the social function of private property is especially relevant in the realm of urban policy and land reform. These issues will be presented and analysed in chapter six.

XIII. ACCESS TO COURTS AND DUE PROCESS

More than 30 of the 78 clauses of Art 5 are related to access to courts and due process, especially in the realm of criminal justice.[93] Similar to what occurs in the realm of the right to equality, in the realm of access to the courts and due process, constitutional provisions and reality diverge considerably.

Among other rights, the Constitution protects universal access to jurisdiction; enshrines the rule that there are no crimes unless previously defined by law, nor are there any penalties unless previously imposed by law; and bans capital punishment (except in the case of declared war) along with life imprisonment, forced labour, banishment and cruel punishments.

Several clauses of Art 5 aim at regulating the rights of prisoners. The Constitution provides that sentences shall be served in separate establishments according to the nature of the offence, the age and sex of the convict, the assurance that prisoners' physical and moral integrity will be respected, and the assurance that female prisoners will be held under conditions that allow them to remain with their children during the nursing period.[94]

The due process clause – no one shall be deprived of liberty or property without due process of law – has several corollaries, such as the provision assuring litigants in judicial or administrative proceedings and defendants in general an adversary system and a full defence, the provision to the effect that evidence obtained through unlawful means is inadmissible in proceedings, and the provision that no one shall be considered guilty until his or her criminal conviction has become final and non-appealable.

Finally, several provisions regulate arrest and release. According to Art 5, LXI to LXVI, no one shall be arrested unless in flagrante delicto

analysis of the challenges of its implementation, see Gabriel Ondetti, 'The Social Function of Property, Land Rights and Social Welfare in Brazil' (2016) 50 *Land Use Policy* 29.

[93] Additionally, clauses LXVIII to LXXIII define the aims and scope of the so-called constitutional remedies, which will be analysed below.

[94] Art 5, XLVIII, XLIX, L. See HC 143641 (2018).

or by written and substantiated order of a competent judicial authority; the arrest of any person and the place where she or he can be found shall be communicated immediately to the proper judge and to someone designated by the arrested person; arrested persons shall be informed of their rights, including the right to remain silent; they have the right to the identification of those responsible for their arrest or interrogation by the police; judicial authorities shall immediately release those illegally arrested; and no one shall be taken to prison or held therein when the law permits provisional liberty, with or without bond.

The enforcement of all these provisions is very heterogeneous. It may be argued that the guarantee of due process within private litigation is reasonably well enforced.[95] However, in the realm of criminal justice the scenario is much more complex. The rights related to arrest and the rights of those who serve their sentences in prison are completely undermined both by the abusive use of force by the police and by the inhuman prison system in Brazil.

The Brazilian police force is one of the most lethal in the world.[96] Moreover, police action in Brazil is frequently based on racial and social profiling: personal searches are almost always performed on non-white and poor persons. Racial and social bias also affects the composition of the prison population in Brazil, since judges frequently base their decisions exclusively on testimonial evidence.

According to the World Prison Brief, Brazil has the third-largest prison population in the world (behind only the United States and China) and more than one-third of this population is composed of pre-trial detainees,[97] for many of whom there are no concrete reasons to justify their continuing imprisonment. In some cases, detainees remain in prison even after having served their sentences. A considerable share of the detainees was convicted for drug trafficking and related crimes; they include more than 25 per cent of male prisoners and more than 60 per cent of women in Brazilian prisons.

[95] However, access to courts and the likelihood of success may still depend highly on access to information, awareness of one's own rights and financial capacity to hire a good lawyer. In this realm, the work of the Public Defender's Office has considerably improved access to the courts in recent decades. See ch 4.

[96] According to the Brazilian Forum of Public Security (*Fórum Brasileiro de Segurança Pública*), 4,223 people were killed by the Brazilian Police in 2016. See Fórum Brasileiro de Segurança Pública, *Anuário Brasileiro de Segurança Pública 2017* (São Paulo, Fórum Brasileiro de Segurança Pública, 2017) 13. See also Daniel M Brinks, *The Judicial Response to Police Killings in Latin America* (Cambridge, Cambridge University Press, 2008).

[97] See http://www.prisonstudies.org/.

Provisions such as those of Art 5, XLIX ('prisoners are assured respect for their physical and moral integrity'), Art 5, LXV ('judicial authorities shall direct immediate release of those illegally arrested'), or Art 5, LXVI ('no one shall be taken to prison or held therein when the law permits provisional liberty, with or without bond'), remain unenforced for a significant number of persons arrested and convicted every day in Brazil. As Rosenn puts it, '[d]espite Brazil's long established constitutional guarantee of habeas corpus, a great many prisoners remain confined in a hugely overcrowded and horrendous prison system when they should be at large'.[98]

In 2015, inspired by decision T-153/1998 of the Colombian Constitutional Court, which had declared an 'unconstitutional state of affairs' in the Colombian prison system, an ADPF was filed before the STF seeking a similar declaration for the Brazilian prison system.[99] The recognition of an unconstitutional state of affairs aims at assessing the case as a structural case, which could justify the adoption of structural remedies, that is, remedies that aim at coordinating the revision of an entire public policy. In a preliminary injunction, the Court did recognise that because of the 'massive and persistent violation of fundamental rights, resulting from structural failures and collapse of public policies, whose modification depends on comprehensive normative, administrative and budgetary measures, the national prison system should be characterised as an "unconstitutional state of affairs"'.[100] Nevertheless, after a long judgment session, the Court rejected almost all demands presented by the plaintiff. Since then, the STF has not shown any willingness to make a definitive decision on the matter, and the prison system in Brazil remains as bad as – or became even worse than – at the time of the preliminary injunction.[101]

Finally, another provision in the realm of due process whose interpretation has time and again been in the agenda of the STF is that of Art 5, LVII, according to which 'no one shall be considered guilty until the

[98] Keith S Rosenn, 'Procedural Protection of Constitutional Rights in Brazil' (2011) 59 *Am J Comp L* 1009, 1017.

[99] ADPF 347 (pending).

[100] ADPF 347-MC (2015).

[101] The Inter-American Court of Human Rights seems to be more active in this realm and has issued a series of provisional measures concerning Brazilian prisons. See, for instance, *Matter of the Penitentiary Complex of Curado regarding Brazil* (2017), *Matter of the Criminal Institute of Plácido de Sá Carvalho regarding Brazil* (2017), *Matter of the Penitentiary Complex of Pedrinhas regarding Brazil* (2014), *Matter of Urso Branco Prison regarding Brasil* (2011), among others.

criminal conviction has become final and non-appealable'. Although the text of this clause is fairly clear, the case law of the Court has frequently swung between a literal and a pragmatic interpretation. The Court has traditionally understood that definitive incarceration can only take place after the conviction has become final and non-appealable.[102] More recently, however – based both on the assumption that sending someone to prison does not violate the presumption of non-culpability and on pragmatic reasoning according to which, because of the wide array of appeals to which a defendant may resort, it may take a long time until a decision becomes final and the statute of limitations will probably expire before a final decision is made – the Court shifted to an interpretation according to which defendants may be sent to prison even before a final conviction.[103] Since impunity is a major concern in Brazilian society, the STF decided to make its own mark in the fight against it, even if this involves weakening a fundamental guarantee in the realm of due process of law.[104]

XIV. NATIONALITY

The general rule for the attribution of Brazilian nationality is the so-called *ius soli*. According to Art 12, I, *a*, everyone born in Brazil is a native-born Brazilian, even if born of foreign parents (unless both were officially serving their country). Brazil has adopted this basic rule since its first constitution.[105]

Of course, this rule is complemented by more specific rules to prevent cases of statelessness. Hence, Brazilian nationality is also granted to those born abroad of a Brazilian father or mother, if one of them were in the service of Brazil or if not, provided they were registered at a proper Brazilian governmental office or came to reside in Brazil and opted for Brazilian nationality at any time after reaching the age of majority.

[102] See, for instance, HC 84078 (2009).

[103] See HC 126292 (2016). A similar interpretation was advanced in the past based on a controversial analogy between the writ of habeas corpus and the extraordinary appeal. See HC 68726 (1991) and HC 72061 (1995).

[104] In 2018, this subject was again on the agenda of the Court and a heated debate spread throughout the country: former President Lula was criminally convicted in the wake of the so-called 'Car Wash Operation', a task force of the Federal Police against corruption schemes. President Lula filed a writ of habeas corpus before the STF to avoid being arrested before his conviction became final and non-appealable. The Court decided against him and he was sent to prison. See HC 152752 (2018).

[105] 1824 Constitution, Art 6.

Brazilian nationality may also be granted by naturalisation. The process of naturalisation is defined by Federal Law 13445/2017. The Constitution, however, establishes rules and criteria for the naturalisation process. The general rule is that foreigners of any nationality residing in Brazil for more than 15 uninterrupted years and without any criminal conviction may request Brazilian nationality. For persons 'whose country of origin is Portuguese-speaking, only one uninterrupted year of residence and good moral character are required' (Art 12, II, a). Moreover, Portuguese permanently residing in Brazil may be granted the 'same rights inherent to Brazilians' (except in cases explicitly provided for in the Constitution itself), provided that Portuguese law grants reciprocal treatment to Brazilians living in Portugal. The equality of rights between Portuguese and Brazilians is currently regulated by the Treaty of Porto Seguro, signed 22 April 2000.

Although Art 12, § 2, establishes that 'the law may not establish any distinction between native-born and naturalised Brazilians', the same article states 'except in the cases provided for in this Constitution'. And the Constitution indeed provides for many types of discrimination between them.

The 1891 Constitution had a native-born-citizen clause like the US constitution,[106] which provided that 'the essential conditions for being elected President or Vice-President of the Republic are … to be Brazilian born …' (1891 Constitution, Art 41, § 3, 1). The next constitution (1934) was drafted in an era of extreme nationalism (not only in Brazil, but worldwide) and expanded to the extreme the list of offices that only native-born Brazilian citizens could hold. According to that constitution, not only the President and the Vice-President of the Republic but also all members of the Chamber of Deputies and Federal Senate, ministers of the federal government, judges of the Supreme Court, and federal judges must be native-born Brazilians.[107] Even some non-governmental activities could only be performed by native-born Brazilians. Naturalised Brazilians could be neither publishers of newspapers nor ship owners or commanders of national ships; in such ships, at least two-thirds of the crew members must be native-born Brazilians. Further, naturalised Brazilians could not perform religious assistance

[106] US Constitution, Article II, Section 1, and Amendment XII.

[107] 1934 Constitution, Art 52, § 5; Art 24; Art 89; Art 59, single paragraph; Art 74; and Art 80.

on military expeditions and they could not even request the revalidation of degrees issued by foreign universities or colleges.[108]

It may be argued that the ensuing Brazilian constitutions never eliminated this nationalist element. All of them contained provisions very similar to those of the 1934 Constitution. And it must be stressed once again that these are not distinctions between Brazilians and foreigners but between two types of Brazilians: the native-born and the naturalised.

Hence, although the current list of positions that only native-born Brazilians may hold is less extreme if compared to that of the 1934 Constitution, it nevertheless remains much longer than that of the 1891 Constitution. Art 12, § 3, still reserves to native-born Brazilians the following positions: President and Vice-President of the Republic; President of the Chamber of Deputies; President of the Federal Senate; Judge of the Supreme Court; positions in the diplomatic service; officers of the Armed Forces; and minister of Defence. Further, Art 89, VII, establishes that the six members of the Council of the Republic who are appointed by the President of the Republic, the Chamber of Deputies and the Federal Senate must be native-born Brazilians. Although this list establishes unjustified distinctions between native-born and naturalised Brazilians, the Brazilian constitutional literature usually does not raise any objection.

In addition to the differences that the Constitution establishes between native-born and naturalised Brazilians, there are positions that both types of Brazilian citizens may hold, but not migrants. The most intuitive of these positions are political offices in general. Only Brazilians (native-born or naturalised) may be elected to executive and legislative political offices. Additionally, migrants cannot vote, not even in local elections, as is increasingly common in other countries.

In May 2017, the new Migration Act (Federal Law 13445/2017) was passed, repealing the Foreigners Act of 1980 (Federal Law 6815/1980). The new law, which is clearly based on human rights values, represents an important advancement in this realm, especially compared with its predecessor, which was enacted during the authoritarian regime and was primarily based on considerations of national security, with provisions that aimed mostly at controlling foreigners rather than granting them rights and access to public goods and services.

[108] 1934 Constitution, Art 131; Art 113, 6; Art 132; and Art 133.

XV. POLITICAL RIGHTS

Art 14 opens the chapter on political rights (Chapter IV of Heading II) with the following declaration: 'Popular sovereignty shall be exercised by universal suffrage, and by direct and secret vote, with equal value for all, and … by plebiscite, referendum and popular bills'. It is a clear attempt to bring together both representative and direct democracy. This provision notwithstanding, representative democracy clearly dominates. Since the promulgation of the 1988 Constitution, besides the plebiscite on the regime and the system of government, provided for by the Constitution itself, no further nationwide plebiscites and only one referendum were held.[109]

Unlike the summoning of plebiscites and referenda, which depends on the will of political institutions, introducing popular bills requires only the mobilisation of civil society. However, this is not an easy task, since popular bills have to be subscribed by 'at least one percent of the national electorate, distributed throughout at least five states, with no less than three-tenths of one percent of the voters of each of these states'.[110] Although attempts to mobilise society to support popular bills are fairly common, since 1988 only a few such bills have been presented to the Chamber of Deputies.

A. The Right to Vote

The electoral franchise is very broad: everyone over 16 years of age is eligible to vote. Brazil is one of the few countries in the world that still has compulsory suffrage: voting is mandatory for those between 18 and 70 years of age and optional for those between 16 and 18, those above 70 years of age, and the illiterate. The rate of attendance at polling booths in Brazil is lower than in some countries where voting is compulsory, especially because failing to vote may be justified without sanctions within 60 days of an election day. Voter turnout in Brazil is on average between 75 and 80 per cent.[111] However, many of those who

[109] Concerning the Firearms and Ammunition Act (Federal Law 10826/2003). This referendum was held on 23 October 2005 and the majority of voters (63.94%) voted against a comprehensive ban on firearms and ammunition for private use.

[110] Art 61, § 2. Since the numbers of registered voters in Brazil in 2014 was 142,822,046, a popular bill must be subscribed by at least 1,428,220 voters.

[111] It may be assumed that voter turnout would be higher if some kind of absentee ballot were allowed, such as postal voting, early voting, or Internet voting. None of these types

go to the polls decide not to cast a valid vote: blank and spoilt ballots are allowed.

Brazil has been using electronic voting machines in all of its elections since 2000. At least potentially, this makes voting easier (especially in a country with a moderate rate of functional illiteracy),[112] elections safer, and vote counting faster. Further, it tends to considerably reduce the number of spoilt ballots (except when the casting of spoilt ballots is deliberate). Finally, the use of voting machines may increase accessibility for voters with some types of disability. Their keys have Braille characters (raised dots) and are equipped with headphones that make it easier for the blind to vote; in addition, photos of the candidates are presented on the screen, which may facilitate their identification by illiterate voters.

Notwithstanding these advantages, electronic voting may have its downsides.[113] The system that has been adopted in Brazil is the direct-recording electronic voting system (DRE), which lacks printed ballots (100 per cent electronic). Printed voting and electronic voting are not mutually exclusive concepts. There are direct-recording electronic voting machines that print the voter's ballot and after confirmation, keep it in a ballot box for future audits, if necessary. The National Congress has enacted several laws providing that voting machines should print a copy of the vote, but this duty has never been implemented: the STF has always struck it down.[114] Elections in Brazil continue to be 100 per cent electronic.

B. The Right to Run for Office

The right to run for political office in Brazil is regulated by Art 14, § 3. Six conditions must be met: Brazilian nationality, full exercise of

of voting are allowed in Brazil. Voting at a different polling station has been allowed since 2000, but only in very limited circumstances.

[112] See, however, the findings of Zucco and Nicolau concerning the counter-intuitive order of voting in Brazil Cesar Zucco and Jairo M Nicolau, 'Trading Old Errors for New Errors? The Impact of Electronic Voting Technology on Party Label Votes in Brazil' (2016) 43 *Electoral Studies* 10.

[113] For a critical account of the electronic voting system adopted in Brazil, see Amílcar Brunazo Filho and Augusto Tavares Rosa Marcacini, 'Legal Aspects of E-Voting in Brazil' in Ardita Driza Maurer and Jordi Barrat (eds), *E-Voting Case Law: A Comparative Analysis* (Farnham, Ashgate, 2015).

[114] See federal laws 10408/2002, 12034/2009, and 13165/2015, along with STF decisions ADI 4543 (2013) and ADI 5889-MC (2018).

political rights, electoral enrolment, electoral domicile in the constituency, political party affiliation, and minimum age, which varies depending on the office.

In addition to establishing the conditions for eligibility, Art 14, §§ 5 to 9, also provide for a complex system of ineligibilities by defining those cases in which a person cannot run for a specific political office (or even for any office at all), although he or she satisfies the general conditions of eligibility. The most important of these provisions are as follows: the heads of executive positions at all levels (President, Governors and Mayors) are eligible only for a single subsequent term; if they want to run for a different office, they must resign from their current office at least six months prior to the election; their spouses and relatives by blood or marriage to the second degree or by adoption are ineligible in the constituency of the incumbent unless they previously held an elective office and are candidates for re-election.

Other cases of ineligibility may be created by federal complementary law, such as Federal Complementary Law 64/1990. However, the most well-known and controversial statute is Federal Complementary Law 135/2010, also known as the Clean Slate Act (*Lei da Ficha Limpa*). The general rule for ineligibility resulting from a criminal conviction (established by the Constitution itself) is that such ineligibility lasts as long as the effects of the conviction. Federal Complementary Law 64/1990 had extended the ineligibility period in some cases (three years after the end of the conviction period). The Clean Slate Act extended both the list of cases of ineligibility and the period (to eight years after the end of the conviction).

C. Loss and Suspension of Political Rights

The Constitution employs three different terms in relation to acts that result in the disenfranchisement of political rights: the deprivation, loss, and suspension of political rights. However, it does not define these terms. Art 15 starts with a general and absolute rule: 'deprivation of political rights is forbidden'. At the same time, however, Art 15 adds that the 'loss' and 'suspension' of such rights may occur only in the five cases it defines: 'I. cancellation of naturalisation by a final and non-appealable judicial decision; II. absolute civil incapacity; III. so long as the effects of a final and non-appealable criminal conviction remain in force; IV. refusal to comply with an obligation imposed upon everyone or to perform alternative service, in accordance with Art 5, VIII; V. administrative dishonesty, according to Art 37, § 4'. Notwithstanding the clear and peremptory wording of Art 15, there are other cases of loss or suspension of political rights that are not mentioned in its five clauses. The clearest example is that of a Brazilian native-born citizen who acquires another nationality by naturalisation, since this implies the loss of Brazilian nationality and consequently the loss of political rights.

XVI. POLITICAL PARTIES

A. Creation and Organisation

The Brazilian Constitution regulates the creation and organisation of political parties under the heading of 'fundamental rights'. Art 17 is the last provision of this heading and is the only provision in Chapter V. It provides that the creation and organisation of political parties is free, but the same article, along with the Political Parties Act (Federal Law 9096/1995) establishes limits on this freedom. Among other things, the Constitution provides that parties must be national (ie, regional and local parties are not allowed in Brazil). Art 7, § 1, of the Political Parties Act defines this national character through a complex formula: a political party is national if it demonstrates the support of voters not affiliated with a political party corresponding to at least 0.5 per cent of the valid votes cast in the last general election for the Chamber of Deputies, distributed throughout one-third or more of the states, with no less than 0.1 per cent of the electorate that voted in each one of them. Only parties that fulfil this condition may be registered before the Superior Electoral Court and run for election. Although this provision establishes a difficult task, namely, to collect millions of signatures throughout at least nine states to register a political party, this has not hindered the creation of several parties since 1988. Shortly before the general elections of 2018, 35 parties were registered before the Superior Electoral Court.

The number of registered parties is not necessarily a problem. The fact that almost all of them have representatives in the National Congress might be. The Brazilian party system is extremely fragmented, and building a government coalition in the legislatures has been a difficult task for every president since 1988.[115] To curb the number of parties, the Political

[115] See ch 3.

Parties Act introduced a legal threshold for the proportional elections for the Chamber of Deputies. However, this threshold was declared unconstitutional by the STF in 2006, before the first election in which it would have been effective.[116]

B. Party Loyalty

Another important concept in the Brazilian party system is so-called party loyalty (*fidelidade partidária*). Although neither the Constitution nor ordinary legislation contain provisions on the matter, and although the STF had previously decided that deputies do not lose their office if they change parties,[117] in 2007, after a decision in the opposite direction made by the Superior Electoral Court, the STF changed its settled case law and decided that the seats belong to the parties, not to the deputies, and that therefore, save for a few exceptions, deputies lose their offices when they leave their parties.[118]

C. Party Financing

The extreme personalisation of the Brazilian electoral system[119] considerably increases the costs of electoral campaigns. Because campaigns are individual, so are (to a great extent) the costs. What one candidate spends usually only helps his or her chances of election. To be sure, every vote cast for a candidate of a given party also increases the electoral chances of the party as a whole and therefore, of every other candidate from that party. However, since the chances of getting one of the seats won by the party depend exclusively on the individual votes each candidate receives, the consequence is that candidates have to perform better than both the candidates of other parties and the candidates of their own party (intra-party competition). The number of opponents is thus extremely high.[120]

[116] See ADI 1351 (2006) and 1354 (2006). For more details, see ch 3.

[117] See MS 20927 (1994).

[118] See MS 26602 (2007), MS 26603 (2007), and MS 26604 (2007). See also ADI 3999 (2008) and ADI 4086 (2008). Later, the STF decided that party loyalty does not apply to elections based on the majoritarian principle (ie, for the heads of the executive branch and the Federal Senate). See ADI 5081 (2015).

[119] See ch 3.

[120] One should not forget that: (1) the number of candidates each party may present is very high (see ch 3), and (2) the size of many Brazilian constituencies is enormous

Additionally, the share of money spent by each candidate varies considerably and the chance of being elected is directly linked to the quantity of money received and spent. According to Speck and Mancuso, '[t]he median amount received by the most-voted candidates for federal deputy is 110 times higher than that received by all other candidates'.[121] In future elections, however, online campaigning, especially the massive use of social media, may considerably change this scenario.

Brazil has adopted a mixed model of party financing.[122] Parties receive money both from private and public sources. Until 2015, there was no restriction on who could donate to political parties. In 2015, however, the STF, in a very controversial decision,[123] declared that donations from corporations were unconstitutional, thus limiting private financing to individuals. The background of this decision was the fact that the biggest corporations in Brazil, especially banks and infrastructure companies, were responsible for more than half of campaign financing, and most of them donate to all parties with a chance of winning. Although the Constitution does not contain any provision on party financing (let alone on who is allowed to donate), the Court argued (among many other things) that Art 14, § 9, which states that federal complementary law shall establish cases of ineligibility to protect 'the normality and legitimacy of elections from the influence of economic power', justifies forbidding corporations from donating. Shortly after this decision, the National Congress passed a new law that (among other things) reinstated permission for corporations to donate to political parties. However, this provision was vetoed by the President of the Republic.

Public money is transferred to political parties through the so-called 'party fund' (*Fundo Partidário*) and, since 2018, also through the highly controversial 'special campaign fund' (*Fundo Especial de Financiamento de Campanha*, FEFC). The latter was created to mitigate the effects of the ban on donations from corporations and is shared among parties

(as Samuels reminds, 'one of Brazil's medium-sized states, Minas Gerais, is the size of France'; see David Samuels, 'Incumbents and Challengers on a Level Playing Field: Assessing the Impact of Campaign Finance in Brazil' (2001) 63 *The Journal of Politics* 569, 571).

[121] Bruno Wilhelm Speck and Wagner Pralon Mancuso, 'A Study on the Impact of Campaign Finance, Political Capital and Gender on Electoral Performance' (2014) 8 *Brazilian Political Science Review* 34, 43.

[122] For an analysis of this model, see Bruno Wilhelm Speck, 'Brazil' in Pippa Norris and Andrea Abel van Es (eds), *Checkbook Elections? Political Finance in Comparative Perspective* (New York, Oxford University Press, 2016).

[123] ADI 4650 (2015).

only in election years. In 2018, it added up to BRL 1,716,209,431.[124] The party fund, in contrast, is shared among parties every year. In 2018, it added up to BRL 888,735,090.[125] According to Art 41-A of the Political Parties Act, the party fund is shared as follows: 95 per cent are allocated in proportion to the votes each party received in the last election to the Chamber of Deputies and the remaining 5 per cent are equally shared among those registered parties that fulfil the 'conditions set forth by the Constitution for accessing the resources of the Party Fund'. Until 2017, every registered party (ie, even parties without representatives in the National Congress) received an equal share of this 5 per cent. However, EC 97/2017 made access to this equal share of resources from the party fund considerably more difficult. According to the new wording of Art 17, § 3, the right to resources from the party fund is granted only to those parties that either: (a) received at least 3 per cent of the valid votes distributed throughout one-third of the federal units (ie, states and federal district) in the election for the Chamber of Deputies, with no less than 2 per cent of the valid votes of each of one of them; or (b) elected at least 15 federal deputies distributed throughout at least one-third of the federal units.

According to the transitional provisions of constitutional amendment 97, these new rules will be enforced only in 2030. Until then, and beginning in 2018, the threshold for accessing these resources will progressively increase every four years.

Finally, it is worth mentioning an additional, albeit indirect, form of party funding with public resources: free access to radio and television time. Every political party in Brazil with at least one representative in the National Congress receives five or ten minutes twice a year to broadcast their ideas on every open television and radio channel (private or public).[126] Additionally, and more importantly, in election years, during the 35 days before the second day before election day, two blocks of 25 minutes on every open TV and radio channel are reserved every day for campaigning. Political parties do not have to pay for the time.

[124] This is the equivalent to €381,108,845 (at the exchange rate of 30 June 2018). Source: Superior Electoral Court http://www.tse.jus.br/eleicoes/eleicoes-2018/prestacao-de-contas-1/fundo-especial-de-financiamento-de-campanha-fefc.

[125] This is the equivalent to €197,356,335 (at the exchange rate of 30 June 2018). Source: Superior Electoral Court http://www.tse.jus.br/partidos/fundo-partidario-1/fundo-partidario.

[126] Constitution, Art 17, § 3; Elections Act, Art 44 to 57.

XVII. TREATIES ON HUMAN RIGHTS

In the original text of the Constitution, Art 5 had two paragraphs in addition to its many clauses. Art 5, § 2, was intended to function as a kind of open door for other, unenumerated fundamental rights. This clause was first adopted by the 1891 Constitution, whose Art 78 provided that '[t]he enumeration of guarantees and rights made in the Constitution shall not exclude other guarantees and rights not enumerated, but resulting from the form of government established and the principles proclaimed by the constitution'. The wording of this provision has been repeated in every Brazilian constitution since then, almost without changes.

The 1988 Constitution maintained this tradition, but opened a second door to unenumerated rights in addition to the 'principles and regime' clause: the 'treaties on human rights' clause. Art 5, § 2, provides that '[t]he rights and guarantees established in this Constitution shall not exclude others derived from the regime and principles adopted by it, *or from international treaties to which the Federative Republic of Brazil is a party*'.

Until 1988, the settled case law of the STF put treaties on a level with ordinary legislation, both of them ranked lower than the Constitution.[127] With the promulgation of the 1988 Constitution, almost everyone assumed that this case law would be overruled because of the clear wording of Art 5, § 2. However, this did not happen. The STF did not change its case law.[128]

In 1992, Brazil incorporated the American Convention on Human Rights (1969) into domestic law. Its Art 7, 7, offers stronger protection for personal freedom because it allows for only one exception to the ban on detention for debt, whereas the Brazilian Constitution allows for two exceptions. Despite the ratification of the American Convention, the STF did not alter its settled case law and continued to enforce detention for debt in the case of unfaithful trustees, which the Convention does not allow.[129]

In 2004, the Judiciary Reform Act introduced a new § 3 to Art 5, according to which 'international treaties and conventions on human rights approved by both houses of the National Congress, in two

[127] See RE 80004 (1977).

[128] See, for instance, HC 72131 (1995), HC 73044 (1996), ADI 1480-MC (1997), HC 75687 (1998), HC 75977 (2000) RE 206482 (2001), RE 253071 (2001), and RE 250812 (2001).

[129] See, for instance, RE 206482 (2001): 'This Court upheld the understanding that … the constitutionality of the civil detention of the unfaithful trustee … persists'.

different voting sessions, by three-fifths votes of their respective members, shall be equivalent to constitutional amendments'. The new § 3 clarified what § 2 implied, but it added a new formal condition: a treaty on human rights will be equivalent to a constitutional amendment if and only if it is approved using the same procedure that is used to pass a constitutional amendment.

However, between the promulgation of the Constitution (1988) and the Judiciary Reform Act (2004), Brazil incorporated several important treaties on human rights into domestic law. None of them were incorporated following the procedure laid down by the new § 3. Until 2004, treaties had been incorporated into domestic law by means of a regular legislative decree of the National Congress, whose approval requires neither a three-fifths majority nor two voting sessions. The question about the hierarchical levels of these treaties incorporated before 2004 arose immediately.

It was only in 2008 that the STF answered this question, when the Court decided four cases related to detention for debt.[130] Although the judges present at the judgment session unanimously decided that the detentions were not legal in any of the cases, their reasoning did not converge. Some judges simply did not take a position on the rank of the American Convention, because they argued that this was not relevant for deciding the case. Some judges argued that treaties on human rights that were incorporated into Brazilian domestic law prior to the Judiciary Reform Act should be considered as having constitutional status.[131] Finally, some judges advocated a rather unorthodox solution (at least in the Brazilian tradition). They argued for an intermediate hierarchic rank called 'supra-legality' (*supralegalidade*): treaties on human rights incorporated into domestic law without following the procedure introduced in 2004 by Judiciary Reform Act ranked below the Constitution but above ordinary legislation.[132] Although the supra-legality thesis was not adopted by the majority of the judges – as a matter of fact, only three judges explicitly endorsed it – it has been considered the official position of the Court on the matter since that time.[133]

In the case of treaties on human rights incorporated into domestic law after 2004 and approved by the procedure described in Art 5, § 3,

[130] See RE 466343 (2008), RE 349703 (2008), HC 87585 (2008) and HC 92566 (2008).

[131] RE 466343 (2008), written opinion of judges Celso de Mello.

[132] RE 466343 (2008). written opinion of judges Gilmar Mendes.

[133] For a detailed analysis of the supra-legality thesis, see Antonio Moreira Maués, 'Supra-Legality of International Human Rights Treaties and Constitutional Interpretation' (2017) 10 *Sur – International Journal on Human Rights* 205.

there is no doubt about its rank as equivalent to constitutional amendments.[134] This means, among other things, that ordinary legislation must comply not only with constitutional provisions but also with the provisions of such international treaties. Consequently, judicial review of legislation now has as a parameter not only the Constitution but also those treaties.[135]

XVIII. THE INTER-AMERICAN HUMAN RIGHTS SYSTEM

The Inter-American Human Rights System is one of the three regional systems for the protection of human rights, alongside the European and African systems. The key elements of the system are the American Convention on Human Rights, the Inter-American Commission on Human Rights, and the Inter-American Court of Human Rights.

A. The American Convention on Human Rights (ACHR)

The American Convention on Human Rights, which in Brazil is usually referred to as the Pact of San José (*Pacto de São José da Costa Rica*), was adopted in 1969 and entered into force in 1978 after being ratified by 11 states. Brazil incorporated the ACHR into domestic law in 1992.

The Convention mainly protects civil and political rights. Chapter III, which is dedicated to economic, social, and cultural rights, has only one article, which provides that the state parties shall adopt measures that aim at progressively realising those rights. This article was later complemented by the Protocol to the American Convention on Human Rights in the area of Economic, Social, and Cultural Rights (first additional protocol, also known as the Protocol of San Salvador), which was adopted in 1988 and entered into force in 1999. Brazil ratified it in 1996.

The second part of the Convention is dedicated to the means of protection and defines the organs of the system: the Inter-American Commission on Human Rights and the Inter-American Court of Human Rights.

[134] As of August 2018, only one treaty was approved following this procedure: the Convention on the Rights of Persons with Disabilities (2009).

[135] The IACtHR and the literature call this 'conventionality control'. See IACtHR, *Almonacid Arellano et al v Chile* (2006), § 124, and *Radilla-Pacheco v Mexico* (2009), § 339.

Brazilian constitutional law has traditionally been a realm in which international treaties have played a rather marginal role. A cursory search of the case law of the STF and Brazilian books on constitutional law reveals a scenario in which international treaties, conventions, and protocols are barely mentioned. In the case law of the STF, the ACHR played a decisive role as *ratio decidendi* only in cases related to the ban on detention for debt, presented above. Even if this scenario is gradually changing and the relationship between constitutional law and international law is growing closer, the STF has always been – and remains – very reluctant in this regard.

B. The Inter-American Commission on Human Rights (IACHR)

Unlike the case of the African Court of Human and Peoples' Rights and the European Court of Human Rights, the Inter-American Court does not hear complaints from individuals. Only the Inter-American Commission and state parties have the right to submit a case to the Court. This means that any individual, group of persons, or nongovernmental entity legally recognised in one member state must lodge petitions with the Commission, which has the power to decide whether or not to submit the case to the Court.

C. The Inter-American Court of Human Rights (IACtHR)

Brazil accepted the jurisdiction of the IACtHR in 1998. From that time to August 2018, the Inter-American Court decided nine cases in which Brazil was a party.[136] In addition to rendering decisions on the merits, the Court has frequently taken provisional measures against Brazil, especially in issues related to the Brazilian prison system.

Brazil's 1998 acceptance of the jurisdiction of the IACtHR did not immediately alter the almost irrelevant role that the case law of this Court has played in the decision-making process of the Brazilian Supreme Court. References to decisions of the IACtHR were virtually

[136] These include the following: *Ximenes Lopes v Brazil* (2006), *Nogueira de Carvalho et al v Brazil* (2006), *Escher et al v Brazil* (2009), *Garibaldi v Brazil* (2009), *Gomes Lund et al. ('Guerrilha do Araguaia') v Brazil* (2010), *Hacienda Brasil Verde Workers v Brazil* (2016), *Favela Nova Brasília v Brazil* (2017), *Xucuru Indigenous People and its members v Brazil* (2017), *Herzog et al v Brazil* (2018). The dates indicate the year in which a judgment on the merits was issued.

non-existent. Even before 1998, that is, even before Brazil had accepted the IACtHR's jurisdiction, the case law of the IACtHR could have played an important argumentative role, especially in decisions related to human rights. The STF frequently refers to foreign precedents as an argumentative tool, but almost never to those of the Inter-American Court. Indeed, references to decisions of the Supreme Court of the United States and of the German Constitutional Court are still much more frequent than references to decisions of the IACtHR.

It is true, however, that there is an identifiable and increasing trend among the judges of the STF to use decisions of the IACtHR as an argumentative tool. According to the STF database, the first time that a decision of the plenum of the Court referred to a decision of the IACtHR was in 2008.[137] Since then, the plenum of the STF referred to precedents of the IACtHR a few dozen times. For a Court that decides tens of thousands of cases every year, this is still very infrequent.[138]

It is worth noting that the increasing number of references to precedents of the IACtHR bears no relation to the increasing number of cases in which Brazil is a party before this Court. These references play an argumentative role and thus are unrelated to compliance with decisions in which Brazil was condemned. Indeed, almost all such citations refer to cases in which Brazil is *not* a party.[139]

Issues related to a lack of compliance with IACtHR decisions in cases in which Brazil is a party still have not been decided by the STF. Perhaps the most paradigmatic case in this realm is the decision in the *Gomes Lund* case.[140] In 2010, six months after the STF decided that the Brazilian Amnesty Law[141] is compatible with the 1988 Constitution,[142] the IACtHR decided that '[g]iven its express non-compatibility with the American Convention, the provisions of the Brazilian Amnesty Law that impedes the investigation and punishment of serious human rights

[137] See ADPF 144 (2008).

[138] For a critical appraisal of what he calls 'qualified openness' of the STF towards the IACtHR, see Tom Gerald Daly, 'Brazilian "Supremocracy" and the Inter-American Court of Human Rights: Unpicking an Unclear Relationship' in Pedro Fortes and others (eds), *Law and Policy in Latin America* (London, Palgrave Macmillan, 2017).

[139] Some of the cited decisions of the Inter-American Court include *'The Last Temptation of Christ' (Olmedo Bustos et al) v Chile* (2001), *Ricardo Canese v Paraguay* (2004), *Tribunal Constitucional v Peru* (2001), *Palamara Iribarne v Chile* (2005), and *Mayagna (Sumo) Awas Tingni Community v Nicaragua* (2005).

[140] *Gomes Lund et al. ('Guerrilha do Araguaia') v Brazil* (2010), series C No. 219.

[141] See ch 1.

[142] See ADPF 153 (2010).

violations lack legal effect. As a consequence, they cannot continue to represent an obstacle … for the identification and punishment of those responsible, nor can they have equal or similar impact regarding other cases of serious human rights violations enshrined in the American Convention that occurred in Brazil'.[143]

Based on this decision, the Federal Public Ministry has attempted to try certain officials who served the authoritarian regime (1964–85). However, these attempts have been blocked by lower courts based on the STF's decision in ADPF 153. Consequently, the IACtHR issued a second decision within a procedure of monitoring compliance with the judgment in which it declared that decisions of Brazilian domestic courts made after the decision on the merits in the *Gomes Lund* case may no longer be based on the STF's decision in ADPF 153; rather, they must comply with the decision of the Inter-American Court.[144]

For the first time, a true conflict between decisions of the IACtHR and decisions of the STF arose. The latter must still decide whether it will uphold its previous decision or adapt it to the decision of the Inter-American Court.[145] That said, the Brazilian Court is clearly postponing a verdict as long as possible. A decision on this matter has been awaited since 2010.

XIX. CONSTITUTIONAL REMEDIES

The Bill of Rights of the Brazilian Constitution includes several so-called constitutional remedies,[146] which are constitutional actions aimed at challenging illegalities and abuses of power that impede the exercise of constitutional rights in some contexts or that are detrimental to the public patrimony, administrative morality, the environment or Brazil's historic and cultural heritage.

[143] *Gomes Lund et al*, § 174. For similar precedents of the Inter-American Court, see *Barrios Altos v Peru* (2001), *Almonacid Arellano et al v Chile* (2006), and *La Cantuta v Peru* (2006).

[144] See *Gomes Lund et al ('Guerrilha do Araguaia') v Brazil*, Monitoring Compliance with Judgment. Order of the Inter-American Court of Human Rights of 17 October 2014, § 18.

[145] On this matter, see Yi Shin Tang, 'International Justice through Domestic Courts: Challenges in Brazil's Judicial Review of the Amnesty Law' (2015) 9 *Int J Transit Justice* 259. See also Fabia Fernandes Carvalho Veçoso, 'Whose Exceptionalism? Debating the Inter-American View on Amnesty and the Brazilian Case' in Karen L Engle and others (eds), *Anti-Impunity and the Human Rights Agenda* (Cambridge, Cambridge University Press, 2016).

[146] Art 5, LXVIII-LXXIII.

A. Habeas Corpus

The writ of habeas corpus (HC) is the oldest constitutional remedy in Brazil. It was introduced by the 1832 Code of Criminal Procedure. In 1891, it attained constitutional status. Art 5, LXVIII, of the 1988 Constitution provides that 'habeas corpus shall be granted whenever a person suffers or is in danger of suffering violence or coercion against his freedom of movement, on account of illegal actions or abuse of power'.

The tradition of having an important constitutional remedy against illegalities and abuses of power runs parallel to a tradition of suspending that remedy several times in the twentieth century either during states of siege or by force of Institutional Acts (such as the AI-5) during the last authoritarian regime (1964–85).

Although access to the writ of habeas corpus has not been suspended since 1988, constitutional text and reality tend to clash in this realm. Brazil has the third-largest prison population in the world (behind only the United States and China). More than one-third of this population is composed of pre-trial detainees, many of whom remain imprisoned for no justifiable reason. Additionally, because of flaws in the justice system, many detainees remain in prison even after having served their sentences. The National Council of Justice found that more than 45,000 detainees were imprisoned longer than they should have been.

The writ of habeas corpus is free of charge and may be filed by anyone in his or her own name or even in the name of a third party, and it may be even be granted *ex officio* whenever a judge becomes aware of illegal coercion impeding a person's freedom of movement.

B. Habeas Data

Habeas data (HD) is a creation of the 1988 Constitution. It quickly spread to many other countries (although not necessarily under the same name), especially in Latin America, including in Argentina, Paraguay, and Peru.

Art 5, LXXII, states that habeas data shall be granted for the following reasons: (a) to ensure knowledge of personal information about the petitioner contained in the records or databases of government or otherwise public agencies; and (b) to correct data whenever the petitioner prefers not to do so through a confidential judicial or administrative process.

The creation of habeas data by the 1988 Constitution was clearly a response to uncontrolled and unchecked data gathering during the authoritarian regime (1964–85). Thus, it is not a surprise that decades after the promulgation of the Constitution, its importance has declined. Moreover, currently the most important data gatherers are not states – they are private corporations. The widespread use of the Internet marks a point of inflexion in the relevance of data protection, especially due to the extensive use of automated personal data processing. However, habeas data does not seem to fit the demands of this new reality. It remains attached to an anachronistic concept of data collection and data processing and is not dynamic enough for the type of data protection that is needed today.[147] Moreover, it is worth noting that neither the Constitution nor the Habeas Data Act (Federal Law 9507/1997) provide for the possibility of deleting personal information stored in databases. Both seem to assume that collecting data as such is not problematic and that problems arise only if the recorded information is wrong or false, in which case it may be corrected. What is now frequently at stake is not whether or not the information is correct, but whether the data should be collected and stored in the first place (not to mention if it should be shared or sold to third parties).

Finally, although Art 1 of the Habeas Data Act widened the concept of public databases, it is controversial as to whether the habeas data could even be used as a means to obtain or correct personal information stored in fully private databases.

C. Writ of Security

The writ of security (MS, *mandado de segurança*) is an original Brazilian constitutional remedy that is in some aspects similar to the *amparo* remedy, which is widespread in Hispanic America.[148] As Rosenn puts it: 'The writ of security is a unique summary constitutional remedy that combines aspects of the Anglo-American writs of mandamus,

[147] For an analysis of the inadequacy of the habeas data in this context, along with an analysis of some alternatives to it, see Danilo Doneda and Laura Schertel Mendes, 'Data Protection in Brazil: New Developments and Current Challenges' in Serge Gutwirth and others (eds), *Reloading Data Protection* (Dordrecht, Springer, 2014).

[148] For a comprehensive analysis of the Latin American *amparo* remedy, including some details on its Brazilian equivalents, see Allan R Brewer-Carías, *Constitutional Protection of Human Rights in Latin America: A Comparative Study of Amparo Proceedings* (Cambridge, Cambridge University Press, 2009).

injunction, prohibition and quo warranto, as well as the motion for summary judgment'.[149]

Art 5, LXIX, provides that 'a writ of security shall be issued to protect a certain and liquid right not protected by habeas corpus or habeas data, when the party responsible for the illegality or abuse of power is a public authority or an agent of a corporate legal entity performing governmental duties'. Its creation responded to the constitutional reform of 1926, which limited the scope of the habeas corpus to personal freedom of physical motion, leaving other rights unprotected by a constitutional remedy. As a foreign observer stated shortly after the creation of the writ of security, it is 'a genuine example of the evolution of a legal institution in response to a practical demand'.[150]

According to the wording of the Constitution, the writ of security protects a 'liquid and certain right' (*direito líquido e certo*) against illegality and abuse of power. The expression 'liquid and certain right' is open enough to permit a wide array of situations to be protected by the writ of security. The constitutional literature in Brazil takes great pains to define it, but these definitions usually do not provide any further guidance. Frequently, it is simply stated that a liquid and certain right is a right whose existence and extension are evident.

The writ of security has been used in a wide array of contexts aimed at attaining many different objectives. They range from the petition of senators against the decision of the Federal Senate that had denied the establishment of an investigative committee, although the request was signed by at least one-third of the senators, to a sick person's demand for a given drug prescribed by a physician.

This last example shows that a 'liquid and certain right' does not imply an absence of controversies related to its existence and extension. Healthcare litigation in Brazil is done mainly through writs of security. In such actions, demonstrating 'liquid and certain' character is usually a very straightforward matter: the right to health is guaranteed by the Constitution, the state has a duty to realise it, the plaintiff has a medical prescription that asserts that she or he needs a given drug, and therefore the state should provide that drug. Although the exact implications of the constitutional provision that grants the right to health are far from clear for either the state or individuals, it is usually

[149] Rosenn (n 98) 1024.

[150] Anyda Marchant, 'Brazilian Writ of Security (Mandado de Seguranca) and Its Relationship to the Extraordinary Remedies of the Anglo-American Common Law: An Object Lesson in Latin American Law Making' (1944) 19 *Tul L Rev* 213, 213.

considered a 'liquid and certain' right that may be enforced by means of a writ of security.

D. Popular Action

Art 5, LXXIII, of the Constitution provides that 'any citizen has standing to bring a popular action to annul an act detrimental to the public patrimony … to administrative morality, to the environment and to historic and cultural heritage'. Its goal is thus to allow citizens to exercise control over the government and administrative acts which supposedly harm the public good. It has been used in several contexts with different goals, and the effects of this type of litigation vary accordingly.

One feature of the popular action (*ação popular*) is worth mentioning. Art 5, LXXIII, does not state that 'everyone has standing' but that 'any citizen has standing' to bring a popular action before a court. In Brazil, the term citizen (*cidadão* or *cidadã*) has a precise legal meaning: citizens are those who are regularly enrolled as voters. Among all the rights set forth in Art 5, this is the only one that can be exercised exclusively by Brazilians. It therefore introduces an implicit exception to the general clause of the head of Art 5, which states that the rights laid down in this article are guaranteed to both Brazilians *and foreigners residing in Brazil*.

E. Writ of Injunction

The writ of injunction (MI, *mandado de injunção*) was a novelty that the 1988 Constitution introduced to the Brazilian constitutional system. According to Art 5, LXXI, it is possible to file a writ of injunction whenever a lack of regulatory legislation makes it impossible to exercise a given constitutional right or freedom.

Shortly after the promulgation of the Constitution, there was a clear divide in both the STF and constitutional scholarship concerning the effects of decisions on writs of injunction. For some time, the STF adopted the view that it could not create new rules and could at most give notice on the matter to the legislature.[151] In 2007, however, the Court decided several writs of injunction related to public servants' right to

[151] The leading case on the matter is MI 107-QO (1989).

strike and changed its settled case law on the subject. Art 37, VII, provides that 'the right to strike [in the Public Administration] shall be exercised in the manner and within the limits defined by specific law'. The law mentioned in this article has never been enacted. For this reason, several trade unions representing public servants from different states filed writs of injunctions that were decided in 2007.[152] The STF decided that since the National Congress did not pass the mentioned law within 20 years of the promulgation of the Constitution, it was legitimate for the Court to issue a provisional regulation that could allow public servants to exercise their right to strike. The Court used, to the greatest extent possible, the provisions of the general law on strikes in the private sector (Federal Law 7783/1989) and complemented them with provisions developed by the Court itself for coping with the peculiarities of strikes in the public sector.

FURTHER READING

Lesser J, *Immigration, Ethnicity, and National Identity in Brazil, 1808 to the Present* (New approaches to the Americas, Cambridge, Cambridge University Press, 2013)

Rosenn KS, 'Procedural Protection of Constitutional Rights in Brazil' (2011) 59 *Am J Comp L* 1009

Speck BW, 'Brazil' in P Norris and A Abel van Es (eds), *Checkbook Elections? Political Finance in Comparative Perspective* (New York, Oxford University Press, 2016)

Telles EE, *Race in Another America: The Significance of Skin Color in Brazil* (Princeton, Princeton University Press, 2004)

[152] See MI 708 (2007), MI 670 (2007) and MI 712 (2007).

6

Beyond Liberal Constitutionalism: Social Rights and the Social and Economic Orders

Social Rights and Social Order – Socioeconomic Rights in Courts – The Environment – Indigenous Peoples – Economic Order

SOCIAL CONSTITUTIONALISM HAS a long tradition both in Latin America and in Brazil. Even though the 1919 German Constitution is frequently identified as the inflexion point that marked the shift from an exclusively liberal constitutionalism to a social constitutionalism, in reality the 1917 Mexican Constitution had already started this shift a few years before. Both constitutions (along with many others) were constantly mentioned by the members of the constituent assembly that drafted the 1934 Brazilian Constitution. Indeed, some provisions of this constitution were very similar to provisions of either the 1917 Mexican Constitution or the 1919 German Constitution, even though the latter was already virtually dead at the time.

Provisions of the Brazilian 1934 Constitution concerning the ban on wage differences based on gender or nationality, the definition of a minimum wage, and the protection against dismissal without just cause (Art 121, 1, *a*, *b*, *g*) are almost a direct translation of Art 123, VII, VI, XXII of the 1917 Mexican Constitution. By the same token, provisions concerning limitations on economic freedom and private property (1934 Constitution, Art 115 and 113, 17) are also very similar to Art 151 and 153 of the 1919 German Constitution.

In addition to illustrating the migration of constitutional ideas from Mexico and Germany to Brazil, the reference to these provisions highlights how the concept of social constitutionalism has broadened over time. The meaning of social constitutionalism in 1934 was surely more limited than it was in 1988 and today. The social character of the

1917 Mexican Constitution, the 1919 German Constitution, and all the Brazilian constitutions from 1934 to 1969 was primarily based on provisions related to social security, social assistance, workers' rights, and state intervention in both economic freedom and private property to promote welfare and social justice.

That said, what the international literature currently refers to as 'social' or 'socioeconomic' rights is something different. Such expressions primarily refer to rights such as the right to education, healthcare, work, housing, food, and transportation, among others. Indeed, in Brazil there has also been a terminological shift. Even though the 1988 Constitution includes workers' rights in the chapter called 'social rights', the expression 'social rights' without further qualifications tends to refer to the first group of rights (education, healthcare, etc).

This does not mean, however, that the original meaning of the social constitutionalism of the first half of the twentieth century is absent from the 1988 Constitution. It only means that there are conceptual and terminological differences that should be stressed. In addition to the divide between social (or socioeconomic) rights and workers' rights, a further divide is that between socioeconomic *rights* on the one hand and social and economic *orders* on the other hand.

I. SOCIAL RIGHTS AND SOCIAL ORDER

The 1988 Constitution was one of the first constitutions in the world that enshrined access to social goods in terms of *rights*, not only of state duties. Art 6 clearly states: 'Education, health, food, work, housing, transportation, leisure, security, social welfare, protection of motherhood and childhood, and assistance to the destitute, are social rights'.[1]

Compared to the long list of freedom rights enshrined in the 78 clauses of Art 5, Art 6 is very concise. It guarantees 12 rights in less than 30 words. However, in addition to Art 6, the Constitution dedicates an entire heading – Heading VIII, 'The Social Order' – to those and other rights. Almost every social right enshrined in the original wording of Art 6 is further regulated in a chapter or section of the heading on the social order, which also has provisions aimed at regulating matters that

[1] The original text of the Constitution provided for only nine social rights. The rights to housing, food, and transportation were added by constitutional amendments EC 26/2000, EC 64/2010 and EC 90/2015, respectively.

do not belong to the traditional idea of social constitutionalism of the first half of the twentieth century, such as the environment, science and technology, indigenous peoples, and even sports.

The following sections will analyse the constitutional provisions related to two socioeconomic rights (health and education) along with the heated debate over their judicialisation.

A. Right to Health

The right to health concisely established in Art 6 is further developed in Arts 196 through 200. Art 196 states that everyone shall have the right to health and that it is a duty of the state to realise that right by means of 'social and economic policies aimed at reducing the risk of illness and other hazards and by universal and equal access to all actions and services for its promotion, protection and recovery'.

The most important concept contained in this provision is that of 'universal and equal access'. This is the core of the Brazilian Unified Health System (SUS, *Sistema Único de Saúde*), whose principles are set forth in Art 198. This system is primarily financed with funds from the social security budget of the Union, states, federal district and municipalities.[2] The term *único* (unified) in the name of the Brazilian public health system does not mean that there is no private system. Indeed, there is such a system, and its existence is guaranteed by Art 199, which provides that healthcare 'is open to private enterprise'.

The creation of the SUS was the outcome of a long struggle for more equality in the access to health services and goods in Brazil, along with more efficiency in system management.[3] It is one of the most ambitious health programmes in the world. There is no other country in the world with more than 100 million inhabitants where access to public hospitals, medical treatments and medicines are granted for free and to everyone (nationals, migrants, residents, non-residents, tourists, etc). There is no doubt that the SUS has been responsible for considerable improvements in health outcomes in Brazil.[4] However, the problems and challenges of such a system are proportional to its size and complexity.

[2] The Unified Health System is regulated in detail by Federal Law 8080/1990.

[3] For a good account of this history, see Jairnilson Paim and others, 'The Brazilian Health System: History, Advances, and Challenges' (2011) 377 *The Lancet* 1778.

[4] See Michele Gragnolati and others, *Twenty Years of Health System Reform in Brazil: An Assessment of the Sistema Único de Saúde* (Washington, DC, The World Bank, 2013).

The system's problems are primarily related to the infrastructure of public hospitals, regional differences in relation to the quality of service, shortages, management problems, and underfinancing (despite the minimum threshold for investments established by Art 198, § 2), among many others.

B. Right to Education

Arts 205 and 206 describe the general objectives and principles of public policies in the realm of education, such as equality of conditions for initial and continuing access to school; freedom to learn, teach, research and express one's thoughts, art and knowledge; pluralism of ideas and pedagogical concepts; the coexistence of public and private institutions; free public education in official establishments; and the democratic administration of public education, among others.

Until 1961, when the first general law on education was enacted, there was no compulsory education in Brazil. Federal Law 4024/1961 established compulsory education of four years. Since then, the period of compulsory education has been progressively increased and Art 208, I, of the Constitution provides for 'free, compulsory elementary education from 4 to 17 years, including assurance of its free offer to all those who did not have access to it at the proper age'.[5] Art 208, II, provides for the 'progressive universalisation of the free high-school education'.

Even though there are children who still do not attend school in Brazil,[6] free public education from primary school to high school is accessible to virtually everyone. Thus, the main problem is educational quality, not access to schools. Even though access to education is nearly universalised, the rate of illiteracy in Brazil is still almost 10 per cent, which is primarily attributable to a persistent high rate of illiteracy among older adults.[7] Moreover, the illiteracy rate is illustrative of ongoing regional inequalities in Brazil. Although the pure illiteracy rates in states of the South and Southeast are mostly under 5 per cent,

[5] See also Federal Law 9394/1996, Art 4, I.

[6] According to the *UNESCO eAtlas of Out-of-School Children*, in 2015, 5% of Brazilian children of primary school age were not in school: see https://tellmaps.com/uis/oosc/#!/tellmap/-528275754.

[7] This rate is much higher – 27% – if one considers both pure and functional illiteracy. Source Index of Functional Illiteracy (INAF, *Indicador de Alfabetismo Funcional*): ipm.org.br/inaf.

in some states of the Northeast and North regions, such as Alagoas and Maranhão, these rates remain higher than 20 per cent.[8]

Hence, even though education can be one of the most powerful means of mitigating inequalities, this transformative potential has not been effectively fulfilled in Brazil. In addition to regional inequalities, the coexistence of public and private educational systems has contributed to maintaining and sometimes even to deepening inequalities, since education in the public schools is – save for a few exceptions – worse than that offered in private schools.

Similar to Art 198, § 2, which establishes a minimum threshold for investments in healthcare, Art 212 provides that '[t]he Union shall apply annually not less than eighteen percent of its tax revenues, and the states, federal district and municipalities at least twenty-five percent of their tax revenues, including revenues resulting from transfers, for maintenance and development of education'. This, however, has not been enough to prevent underfinancing and the low quality of public education in Brazil.

II. SOCIOECONOMIC RIGHTS IN COURTS

In recent years, there has been a vivid debate among legal academics and practitioners about how the law and legal institutions (especially courts) can contribute to improving the realisation of socioeconomic rights. Judicial activism is particularly striking in this realm, especially when the right to health is at stake. Judges around the country have been granting access to medicines and medical treatments to people who do not have access to them.

The literature on the effects of litigation in the realm of socioeconomic rights is vast and there are profound disagreements.[9] I will use healthcare litigation as a paradigmatic example because it is the most important example in the realm of social rights. Whenever necessary, examples of other rights will also be mentioned.[10]

[8] Source: Brazilian Institute of Geography and Statistics (IBGE): https://www.ibge.gov.br/estatisticas-novoportal/sociais/educacao/19897-sintese-de-indicadores-pnad2.html?edicao=9129&t=series-historicas.

[9] A considerable part of this literature is written in English and therefore is accessible to those who want a more detailed account of the issues and arguments at stake.

[10] For an analysis that includes other socioeconomic rights, see Octavio LM Ferraz, 'Between Activism and Deference: Social rights adjudication in the Brazilian Supreme Federal Tribunal' in Helena Alviar García and others (eds), *Social and Economic Rights in Theory and Practice: A Critical Inquiries* (New York, Routledge, 2015).

It is an undisputed fact that the public health system has improved in recent decades (just as it is an undisputed conclusion that there remains much to be done). Among jurists, disagreements primarily arise when assessing the role that courts have played in these improvements. Although this dispute is not unique to Brazil, some features of healthcare litigation and the Brazilian judicial procedure make the debate even more controversial. The most important of these features are: (a) the individual character of the healthcare litigation: each demand for drugs and medical treatments before the courts is usually filed by only one individual;[11] (b) the fact that only the plaintiff directly benefits from the effects of a judicial decision (*inter partes* effects) irrespective of whether there are other persons in the same situation; and (c) the lack of a system of binding precedents that could expand the effects of one decision to all similar cases.

Especially because of these features, many have argued that social rights litigation unduly allocates scarce goods to individuals who have access to information and resources for bringing their cases before a court, and therefore, such litigation interferes with public policies that are designed to be evenly enforced. As a result, healthcare litigation potentially 'makes the Brazilian public health system less fair and efficient'.[12] However, part of the literature on this issue argues that in spite of the features presented above (individual claims, *inter parte* effects, no binding precedents), healthcare litigation potentially improves the outcomes of the public health system both directly[13] and indirectly, either by creating awareness concerning issues that might otherwise be neglected by the political branches or by exerting pressure on the political branches to be more transparent and accountable.[14]

[11] For an analysis of healthcare litigation beyond the demand of drugs or medical treatments, see Ana Paula de Barcellos, 'Sanitation Rights, Public Law Litigation, and Inequality: A Case Study from Brazil' (2014) 16 *Health and Human Rights Journal* 35.

[12] Daniel Wei L Wang, 'Right to Health Litigation in Brazil: The Problem and the Institutional Responses' (2015) 15 *Human Rights Law Review* 617, 619. See also Octavio LM Ferraz, 'Brazil – Health Inequalities, Rights and Courts: The Social Impact of the Judicialization of Health' in Alicia Ely Yamin and Siri Gloppen (eds), *Litigating Health Rights: Can Courts Bring More Justice to Health* (Cambridge, Harvard University Press, 2011); Virgílio Afonso da Silva and Fernanda Vargas Terrazas, 'Claiming the Right to Health in Brazilian Courts: The Exclusion of the Already Excluded?' (2011) 36 *Law & Social Inquiry* 825; Ana Luiza Chieffi and others, 'Legal Access to Medications: A Threat to Brazil's Public Health System?' (2017) 17 *BMC Health Services Research* 499.

[13] See João Biehl and others, 'The Judicialization of Health and the Quest for State Accountability: Evidence from 1,262 Lawsuits for Access to Medicines in Southern Brazil' (2016) 18 *Health and Human Rights Journal* 209.

[14] See, for instance, Flávia Piovesan, 'Brazil: Impact and Challenges of Social Rights in Courts' in Malcolm Langford (ed), *Social Rights Jurisprudence: Emerging Trends in International and Comparative Law* (Cambridge, Cambridge University Press, 2008).

The STF convened a public hearing to discuss this matter in 2009, and the National Council of Justice (CNJ) created a working group dedicated to the subject; that group has published recommendations that should help judges throughout the country both to decide cases related to the right to health and to mitigate the uncontrolled impact of judicial decisions on the public policies proposed by the political branches. The most important of those recommendations are that courts should: (a) obtain technical support from physicians and pharmacists to help judges assess the clinical evidence presented by litigants; (b) advise judges: (i) to analyse cases based on complete and comprehensive information; (ii) to avoid granting either drugs that are not registered with the National Health Surveillance Agency (ANVISA) or experimental drugs; and (iii) to consult (whenever possible) the health authorities before making an interim decision; (c) to include health law legislation as a subject to be examined in the public entrance exams for judges; and (d) to require judges to visit public health units.[15]

III. THE SOCIAL ORDER BEYOND SOCIAL RIGHTS: THE ENVIRONMENT AND INDIGENOUS PEOPLES

A. The Environment

In addition to being home to the largest rainforest in the world, Brazil also has more than 10 per cent of the world's renewable freshwater resources and 13 per cent of the world's biota (an estimated total of 1.8 million species).[16] The challenges of protecting these resources are as substantial as the resources themselves. Economic interests and environmental protection are in constant tension.

The chapter on environmental protection of the 1988 Constitution has only one article: Art 225. However, this article has been responsible for important improvements in this area. Moreover, if one bears in mind that the Constitution was drafted in the 1980s, it is possible to argue that this article – which was the result of the long engagement of several organised civil society groups in favour of more effective protection of the environment in Brazil – was quite ahead of its time. Since then, several constitutions in Latin America (eg, the constitutions of Bolivia

[15] CNJ, Recommendation 31/2010. For a comprehensive account of this recommendation and the public hearing held in the STF, see Wang (n 12).

[16] See Thomas M Lewinsohn and Paulo Inácio Prado, 'How Many Species Are There in Brazil?' (2005) 19 *Conservation Biology* 619.

and Ecuador, among others) have enshrined environmental protection among their provisions.

Similar to other subjects regulated in the heading of the social order, Art 225 uses the language of rights, not merely of state duties or public interest. It states: 'Everyone has the right to an ecologically balanced environment, which is an asset of common use and essential for a healthy life. The Government and the community have a duty to defend and to preserve the environment for present and future generations'. Its seven clauses define a series of governmental duties for the enforcement of this right.

Based on these constitutional provisions, advanced environmental legislation has been enacted since 1988. However, as Drummond and Barros-Platiau put it, 'much remains to be done in terms of enforcement and compliance, especially in the case of economic actors'.[17] The range of subjects regulated by this legislation is wide and includes animal protection, genetically modified organisms, environmental crimes, and of course, water resources and protection of the Brazilian forests.

i. The Forest Code

The discussion about and enactment of the Brazilian Forest Code in 2012 is a good example of the challenges for environmental protection in Brazil, along with the variety of players and strategies involved. Civil society was highly mobilised not only during its discussion and voting in Congress but also after its approval, when a strong campaign was launched to convince the President of the Republic of vetoing provisions considered detrimental to the environment, especially those related to alleged amnesties for past deforestation. The President did veto some (but not all) of those provisions. Later, the struggle moved to the judicial arena when the Federal Public Ministry (one of the main institutional players in the environment protection[18]) and political parties filed constitutional actions before the STF. Left-wing parties and the Public Ministry challenged the constitutionality of several provisions, while right-wing parties traditionally associated with interests of big landowners and agribusiness demanded the declaration of the constitutionality of those provisions. These cases were decided only in 2018, and even

[17] José Drummond and Ana Flávia Barros-Platiau, 'Brazilian Environmental Laws and Policies, 1934–2002: A Critical Overview' (2005) 28 *Law & Policy* 83.

[18] See, for instance, Lesley K McAllister, *Making Law Matter: Environmental Protection and Legal Institutions in Brazil* (Stanford, Stanford Law Books, 2008).

though several judges emphasised that several provisions of the Forest Code were less protective of the environment than they ideally should be, the Court took an unusually deferential position vis-à-vis the legislature and upheld the constitutionality of almost all of them.[19]

ii. Animal Rights

The Constitution does not employ the term animal *rights*, but nevertheless protects them by forbidding 'all practices that … subject animals to cruelty'.[20] Even before the enactment of the Environmental Crimes Act (Federal Law 9605/1998), which defines abusing, mistreating, injuring or mutilating wild, domestic or domesticated animals, whether native or exotic, as a criminal offence, the STF had struck down as unconstitutional state laws permitting events that involved cruelty against animals (such as roosters and bulls) under the justification of promoting traditional Brazilian customs.[21]

In 2016, a Court decision striking down a law of the state of Ceará that permitted the so-called *vaquejada*, a sort of rodeo in which a bull is chased and pulled to the ground by its tail,[22] caused a backlash in the National Congress, which approved a constitutional amendment (EC 96/2017) that added a § 7 into Art 225, providing that for the purposes of the provision in the final part of Art 225, § 1, VII, 'sporting practices that use animals shall not be considered cruel provided they are cultural manifestations, as set forth by Art 215, § 1 … registered as part of the Brazilian intangible cultural heritage, and regulated by specific law which shall assure the welfare of the involved animals'.

One could argue that the balancing that the STF has always struck between animal protection and the protection of popular culture, which has consistently pointed to the prevalence of the former over the latter, is made difficult or even blocked by the explicit language of the new Art 225, § 7. However, since what has always been at stake is the welfare

[19] See ADC 42 (2018), ADI 4901 (2018), ADI 4902 (2018), ADI 4903 (2018) e ADI 4937 (2018).

[20] Art 225, § 1, VII.

[21] See RE 153531 (1997). After the enactment of the Act, see ADI 3776 (2007), and ADI 1856 (2011). For a detailed presentation of the arguments of some of these (and other) decisions, along with the legislation on animal welfare in Brazil, see Tagore Trajano de Almeida Silva, 'Brazilian Animal Law Overview: Balancing Human and Non-Human Interests' (2010) 6 *J Animal L* 81, 87–100.

[22] ADI 4983 (2016). For a short description of this decision, see Luís Roberto Barroso and others, 'Developments in Brazilian Constitutional Law: The Year 2016 in Review' (2017) 15 *Int J Const Law* 495, 503.

of animals – otherwise there would be no need for a balance – the new § 7 adds very little (if anything) to the interpretations and decisions in such cases. It may even be argued that the backlash backfired and that only sporting practices that are registered as part of the intangible Brazilian cultural heritage may use animals, and even then, only if their welfare is assured.

There are still no relevant STF decisions concerning animal welfare besides those involving popular festivals. The Court still has not decided cases involving the protection of animals in the realm of religious freedom, for instance, such as a case related to ritual slaughter (such as the Jewish *shechita* or the Islamic *dhabihah*) or animal sacrifices (such as those within the Afro-Brazilian religion *Candomblé*). The first (ritual slaughter) is explicitly allowed by Decree 9013/2017, and its constitutionality has not been challenged before the STF. There is no federal legislation on animal sacrifice, but there is at least one pending case on the matter on the Court's docket.[23]

B. Rights of Indigenous Peoples

In countries in which the dominant population is not native, relations with indigenous peoples tend to be very delicate. The case of Brazil is no exception: the relationship has usually been marked by conflicts, violence, domination and oppression. Indigenous communities have been exterminated, indigenous persons have been enslaved, and traditions, culture, and languages have been destroyed. To be sure, there has also been less violent and even collaborative relationships. But domination has clearly prevailed, always.

At the same time, in the process of building a nation state in the nineteenth century, indigenous mythology played a role in the attempt to forge a Brazilian national identity. Just as many nationalist movements in Europe resorted to immemorial traditions – when not invented, usually exaggerated – and symbolic myths to advance their case for building nation states, Brazilian national identity should be the result of the encounter between two ancient traditions: the indigenous and the Portuguese.[24] In this realm, Brazilian Romanticism, especially in

[23] See RE 494601 (pending).

[24] That black African traditions did not take part in this imaginary forging of a new nation, even though at least one-third of Brazil's population were of black African descent, is not a surprise, since a considerable portion of the black population was enslaved.

literature, was clearly engaged in building a new national identity. Key works in this realm were José de Alencar's *The Guarany* (1857) and *Iracema* (1865).[25] The fact that the relationship between white and indigenous peoples in Brazil was, to say the least, far from harmonious did not seem relevant to the white elite engaged in forging a national identity.

Until 1988, the explicit and official objective in relation to indigenous peoples had been their integration into the 'national communion'. Hence, although plain extermination of indigenous peoples ceased to be a state policy quite early, their 'integration into the national communion' is substantially similar to extermination. Although people are not exterminated, cultures, traditions and languages are.

The 1988 Constitution is undoubtedly an inflexion point in this history. This does not mean that the situation of indigenous peoples in Brazil is exemplary, but there is no doubt that the Constitution established the conditions for improving their legal and factual situation. Although only two articles are dedicated to indigenous peoples, they seek to address some of the most problematic issues in this realm, about which the previous Brazilian constitutions had always remained silent. Moreover, 'integration into national communion' was definitely abandoned.

This is clearly identifiable from the outset: the head of Art 231 establishes that indigenous peoples 'shall have their social organisation, customs, languages, creeds and traditions recognised, as well as their original rights to the lands they traditionally occupy; the Union has the responsibility to demarcate these lands and to protect and ensure respect for all their property'. The §§ 1 to 7 of Art 231 regulate the right to property to those lands. Art 232 provides that indigenous persons, indigenous communities and organisations have standing to defend their rights and interests before the judiciary (with the Public Ministry intervening at all stages of the proceedings).

The Brazilian Constitution was a milestone in both Brazilian and Latin American history. Until the late 1980s, no Latin American constitution was as concerned with indigenous peoples as the Brazilian 1988 Constitution. However, much has changed since that time. The

See ch 1. On this matter, see Lilia Moritz Schwarcz, 'A Mestizo and Tropical Country: The Creation of the Official Image of Independent Brazil' (2006) 80 European Review of Latin American and Caribbean Studies 25.

[25] For a translation of *Iracema*, see José de Alencar, *Iracema, the Honey Lips: a legend of Brazil* (London, Isabel Burton tr, Bickers & Son 1886). *The Guarany* was later turned into an opera by Carlos Gomes (1870).

constitutions of Colombia (1991) and Bolivia (2009) are probably the best examples of this ongoing change.

From a legal perspective, although the effectiveness of constitutional and legal provisions is often undermined by strong and conflicting political and economic interests, it remains possible to argue that the situation has changed for the better.

i. Land

Art 20, XI, provides that the lands 'traditionally occupied' by indigenous peoples are property of the Union, while Art 231, § 2, establishes that the lands traditionally occupied by them are destined for their permanent possession, and they shall be entitled to the exclusive usufruct of the riches of the soil, rivers and lakes existing thereon. Those lands are also 'inalienable and non-transferable,' and the rights thereto are 'non-derogable'.

The relationship of the indigenous peoples to their lands is not easy to grasp in Western legal terms, especially through the concept of private property. The Constitution therefore does not grant the property on these lands to them. The lands *belong* to the indigenous peoples, but the property upon them is held by the Union. Crucial to this realm is that this possession is permanent and that indigenous peoples have exclusive rights on their lands.[26]

The Union has the responsibility of demarcating the lands mentioned in Art 231. One central issue is the need to define what the term 'lands traditionally occupied' by indigenous peoples means. This is the most important concept both in Art 231 and in Art 21, XI. Enforcement of the right of indigenous peoples to their lands strongly depends on the interpretation of this expression. Since it is simply impossible to understand the term as the lands indigenous peoples occupied before the arrival of the Portuguese in 1500, a different meaning of 'traditionally occupied' must be defined. In some recent decisions, the STF has understood 'traditionally occupied' as 'occupied on 5 October 1988'.[27] According to this rationale, lands that are traditionally occupied by indigenous peoples are

[26] It should be noted, however, that Art 231, § 3, authorises the exploitation of water resources, including their energy potential, and prospecting and mining of mineral wealth on indigenous lands. This, however, depends on the authorisation of the National Congress 'after hearing from the communities involved' and most importantly, provided that in the case of mining, these communities can participate in the results of that exploitation.

[27] See Pet 3388 (2009).

those that they occupied on the day the Constitution was promulgated, and these (and only these) lands may be demarcated as belonging (in the sense explained above) to them. The judge rapporteur of the decision in Pet 3388 used a metaphor according to which one should assume that a 'radiography' of indigenous land occupation was taken on 5 October 1988 and that this 'radiography' shall be considered the ultimate criterion for demarcating those lands. The Court struck down, *inter alia*, the demarcation of the indigenous lands of *Guyraroká*, where members of the ethnic group *Guarani Kaiowá* had lived for 200 years until the middle of the twentieth century, when farmers forced them to leave. The Court argued that because the *Guarani Kaiowá* did not live on the lands at the time the Constitution was enacted, the demarcation should be declared void.[28]

This criterion is problematic for at least four reasons: (a) because the Constitution itself does not mention it;[29] (b) because the fact that an indigenous community occupied a portion of land on that date does not mean that it had traditionally occupied it – it may be the case that they had traditionally occupied other lands but were forced to move to where they were on 5 October 1988; (c) because if the Constitution can be considered a turning point in the realm of indigenous rights, a 'radiography' taken on the date of its promulgation reflects the past, which has usually involved forced displacement (either officially by the government or *de facto* by farmers and miners); and directly linked to this fact, (d) because the Constitution was promulgated after more than 20 years of an authoritarian regime during which forced displacement was frequent. Hence, taking a 'radiography' of this moment to use as a criterion for future demarcation seems to be completely at odds with a constitution that wants to change reality, not maintain the status quo.

The STF accepts only one exception to the cut-off date of 5 October 1988: if an indigenous community was displaced from its land before the date, but had resisted and was still resisting. This resistance to forced displacement must be demonstrated by the indigenous community itself, by means of factual evidence or by means of a lawsuit that was both filed before and still pending on 5 October 1988.[30] In opposition to this

[28] See RMS 29087 (2014).

[29] This argument is even stronger if one bears in mind that the Constitution explicitly establishes the date of its publication as a criterion for legal decisions in 15 different articles, but not in Art 231.

[30] See ARE 803.462-AgR (2014), which struck down the demarcation of the indigenous land *Limão Verde*.

interpretation, Judge Luís Roberto Barroso argued that it does not seem reasonable to make the demonstration of the existence of a land conflict dependent on the filing of a legal action, because this 'would imply interpreting the behaviour of indigenous communities in the light of our customs and institutions'.[31]

ii. Language

According to the 2010 Census, 274 indigenous languages are spoken in Brazil.[32] The intensity of use of these languages varies considerably. Some of them are spoken by tens of thousands of people. However, many of them are spoken by less than 100 – or sometimes less than 50 – people. Many are at risk of extinction.

Most of these languages belong to two language trees: *Tupi* and *Macro-Je*. However, there are at least 19 language branches that do not belong to these trees, and in some of these branches there is only one language (isolated language). Notwithstanding its linguistic diversity, Brazil has only one official language: Portuguese.

Still, albeit in a very limited way, the Constitution recognises this linguistic diversity. In addition to Art 231, Art 210, § 2, provides that 'regular elementary education shall be given in the Portuguese language, assuring to indigenous communities the use of their native languages and their own learning methods'.

In recent years, some municipalities whose populations are largely composed of indigenous persons have adopted the strategy of designating two (or even more) official languages. The first example of this was the municipality of São Gabriel da Cachoeira, in the state of Amazonas, which adopted the *Nheengatu*, *Tukano* and *Baniwa* languages, along with Portuguese, as its official languages.[33] According to Municipal Law 145/2002, this implies, among other things, that the municipality is committed to 'provide the basic public services in public offices in the official language and in the three co-official languages, orally and in writing'. The compatibility of this type of provision with Art 13 of

[31] See ACO 362 (2017). Judge Barroso, who is the successor of judge Ayres Britto as judge rapporteur in the ancillary decisions in Pet 3388, has argued that the cut-off date criterion established in the main decision of that case is not a universal criterion to be replicated in every case and controversy. See Pet 3388-ED (2013).

[32] Source: IBGE https://indigenas.ibge.gov.br/.

[33] Municipal Law 145/2002, São Gabriel da Cachoeira-AM.

the Constitution, which establishes only one official language, is not entirely clear. Even if one assumes that it is indeed possible to establish local official languages, it remains unclear whether this power belongs to the municipalities, since the constitutional articles that establish federal power-sharing did not contain any provision on language issues. There is no doubt, however, that in several municipalities the adoption of co-official languages may be a measure that has positive effects.

iii. Social Organisation and Customs

The recognition of indigenous social organisations and customs may create tension between legal systems that are not entirely compatible with one another. Many of the fundamental rights enshrined in the Brazilian Constitution – and in many constitutions of the world – are based on Western values that are not necessarily shared by indigenous peoples. There are many cases in which equality, freedom, and even the right to life are not recognised by indigenous communities in the same fashion as they are in liberal democracies.

This clash of traditions is especially clear when the violation of any of these fundamental rights is considered a criminal offence in the Western tradition. In these cases, not only the weight given to values such as life or freedom but also the forms of punishment for committing such violations may in many indigenous communities depart considerably from the official Brazilian legal system. What may be acceptable and commonplace in Western societies, such as restricting individual liberty through incarceration, may be unacceptable in some indigenous communities; what may be the norm in some of these communities, such as corporal punishment, may be considered cruel and therefore forbidden by Art 5, XLVII, of the Constitution.

Although extreme cases – especially related to the life of newborns[34] – are frequently used as arguments for the impossibility of recognising indigenous customs that are incompatible with the Bill of Rights of the Constitution, the fact is that most cases of conflicting values and procedures are much less dramatic. Respecting indigenous customs to the greatest extent possible is thus a constitutional duty. Furthermore, it is

[34] For an analysis of some of these cases, see Rita Laura Segato, 'May Every People Weave the Threads of Their Own History: Juridical Pluralism in Didactical Dialogue with Legislators' (2014) 1 *Revista DireitoUnB* 65. See also Marcelo Neves, *Transconstitutionalism* (Oxford, Hart, 2013) 136–44.

also a duty that is derived from the incorporation into Brazilian domestic law of the Convention concerning Indigenous and Tribal Peoples in Independent Countries (ILO Convention 169). Especially relevant in this context is Art 9 of the Convention: 'Article 9. 1. To the extent compatible with the national legal system and internationally recognised human rights, the methods customarily practised by the peoples concerned for dealing with offences committed by their members shall be respected; 2. The customs of these peoples in regard to penal matters shall be taken into consideration by the authorities and courts dealing with such cases'.

C. Quilombolas

Quilombos were settlements founded by runaway slaves from the seventeenth to the nineteenth centuries. The inhabitants of these quilombos were called *quilombolas* (maroons). Especially in the seventeenth and eighteenth centuries, the *quilombos* played an important role in the resistance against slavery. Some of them had had several thousand inhabitants and resisted for long periods against the efforts of the Portuguese colonial power to defeat them. The most well-known of the *quilombos* was Palmares, whose last leader, Zumbi, was one of the most important figures in the fight against slavery and has been a symbol for the struggle for race equality in Brazil until today. He was killed and decapitated by the Portuguese in 1695; since 2011, the anniversary of his death, 20 November, has been officially considered the 'day of black awareness', which is a holiday in several municipalities and states.

Unlike the land rights of indigenous peoples, which are provided for in detail in the heading on the social order, the land rights of the *quilombolas* are provided in a very concise fashion by Art 68 of the ADCT, which establishes that the remnants of the *quilombola* communities who are occupying their lands are entitled to these lands and the state shall grant them the appropriate deeds.[35]

In 2003, the President of the Republic issued Decree 4887/2003, which aimed to regulate the process of demarcating the lands of the *quilombolas* and identifying the members of these communities. This decree

[35] For an account of one of the struggles that led to the approval of this constitutional provision, see Flávio Gomes and Daniela Yabeta, 'Other Legacies, Heritage, and Memories of Emancipation: Peasantry, Quilombolas, and Citizenship in Brazil (nineteenth to Twenty-First Centuries)' (2017) 10 *African and Black Diaspora: An International Journal* 162.

replaced Decree 3912/2001, which had set forth more restrictive criteria for the recognition of the right to the *quilombo* lands and had established two important cut-off dates: (i) only those lands occupied by *quilombos* in 1888, which (ii) were still occupied by *quilombola* communities on 5 October 1988, would fall into the scope of Art 68 of the ADCT. Decree 4887/2003 rejected these cut-off dates.

This decree was challenged before the STF both on formal and on substantial grounds. The plaintiff argued firstly that Art 68 of the ADCT should have been regulated by federal law, not an executive decree. In addition to this formal ground, the plaintiff also challenged the most important criterion for defining who is entitled to the lands and to which lands they are entitled: Decree 4887/2003 defines as its central criterion both the self-declaration (as the remaining member of a *quilombola* community) and the self-assignment of the lands occupied by these communities.[36] The STF rejected all of the plaintiff's arguments and ruled that Decree 4887/2003 is fully compatible with the Constitution.[37]

IV. THE ECONOMIC ORDER

Heading VII of the Constitution ('The Economic and Financial Order') clearly follows the tradition that Mexico inaugurated in 1917. Its provisions regulate economic freedom and private property (urban or rural) to foster equality, social justice and national development. When the Constitution was promulgated, the provisions of Heading VII were quite interventionist and protectionist. Many economic activities and public services were considered a state monopoly, such as oil (prospecting, transporting, and refining) and natural gas, telecommunication, and transportation of goods both in the coastal trade and in internal navigation. Additionally, the government should give preferential treatment to Brazilian enterprises with domestic capital. All these articles have been amended, especially in the 1990s, in the wake of economic liberalisation and the privatisation of state-owned enterprises that occurred during the government of President Fernando Henrique Cardoso.

[36] This latter criterion, however, should be complemented by studies conducted by the executive branch (Art 3).

[37] See ADI 3239 (2018).

A. Principles of the Economic Activity

The general principles of the economic activity are set forth in Art 170, which establishes that the economic order, 'founded on the appreciation of the value of human labour and free enterprise, is intended to assure everyone a dignified existence, according to the dictates of social justice'. The same article lays down several principles that the economic order should respect and promote. The issue of whether these principles have been constraining economic activity in Brazil since 1988 is a controversial one. It seems that, to a great extent, they have not. This is not a surprise. As one commentator argued shortly after the promulgation of the 1988 Constitution, a great many of the provisions concerning the economic order 'are merely rhetorical, and no attention was paid to the problem of how to implement them … [I]nstead we have a reiteration of general principles of human dignity and social justice'.[38] Except for those objectives that are regulated in more details in other constitutional provisions or by ordinary legislation – such as consumer and the environmental protection – the so-called principles of the economic order have not served to limit or at least regulate economic activity.

This does not mean that there are no laws or judicial decisions that limit economic activity to promote other rights or goals. It means only that the majority of such laws and judicial decisions have no relation to the major principles and goals set forth in Art 170, such as to foster national sovereignty, to reduce social or regional inequalities or to promote full employment. Some of the decisions that the STF itself understands as representative of its case law in the realm of the economic order are telling. The Court uses great rhetorical strength and emphasises the relevance of the principles of economic activity to uphold laws with marginal relevance, such as those that grant half-price tickets to students in cinemas or theatres[39] or prohibit the installation of filling stations in the parking lots of supermarkets and shopping malls,[40] for instance.

B. Urban Policy

The heading on the economic order includes an entire chapter dedicated to urban policy. Art 182 states that urban policy should be carried out by

[38] Fabio Konder Comparato, 'The Economic Order in the Brazilian Constitution of 1988' (1990) 38 *Am J Comp L* 753, 769.
[39] See ADI 1950 (2005).
[40] See RE 597165-AgR (2015).

the municipal government 'according to general guidelines set forth by law' and should aim at fully realising the social function of the cities and ensuring the well-being of its inhabitants. The law mentioned in Art 182 is Federal Law 10257/2001, known as the City Act (*Estatuto da Cidade*).[41]

In the realm of urban policy, the criteria established by the Constitution for assessing compliance with the social function of private property are much more general than those set forth in the realm of rural policy. Art 182, § 2, simply states that urban property fulfils its social function if it meets the fundamental requirements for the city's ordering, as set forth in the urban master plan. This means that this compliance is context-dependent and what fulfils the requirements of an urban master plan in one city does not necessarily fulfil those of other cities.

C. Land Reform

The debate on land reform was one of the most heated during the Constituent Assembly of 1987–88. Just as wealth in general is very unequally distributed in Brazil, so is land. Large privately owned land still comprises a large share of the privately owned rural land in Brazil. Properties with more than 2,000 hectares correspond to less than 2 per cent of the total amount of properties but to more than 40 per cent of the total area of privately owned rural properties.[42] At the same time, several thousand families have no access to rural land.

The heading on the economic order has a chapter dedicated to rural policy and land reform. The main features of the provisions on land reform are as follows: (a) the power to expropriate land for purposes of land reform belongs to the Union; (b) only properties that do not fulfil their social function may be expropriated; (c) compensation for expropriation is not paid in money, but in agrarian debt bonds redeemable in up to 20 years, starting from the second year after issuance; (d) neither small and medium-sized rural properties (provided that their owners do not possess other properties) nor productive property of any size may be subject to expropriation for agrarian reform purposes; (e) the definitions

[41] For an analysis of the challenges in the implementation of the City Act, see Raquel Rolnik, 'Ten Years of the City Statute in Brazil: From the Struggle for Urban Reform to the World Cup Cities' (2013) 5 *International Journal of Urban Sustainable Development* 54. See also Edesio Fernandes, 'Urban Planning at a Crossroads: A Critical Assessment of Brazil's City Statute, 15 Years Later' in Gautam Bhan and others (eds), *The Routledge Companion to Planning in the Global South* (London, Routledge, 2018).

[42] Source: National Institute for Settlement and Land Reform (*Instituto Nacional de Colonização e Reforma Agrária – INCRA*): www.incra.gov.br.

of small and medium-sized properties and the definition of productive property are provided by federal law; (f) the social function is met when rural property simultaneously complies with the following requirements: (i) rational and adequate use; (ii) adequate use of available natural resources and preservation of the environment; (iii) compliance with provisions regulating labour relations; and (iv) exploitation that favours the well-being of owners and workers.

One of the most important controversies in the interpretation of the provisions concerning land reform is related to Art 185, II. This article states that productive properties will not be subject to expropriation for the purpose of land reform. The central question in this context is as follows: what if a productive property does not comply with its social function because, for instance, it does not meet the conditions of environmental protection or labour law regulations? In such cases, the rural property does not comply with its social function. Art 184 provides that properties that do not comply with their social function may be subject to expropriation for land reform purposes, but Art 185, II, seems to block this consequence when the property at stake is productive. In a nutshell: productive properties may not be expropriated for land reform purposes even if they do not comply with their social function.

This does not mean that owners of properties that do not comply with their social functions cannot be punished if they violate the legislation concerning environmental protection or labour relations. It does not even mean that such properties may not be expropriated. It only means that a possible expropriation should follow the general rules for expropriation for social interest laid down by Art 5, XXIV, according to which compensation must be just, prior and in cash, not in agrarian debt bonds redeemable in up to 20 years. This has also been the interpretation of the STF.[43]

FURTHER READING

Davis SH, *Victims of the Miracle: Development and the Indians of Brazil* (Cambridge, Cambridge University Press, 1977)

Ferraz OLM, 'Brazil – Health Inequalities, Rights and Courts: The Social Impact of the Judicialization of Health' in AE Yamin and S Gloppen (eds), *Litigating Health Rights: Can Courts Bring More Justice to Health* (Human rights practice series, Cambridge, Harvard University Press, 2011)

[43] See, for instance, MS 22193 (1993).

Hemming J, *Die If You Must: Brazilian Indians in the Twentieth Century* (London, Macmillan, 2004)
Hoffmann FF and Bentes FRNM, 'Accountability for Social and Economic Rights in Brazil' in V Gauri and DM Brinks (eds), *Courting Social Justice: Judicial Enforcement of Social and Economic Rights in the Developing World* (Cambridge, Cambridge University Press, 2008)
Lopes JR de L, 'Brazilian Courts and Social Rights: A Case Study Revisited' in R Gargarella, P Domingo, and T Roux (eds), *Courts and Social Transformation in New Democracies* (Aldershot, Ashgate, 2006)
McAllister LK, *Making Law Matter: Environmental Protection and Legal Institutions in Brazil* (Stanford, Stanford Law Books, 2008)

7

Federalism: Cooperation and Increasing Centralisation

Allocation of Powers – Legislative Powers – Policy Powers – Member States – Municipalities – Federal Intervention

DURING THE EMPIRE (1822–89), Brazil adopted a unitary form of state. This was a central concern after independence from Portugal because of the need to, among other things avoid territorial fragmentation, as had occurred throughout Spanish America. Although federalist ideals were far from absent, concrete opportunities to adopt a federal division of powers arose only with the decline of the monarchy and the strengthening of republican movements. With the proclamation of the republic (1889) and the first republican constitution (1891), two main foundations of the Brazilian republican state organisation were established: the presidential system and the federal system. Despite changes in their configuration throughout the twentieth century, these systems remain the main constitutional and institutional features of contemporary Brazil. The 1891 Constitution defined the federal form of state as an 'eternal clause', that is, protected against amendments; the 1988 Constitution maintained this tradition.[1]

Developments in Brazilian federalism clearly followed the political, institutional and constitutional turbulence of the twentieth century.[2] Since its beginning – dual and non-cooperative – until the current model, there have been several oscillations and disruptions in the federal design in Brazil. Especially in the authoritarian periods (1937–45 and 1964–85) it could be argued that Brazilian federalism was rather nominal, since the member states did not have enough political and legislative autonomy to characterise the system as federal.

[1] Art 60, § 4, I. See ch 8.
[2] See ch 1.

The federalism established by the 1988 Constitution is – at least potentially – an example of cooperative federalism. For the first time in Brazilian constitutional history, several powers (political, administrative and legislative) are shared among different authorities on different levels.[3] These powers are shared not between the Union and the member states only, as is customary in federal countries: the Constitution included the municipalities in the federal division of powers.

Before going any further, some terminological issues must be considered to avoid misunderstandings: (a) What is elsewhere usually called the 'central government' will be referred to as the 'Union' (*União*). Although this term may refer to different things in other countries, it has long been used in Brazil to refer to the central and sovereign authority. Calling this authority the 'central government', as is common in other federations, would be confusing because in the Brazilian tradition the term 'government' is restricted to the executive branch, and references to Union in the Constitution encompass all central authorities, irrespective of the branch to which they belong. (b) The constituent units of the Brazilian federation will be referred to as either 'member states' (*estados membros*) or simply 'states' (*estados*). In addition to the 26 Brazilian states, there is a federal district (*Distrito Federal*, DF) in which the capital, Brasília, is located. (c) Finally, the local units within the states will be referred to as municipalities (*municípios*). Similar to the term 'Union', 'municipality' also means different things in different countries. In his translation of the Brazilian Constitution, for instance, Rosenn uses the term 'county' for *município*.[4] Although it is true that Brazilian *municípios* include both an urban and a rural territory and may therefore be larger than municipalities in other countries, which are frequently only an urban administrative unit, in this realm there is also no terminological uniformity. Furthermore, the term 'county' means different things in different countries. Thus, even if it may sometimes sound odd to use the term 'municipality' to refer to units that have an enormous area,[5] the term municipality will be nevertheless used here not only because municipality and *município* are cognates but also because in virtually all texts on the Brazilian political system, municipality is the term used to refer to *município*.

[3] Although it is true that some kind of power-sharing has existed since the 1934 Constitution, a comprehensive system of power-sharing was introduced for the first time by the 1988 Constitution.

[4] See his translation of the 1988 Brazilian Constitution in the project *Oxford Constitutions of the World* (oxcon.ouplaw.com).

[5] The case of the municipality of Altamira (the largest in Brazil), although an outlier, may be illustrative: it has an area of 159,533 square kilometres (ie, it is larger than England).

I. CENTRALISATION AND DECENTRALISATION UNTIL 1889

Federalist ideals in Brazil did not suddenly arise in 1889 with the creation of the republic. Even before Brazil's 1822 declaration of independence, there were strong federalist movements, even if this term was not necessarily used. Moreover, the distribution of power in Brazil since the arrival of the Portuguese occurred over time in a series of waves of centralisation and decentralisation.[6] The Portuguese first decided on a highly decentralised model, the hereditary captaincies; later, the captaincies were subordinated (at least in theory) to a Governorate General; during the Iberian Union, this governorate general was extinguished and two states were created – the State of Brazil and the State of Maranhão; in 1815, a United Kingdom of Portugal, Brazil and The Algarves was created.

The decentralisation of power during the colonial period facilitated the emergence of distinct regional identities, along with local elites who had very different and particular interests. These regional identities became especially salient at the time of independence, something that the official historiography had long striven to deny, as though both the process of independence and the decision to create a unitary state were the general will of the nation. Many argued that sovereignty belonged to the provinces, which could (but not necessarily should) unite in federal or confederate ties. The most concrete examples of this strain of thought were undoubtedly the Pernambuco Revolt of 1817 and the Confederation of the Equator of 1824. Some also advocated a federal republic, following the example of the United States.

In any case, the use of terms such as federation, confederation, republic and even democracy did not follow any clear identifiable pattern, and this confusion was strategically used by the advocates of a strong, unitary and centralised regime to repress any federalist movement in Brazil. According to them, federalism was necessarily connected with territorial fragmentation, secession and republicanism. The example of the fragmentation of Colonial Spanish America and all the political conflicts and wars associated with it only reinforced the argument for a monarchical and unitary state.

Although during the constituent debates of 1823 there were some proposals to adopt the federal form of state, none of them had any chance of success. With the dissolution of the Constituent Assembly by Emperor Pedro I[7] and the enactment of a rather centralising constitution

[6] See ch 1.
[7] See ch 1.

drafted under his personal supervision, federalist ideals seemed to have been definitively defeated.[8]

Nevertheless, in 1834, during the Regency period, a constitutional reform – known as Additional Act (*Ato Adicional*) – extinguished the Council of State, a key organ in the political centralisation of the Empire, transformed the old general councils into elected provincial legislatures and established a tax sharing system between the central power and the provinces, creating some political, administrative and fiscal decentralisation within the unitary state.

Whether coincidentally or not, it was also during this period that countless uprisings broke out around the country, many of them with a federalist or even secessionist character.[9] In 1840, the Additional Act was profoundly modified by a law that in theory should only establish criteria for its interpretation but that in practice promoted a major centralising reform, especially by means of an extensive decrease in the powers of provincial legislatures. In 1841, the Council of State was reinstated and the Code of Criminal Procedure of 1832 – which promoted the decentralisation of the system of justice even before the political and administrative decentralisation proposed by the Additional Act of 1834 – was reformed to curb the decentralisation in this realm. This was the beginning of what is known as the Return (*Regresso*), a conservative and centralising reaction to the liberal and decentralising experiences of the 1830s.

It was only in 1870 that federalist ideals regained political momentum in Brazil. That year, two seminal texts of the federalist movement were published: the Republican Manifesto and *A Província* (The Province), a book written by Tavares Bastos. The accusations against the monarchy made by the former were less directed against the regime than against the form of state; it can be argued that the text was above all a federalist manifesto. The latter is probably the most important book in defence of the federalist ideal written in Brazil.

The adoption of the federal form of state took place only 19 years after the publication of these two texts, with the proclamation of the Republic of Brazil. One reason for the proclamation of the republic

[8] But not throughout the country. The Confederation of the Equator, which began in the province of Pernambuco shortly after the dissolution of the Constituent Assembly, was a first demonstration that the unitary ideal did not enjoy unrestricted support, especially in the northern provinces.

[9] See Leslie Bethell and José Murilo de Carvalho, '1822–1850' in Leslie Bethell (ed), *Brazil: Empire and Republic, 1822–1930* (Cambridge, Cambridge University Press, 1989) 68.

was the inability of the Empire to realise that the progressive movement towards federalism was virtually inevitable. Some of the main supporters of federalism were actually monarchists. However, many of them eventually changed sides and supported the republican cause when they realised that the federal form of state would never be adopted under the Empire.

II. ALLOCATION OF POWERS UNDER THE 1988 CONSTITUTION

The federal power-sharing model adopted by the 1988 Constitution is based on several criteria. The constitutional literature refers to at least four of them. *Exclusive* powers are granted by Art 21 and 22 to the Union, by Art 25, § 2, to the states, and by Art 30, I, to the municipalities. *Residual* powers are granted to the states by Art 25, § 1. *Common* powers are defined in Art 23. Finally, *concurrent* powers are defined in Art 24.

The same articles may also be classified following a different divide, namely, between legislative and policy powers.[10] From this perspective, Arts 21 and 23 allocate policy powers, whereas Arts 22, 24, 25, § 1, and 30, I, allocate legislative powers.

A. Exclusive Powers

Although it is true that all three levels of authority hold some type of exclusive power, the Constitution allocates those powers very unevenly. While the states have only one exclusive power (the exploration of local services of piped gas) and the municipalities hold a general exclusive power for 'legislating upon matters of local interest', the Constitution establishes a list of more than 50 subjects upon which only the Union may legislate (for instance, civil, commercial, criminal, procedural, electoral, and labour law; traffic and transportation; nationality; citizenship and naturalisation; social security; and commercial advertising). In addition to the exclusive legislative powers defined by Art 22, the Union holds several exclusive policy powers granted by Art 21, such as the power to maintain relations with foreign states, declare war, and issue currency, among others.

[10] The distribution of fiscal powers is defined elsewhere in the Constitution.

Finally, the power to levy taxes and the system of revenue-sharing are also explicitly and extensively regulated by the Constitution and several exclusive powers are allocated to the Union, the states, the federal district, and the municipalities. This allocation is not performed in the heading dedicated to the federal design but by Arts 153 to 162, which belong to Heading VI of the Constitution.

B. Residual Powers

Initially, residual powers were the key to Brazilian federalism. The 1891 Constitution stipulated in Art 65, 2, that the member states had each and every power and rights that were not explicitly or implicitly denied by the Constitution. Similar formulas have been adopted by every subsequent Brazilian constitution. The 1988 Constitution, in Art 25, § 1, also provides that the powers not forbidden to the states by the Constitution are granted to them. However, although the formula has been unchanged since 1891, its meaning has changed considerably since then.

C. Common Powers

Common powers are those that are shared by all levels of authority (the Union, states, municipalities and the federal district) without any further qualification. They are not legislative, but policy powers. These include the duty to ensure that the Constitution, the laws and democratic institutions be respected; the duty to protect documents, works and other assets of historical, artistic or cultural value; the duty to provide the means of access to culture, education, and science; and the duty to preserve the forests, fauna, and flora, among others.

Notwithstanding the fact that the duties defined in Art 23 are common powers that may be exercised without any hierarchy or division of labour between the different levels of authority, the Constitution nevertheless provides that federal complementary laws may establish 'rules for the cooperation between the Union and the states, the federal district and the municipalities'. Until now, only one federal complementary law has been enacted with this purpose (Federal Complementary Law 140/2011); its scope is limited to environmental issues. Although it provides for different forms of cooperation, this complementary law clearly ascribes a central role to the Union.

D. Concurrent Powers

The so-called concurrent powers are without any doubt those that have resulted in the most important controversies in the Brazilian federal design. Art 24 provides that the Union, the states and the federal district[11] have concurrent power to legislate on matters such as, *inter alia*, tax law, financial law, economic law and urban planning law, production and consumption, education, culture, teaching and sports, social security and healthcare.

Unlike the case of common powers – within which all levels of authority have equal powers – Art 24, §§ 1 to 4, establishes that the powers of the Union shall be limited to the establishment of general rules and that the states have the power to supplement those general rules. Additionally, the same article establishes that in the absence of federal legislation defining general rules, the states shall exercise full legislative power to provide for their peculiarities and finally, that ensuing federal legislation establishing general rules on a given matter abrogates state legislation to the extent that it is contrary to those new general rules.

III. LEGISLATIVE POWERS

There are at least three problematic issues related to the interpretation of the provisions presented in the previous section: (a) to define the boundaries of exclusive powers; (b) to grasp the relationship between general and supplementary rules within concurrent powers; and (c) to comprehend the meaning of 'local interest' so as to establish the limits of the powers of municipal authorities.

These challenges may be divided into two categories, which may be called *semantic* and *formal* uncertainties.[12] These uncertainties are not purely academic debates. Their consequences may be especially apparent in the case law of the STF: controversies about federal power sharing account for a considerable share of the constitutional actions decided by the Court.

[11] The municipalities are not mentioned in Art 24. Nevertheless, based on the wording of Art 30, II, which provides that municipalities have the power to 'supplement federal and state legislation', some authors argue that the municipalities may also legislate upon the subjects specified in Art 24, and this interpretation has also been followed by the STF. See, for instance, RE 194704 (2017) and RE 586224 (2015).

[12] The reasoning and examples used in the ensuing text are based on Virgílio Afonso da Silva, 'Federalismo e articulação de competências no Brasil' in Guy Peters and Jon Pierre (eds), *Administração pública: coletânea* (Brasília/São Paulo, ENAP/UNESP, 2010).

A. Semantic Uncertainty

Semantic uncertainty simply refers to the difficulty of defining the precise meaning of the terms and expressions used in the Constitution. In this sense, it is not peculiar to the federal design as such, but a general interpretive issue that is pervasive in the law. In the case of Brazilian federalism, this uncertainty is especially related to the interpretation of the articles that define exclusive powers. Thus, even though there is no doubt that only the Union may legislate in the area of private law, the very limits of the term 'private law' are not always clear. Since the definition of which powers each authority holds depends on the interpretation of such open-ended concepts, these interpretive doubts lead to uncertainty about the allocation of powers.

Besides the troublesome task of defining the boundaries of legal terms, this semantic uncertainty is associated with a further obstacle. A simple example may illustrate the problem. Although private property is traditionally considered a subject within the scope of private law,[13] this cannot mean that every piece of legislation that regulates the use of private property is automatically to be considered legislation upon private law and therefore a power to be exercised exclusively by the Union. In 2006, the city of São Paulo enacted a municipal law known as the 'Clean City Act' (*Lei Cidade Limpa*, São Paulo Municipal Law 14223/2006). Among other things, the law regulates the size of business signboards and forbids almost any kind of external advertising in the city, especially on billboards. Apart from indirectly regulating commercial advertising, which falls within the exclusive power of the Union, to the extent that the statute forbids billboards even on private buildings, it clearly regulates the use of private property. However, it has been argued that the city of São Paulo has the power to legislate on the subject because it is a matter of 'local interest', as provided for by Art 30, I.

It is not difficult to notice that the Constitution employs two different – and incompatible – criteria for allocating exclusive legislative powers. The exclusive powers held by the Union are based on a substantive criterion: certain matters may only be regulated by the Union. In contrast, the exclusive legislative powers held by municipalities are clearly interest-based: municipalities may legislate upon matters of local interest.

[13] For the purposes of this example, the fact that the private property 'shall comply with its social function' (Art 5, XXIII) is not relevant.

Therefore, a subject may clearly fall within the scope of private law (and hence within the power of the Union) and at the same time be of local interest (and hence within the power of the municipalities). The STF has never concerned itself with the task of developing standards to cope with this type of difficulty (indeed, the Court does not even seem to be aware of this problem).

B. The Formal Uncertainty

A different challenge for the interpretation of the constitutional provisions on federal power-sharing occurs not within the allocation of exclusive powers but within the allocation of concurrent powers. The main reason for these controversies is the constitutional provisions found in Art 24, §§ 1 and 2: § 1 provides that within the matters that are the subject of concurrent powers, the power of the Union shall be limited to the establishment of general rules, and § 2 provides that the states have the power to supplement these general rules.

The definition of what is general and what is supplementary is the core of the problem. The literature on this subject clearly falls short of providing useful criteria to make this distinction. What constitutional scholars – and the case law of the STF – usually do is simply substitute the terms 'general' and 'supplementary' for synonyms, which clearly does not help solve the problem.

I am not arguing that there are clear criteria on which the distinction between general and supplementary rules may be based. Indeed, it seems that there are not, that is, there are no criteria that can solve in advance the tension between the powers of the Union and the powers of the states within the scope of concurrent legislation. Within the universe of every possible legal norm, there are no watertight definitions of what is general and what is specific. Rather, there is a continuum of possibilities between two (hypothetical) extremes: absolute generality and absolute specificity. Everything in between will be more general in relation to one side of the continuum and more specific in relation to the other side of the continuum.

One could surely argue that a geographic-based criterion could solve the problem. If a given subject relates exclusively to one state, the matter should thus be regulated by this state. If the issue has national relevance, it should thus be regulated by the Union. Though intuitive and apparently plausible, this geographic criterion has no direct relationship with the constitutional dichotomy between general and supplementary rules because it says nothing about the content of the laws to be enacted, only their geographic scope. Consequently, if the Union legislates on a given matter in such a detailed manner that there remains no margin for the states to complement, supplement or adapt this legislation to cope with their regional peculiarities, the regulation could not really be considered substantially general, even though it is geographically general (because it aims to provide rules for the whole country).

The considerations above suggest that it is not possible to establish an abstract criterion to distinguish what is general from what is supplementary. Although not explicitly (and sometimes also not consistently), the STF has been coping with this impossibility simply by deciding that state legislation must comply with federal legislation. In doing so, the Court does what it repeatedly states it cannot and should not do – namely, check the compatibility of two ordinary pieces of legislation (Union and state)[14] – and does not do what it claims it should do, namely, check whether the provisions in the federal law are general and those in the state law are supplementary.

Consequently, whenever the Union decides to regulate a given subject uniformly throughout the country, the provisions of such regulations are considered general, and the states may only exercise their power within the space left unregulated (if any). The Court virtually never declares a federal law unconstitutional on the grounds that its provisions are incompatible with the concept of general norms.[15]

At least two objections could be raised against this approach.

It could be argued that the Union would hold a power that no other authority holds, namely, the exclusive power to define the limits of its own power. Further, if the Union alone could decide what is general and what is not, this actually means that it has the exclusive power to exhaustively regulate a given subject whenever it considers it politically convenient to do so. This arguably undermines the very idea of concurrent powers.

[14] See, for instance, ADI 252 (1997), ADI 1540 (1997), ADI 2344-QO (2000), ADI 2876 (2009).

[15] In a series of recent decisions on the manufacturing and use of asbestos products and health protections, the Court declared some provisions of a federal law unconstitutional (Federal Law 9055/1995) and upheld state and municipal laws that were incompatible with it. These decisions, however, were not based on federal power-sharing, but on substantive grounds alone. See ADI 3356 (2017), ADI 3357 (2017), ADI 3937 (2017) and ADPF 109 (2017). See also ADI 3406 (2017), ADI 3470 (2017), and ADI 4066 (2017).

IV. POLICY POWERS

Arts 21 and 23 define a series of non-legislative powers and allocate them exclusively to the Union and to all levels of authorities, respectively, within the Brazilian federation – Union, states, federal district and municipalities. The latter are called *common* powers.

The relationship between the Union, states and municipalities in the realm of public policies is not exclusively defined by Art 23. Many provisions concerning public policies may be found throughout the Constitution, especially in its Heading VIII (Social Order), in which the general principles for public policies on, *inter alia*, healthcare, social security, social assistance and education are defined. Still, the national coordination of these and other policies largely depends on the provisions of Art 23, which establishes that the powers on many of these matters are jointly shared by all levels of authority within the federation. The definition of these powers as common to all levels of authority without any kind of division of tasks (not even in very general terms) leads to the question of how to coordinate the execution of policy within the federation.

Dispersion of power may bring about both gaps and overlaps in policy execution. In both cases, there may also be disputes between different levels of government. Whether and to what extent these gaps, overlaps and disputes occur primarily depend on the existence of means for fostering coordination within a federation. In Brazilian federalism, it may be argued that the ability to coordinate the execution of multilevel policies varies considerably. In some areas – the most important example is probably healthcare, through the National Unified Healthcare System (*Sistema Único de Saúde*, SUS) – the Union has been able to coordinate policy execution in the states and municipalities, whereas in some other areas this ability is clearly weaker.

It may be argued that good federal coordination in the execution of public policies is more likely to succeed when the Union can provide some form of incentives for states and municipalities, especially when these incentives include some form of cash transfer.

V. THE STATES IN THE BRAZILIAN FEDERALISM

The Brazilian federation is composed of 26 states and a federal district. The Constitution does not name the states that constitute the federation (with the exception of the states that were created by the 1988

Constitution itself, which are mentioned in Art 13 and 14 of the ADCT). Neither is there a special act or federal law that does this. The territorial boundaries of each state are recognised in several documents and domestic agreements between the states themselves, usually following the technical expertise of the Brazilian Institute of Geography and Statistics (IBGE). Historically, such boundaries have later been confirmed in different types of national laws, such as decree-laws, ordinary laws and even constitutional provisions.[16] However, even today there are controversies concerning the boundaries between some states and many controversies concerning the boundaries between municipalities.

A. The Role of the States in the Brazilian Federalism

With the promulgation of the 1988 Constitution, some authors pointed to an alleged strengthening in the position of the states within the Brazilian federal system. Even though this is surely true in several aspects, it does not seem to be true in the field of legislative and policy powers[17] for at least the following reasons: (a) in the area of legislative powers, while Art 22 provides for a list of more than 50 subjects upon which only the Union may legislate, the states have only one exclusive power, which is related to the services of piped gas; (b) in the area of policy powers, there are also strong incentives for the states (and the municipalities) to follow the policies defined by the Union.

Still, one could expect that even if the allocation of powers may privilege the Union, the states at least have autonomy in deciding how they organise themselves internally, since in this realm they are not competing with a strong central authority. According to Art 25, the states 'are organised and governed by the constitutions and laws that they may adopt, observing the principles of this Constitution'.

The Constitution itself does not impose unreasonable limits on the political self-organisation of the states. It only limits the political self-organisation of the states when it defines the number of deputies in

[16] See, for instance, Art 12, § 5 of the ADCT, which provides as follows: 'The current borders of the state of Acre with the states of Amazonas and Rondônia are recognised and confirmed, in conformity with the cartographic and geodesic surveys conducted by the Tripartite Commission composed of representatives of these states and of the specialised technical services of the Brazilian Institute of Geography and Statistics'.

[17] For a similar conclusion, see Marta Arretche, 'Demos-Constraining or Demos-Enabling Federalism? Political Institutions and Policy Change in Brazil' (2013) 5 *Journal of Politics in Latin America* 133.

the state legislatures, the duration of the term of state deputies and the electoral system used for their election, and the duration of the term of state governors. Additionally, according to Art 34, VII, *a–e*, states must do the following: (a) adopt a republican, representative, and democratic regime; (b) protect individual rights; (c) respect municipal autonomy; (d) perform the rendering of accounts of public administration; and (e) comply with the minimum level of investments established by the Constitution in education and public health.

The real source of limitations on the autonomy of the states is the case law of the STF. In its interpretation of Art 25, the Court developed the so-called *symmetry principle*. Despite its name, this principle has no relation whatsoever with the most widespread use of the term symmetry in federal studies.[18] The symmetry principle developed by the STF consists of a very broad interpretation of the duty of state constitutions to comply with the 'principles of this [federal] Constitution' (as provided in Art 25). The Court does not offer any precise definition of this so-called duty of symmetry, so it is always free to decide whether or not state constitutions comply with the federal Constitution.

Since 1988, the STF has struck down several provisions of state constitutions on the ground that they are inconsistent with the principles of the federal Constitution.[19] As a result, the provisions concerning the organisation of executive and legislative powers are virtually the same throughout the country. In several respects, Brazil's state constitutions are mere copies of the federal Constitution. Although the states have never really attempted to clearly depart from the main institutional design adopted by the Union, several state constitutions do have provisions that do not follow their equivalent in the federal Constitution. The STF is eager to strike down such 'deviations', even if they do not really imply non-compliance with the 'principles' of the federal Constitution.

Some examples may illustrate how the Court interprets this duty of symmetry. The Court decided that the amendment procedure of state constitutions must be the same as that of the federal Constitution. The federal Constitution establishes that for it to be amended, three fifths of the National Congress must approve the amendment proposal. The Constitution of the state of Espírito Santo established a higher quorum

[18] See Charles D Tarlton, 'Symmetry and Asymmetry as Elements of Federalism: A Theoretical Speculation' (1965) 27 *The Journal of Politics* 861.

[19] See, for instance, ADI 102 (2002), ADI 452 (2002), ADI 486 (1997), ADI 678 (2002), ADI 1304 (2004), ADI 1391 (2002).

(four fifths) for approving amendments, and this provision was declared unconstitutional by the STF.[20]

The same strict interpretation applies to the law-making process of state laws, which according to the STF, cannot depart from the national model. For this reason, the court decided that since the federal Constitution establishes that legislation in some areas can only be initiated by the President of the Republic, the same should occur within the states: in exactly the same areas, only the Governor may initiate legislation.[21]

B. Legally Weak, but Politically Robust?

In light of what has been presented so far, it seems plausible to argue that at least from the perspective of constitutional law, Brazil's states – and especially their state legislatures – have quite limited power and autonomy. From this perspective, Brazilian federalism cannot be considered robust.

This does not mean, however, that the states play no role in the Brazilian federal system. It means only that this role does not rest upon the legislative powers granted to the states by the Constitution. That said, the states do play a role in the legislative arena. However, this role is based rather on political reasons, not on legal features of the system. The main players in this context are not the state assemblies – which are incapable of challenging the National Congress in a dispute for spheres of legislative autonomy – but the state Governors, who have traditionally been strong players in Brazilian federalism ever since its beginning in the late nineteenth century.[22] Nevertheless, even these traditional players have been losing influence in some areas, especially in less affluent states, due to their financial dependence from the Union, which in some contexts may even bypass subnational players in the enforcement of public policies, especially through conditional cash transfer programmes.[23]

[20] See ADI 486 (2006).

[21] See ADI 102 (2002). See also ADI 1304 (2004) and 1391 (2002).

[22] For more details on the role of state governors, see David Samuels and Fernando Luiz Abrucio, 'Federalism and Democratic Transitions: The "New" Politics of the Governors in Brazil' (2000) 30 *Publius* 43; José Antonio Cheibub and others, 'Political Parties and Governors as Determinants of Legislative Behavior in Brazil's Chamber of Deputies, 1988–2006' (2009) 51 *Latin American Politics and Society* 1; and David Samuels, 'The Gubernatorial Coattails Effect: Federalism and Congressional Elections in Brazil' (2000) 62 *Journal of Politics* 240.

[23] See, for instance, Tracy Beck Fenwick, 'Avoiding Governors: The Success of Bolsa Família' (2009) 44 *Latin American Research Review* 102; André Borges, 'The Politi-

C. Changing Territorial Boundaries

According to the Constitution, states 'may merge into each other, subdivide, or split to be annexed to others, or form new states'.[24] For this to occur, it is required to obtain both the approval of the population that is directly interested[25] (as expressed through a plebiscite) and the approval of the National Congress (by means of a complementary law). The result of the plebiscite is only binding when the proposal is rejected by the voters, that is, in this case, the National Congress cannot decide otherwise. However, if the proposal is approved in the plebiscite, the National Congress can still decide against splitting or merging.

Since 1988, there has been only one attempt to change the boundaries of a state: in 2011, a plebiscite concerning the subdivision of the state of Pará[26] into three states was held, but the population voted against the proposal. Thus, the boundaries of the Brazilian states have been the same since the enactment of the 1988 Constitution.

VI. A THREE-TIERED FEDERATION: MUNICIPALITIES

One of the most important innovations in the federal design introduced by the 1988 Constitution was the explicit inclusion of the municipalities as a constituent unit. This is announced in Art 1 as follows: 'The Federative Republic of Brazil, formed by the indissoluble Union of the States and Municipalities as well as of the Federal District …'. This is reinforced by Art 18, which provides that '[t]he political and administrative organisation of the Federative Republic of Brazil comprises the Union, the States, the Federal District, and the Municipalities, all autonomous, as provided for in this Constitution'.

cal Consequences of Center-Led Redistribution in Brazilian Federalism' (2011) 46 *Latin American Research Review* 21. See also Diogo R Coutinho, 'Decentralization and Coordination in Social Law and Policy: The Bolsa Família Program' in David M Trubek and others (eds), *Law and the New Developmental State: The Brazilian Experience in Latin American Context* (Cambridge, Cambridge University Press, 2013).

[24] Art 18, § 3.

[25] According to Federal Law 9709/1998 (Art 7), 'population directly interested' means the population of the entire state (in the case of splitting), or states (in the case of merging and splitting followed by annexation). This provision was challenged before the STF, which upheld it. See ADI 2650 (2011).

[26] Pará is located in Northern Brazil and is the second-largest Brazilian state, with 1,247,954 square kilometres.

The autonomy of the municipalities has several features: (1) municipalities have their own constitution, called 'organic law'; (2) both the head of the executive branch and the local legislature are directly elected; (3) municipalities have the exclusive power to legislate on matters of local interest, and they also have common policy powers, which they share with the Union and the states; and (4) municipalities have their own administrative structure, financed at least partially by local tax revenues.[27]

Both the head of the executive branch (*prefeito*) and the municipal legislature (*câmara municipal*) are elected for a four-year term. Despite their power of self-organisation and self-government, the size of the local legislatures is strictly regulated by the Constitution, which establishes 24 different assembly magnitudes, ranging from nine to 55 representatives according to the population of the municipalities.

The rules for creating of new municipalities are defined in Art 18, § 4, and are very similar to those regulating the creation of new states: it requires the approval of the populations of the municipalities involved (via plebiscite) and subsequent approval by the state legislature. However, Art 18, § 4, establishes two limitations that are not present in the procedure for creating new states. The creation of new municipalities may only occur: (1) in certain periods determined by federal complementary law; and (2) after the publication of studies showing the feasibility of the new municipality.

These two conditions did not appear in the original wording of Art 18, § 4. They were introduced by a 1996 constitutional amendment (EC 15/1996) whose goal was to pace the creation of new municipalities. Between 1988 and 1996, more than a thousand new municipalities were created in Brazil. However, the federal complementary law mentioned in the new wording of Art 18, § 4, still has not been enacted. This legislative omission led many states to regulate the process of creating new municipalities through state law, even though the Constitution requires a federal complementary law for this purpose. Therefore, even after 1996, new municipalities continue to be created in Brazil.

The case law of the STF on this matter is rather unorthodox. With respect to the municipalities created after 1996 – which therefore did not satisfy the new requirements set forth in Art 18, § 4 – the Court recognised

[27] In reality, more than 80% of the municipalities in Brazil are highly dependent on transfers from the states and the Union. In those municipalities, such transfers comprise more than 75% of the municipal budget. Source: Brazilian National Treasury (www.tesouro.fazenda.gov.br).

what it called 'the normative force of the facts' and upheld their creation even though the constitutional requirements were not met.[28] The Court argued that the impossibility of meeting the constitutional requirements was due to the omission of the National Congress from enacting the necessary federal complementary law.[29] Definitive recognition of the municipalities created after 1996 came with a 2008 constitutional amendment (EC 57/2008) adding Art 96 to the ADCT, which provides that the creation of new municipalities by state laws 'that have been published by 31 December 2006 are validated, taking into account the requirements established in the respective state legislation at the time of their creation'. Since that date, no new municipality has been created in Brazil.

VII. THE FEDERAL DISTRICT

In addition to recognising the municipalities in the federal design as a third order of government, the Constitution changed the status of the federal district in which the federal capital – Brasília – is located. From 1763 to 1960, the capital of Brazil was Rio de Janeiro. Brasília was conceived and built in the second half of the 1950s and officially founded on 21 April 1960. The idea of moving the capital from the coast to the interior was an old one. Art 3 of the 1891 Constitution had already provided that '[a] territory of 14,400 square kilometres shall be marked off in the central plateau of the republic, as the property of the Union, and in this territory shall be established the future federal capital'. Similar provisions are found in the 1934 and 1946 Constitutions. But it was only in the second half of the 1950s (under the government of President Juscelino Kubitschek) that this idea materialised. The city was planned by Lúcio Costa and its most important buildings were designed by Oscar Niemeyer. The landscape architect was Roberto Burle Marx. Since 1987, the city has been considered a UNESCO World Heritage Site.[30]

[28] See, for instance, ADI 2240 (2007), 3316 (2007), 3489 (2007) and 3689 (2007).

[29] It is necessary to mention, however, that the National Congress approved such a federal complementary law twice (in 2013 and 2014), but the President of the Republic vetoed it on both occasions.

[30] According to UNESCO, 'Brasilia is a singular artistic achievement, a prime creation of the human genius, representing, on an urban scale, the living expression of the principles and ideals advanced by the Modernist Movement and effectively embodied in the Tropics through the urban and architectural planning of Lucio Costa and Oscar Niemeyer' (http://whc.unesco.org/en/list/445).

Until 1988, although the federal district had been considered part of the Brazilian federal design and always had representatives in the Federal Senate as well as deputies who were elected within its territory, its power of self-government and self-organisation was very limited. Since 1988, the federal district has had the same power of self-government as the states, including the power to directly elect a governor and a legislature. Furthermore, since the federal district is not subdivided into municipalities, it holds not only the legislative powers allocated to the states but also the legislative powers allocated to the municipalities.

VIII. FEDERAL TERRITORIES

Several articles in the Constitution refer to the so-called 'federal territories' or simply 'territories'. Previous Brazilian constitutions mentioned these federal territories as a constituent unit of the Brazilian federation, something that strictly speaking, they have never been. The 1988 Constitution explicitly changed this, and its Art 18, § 2, provides that 'Federal Territories are part of the Union, and their creation, transformation into states, or re-integration into their state of origin shall be regulated by complementary law'. The most important feature of these federal territories – a feature that derives from the fact that they belong to the Union – is their non-autonomous character, since they are organised by federal law. The governors of federal territories are not directly elected, but nominated by the President of the Republic and confirmed by the Federal Senate. Nevertheless, if a territory has more than 100,000 inhabitants, it may have an elected legislature.

Despite these (and other) provisions on the matter, since 1988 there have been no federal territories in Brazil. At the time of the promulgation of the 1988 Constitution, there were three federal territories: Amapá, Roraima and Fernando de Noronha. The Constitution converted the first two of those territories into states and integrated the third into the state of Pernambuco.[31] Other states that are currently part of the Brazilian federation were also non-autonomous federal territories at one time.

Thus, until 1988 the area occupied by all states and the federal district had always been less than the overall area of the country. Since the states and the federal district now occupy the entire area of the country, the creation of a new federal territory can only be achieved either by converting an existing state into a territory or by splitting a state and converting

[31] Respectively, Art 14 and 15 of the ADCT.

part of it. The procedure for the creation of new federal territories is the same that is required for the creation of new states.

IX. FEDERAL INTERVENTION

The final constitutional provisions that belong to the core of the Brazilian federal design are those that regulate the process of federal intervention in states and state intervention in municipalities. As expected in a federal system, the general rule established by these articles is that of non-intervention.[32] However, there are exceptional situations that may justify the Union's intervention in the states and the states in the municipalities. In the first case, the Union is allowed to intervene in the states, among other things, to 'maintain national integrity', to 'repel a foreign invasion or invasion of one unit of the federation into another', to 'guarantee the unimpeded functioning of any of the branches of government in the units of the federation', or to ensure that the states: (a) adopt a republican, representative, and democratic regime; (b) protect individual rights; (c) respect municipal autonomy; (d) render the accounts of public administration; and (e) comply with the minimum level of investments established by the Constitution in education and public health.

Art 36 regulates the procedure for federal intervention, which may involve a multiplicity of persons and institutions, both as applicants and as the authorising authority. The main actors in this realm are the President of the Republic and the National Congress. In almost every case of intervention described in Art 34, the procedure is rather straightforward: the President of the Republic requests the intervention,[33] the National Congress approves or rejects it; in the former case, the President of the Republic executes the intervention. The measures that may be undertaken are not established by the Constitution in advance and will depend on the situation that justified the intervention. In any case, however, the President of the Republic must submit his or her decree of intervention for consideration by the National Congress, and this decree must 'specify the extent, period and conditions of enforcement and … if applicable … appoint the intervenor'.[34]

[32] Art 34: 'The Union shall not intervene in the states or in the federal district'; Art 35: 'A state shall not intervene in its municipalities'.

[33] After hearing both the Council of the Republic (Art 90, I) and the National Defence Council (Art 91, § 1, II).

[34] Art 36, § 1.

From 1988 to 2018, there were no cases of federal intervention in the states. In February 2018, however, the President of the Republic decreed an intervention in the state of Rio de Janeiro, allegedly to address the 'serious impairment of public order'.[35] This intervention was limited to the area of public security, although the Constitution does not explicitly provide for a partial intervention.

X. THE FEDERAL SENATE

As is usual in federal States, Brazil has a bicameral legislature. States are equally represented in the Federal Senate with three senators, who are elected by a plurality vote for an eight-year term. Since senators are directly elected and tend to act following their party lines, and since the Federal Senate has – with a few exceptions – the same powers as the Chamber of Deputies, it is difficult to argue that the Senate represents a true federalist element within the National Congress. Additionally, because of the peculiarities of the Chamber of Deputies' electoral system, the representation of regional interests is sometimes pursued more intensely in the Chamber of Deputies than in the Senate.

FURTHER READING

Arretche M, 'Demos-Constraining or Demos-Enabling Federalism? Political Institutions and Policy Change in Brazil' (2013) 5 *Journal of Politics in Latin America* 133

Mainwaring S, 'Multipartism, Robust Federalism, and Presidentialism in Brazil' in S Mainwaring and MS Shugart (eds), *Presidentialism and Democracy in Latin America* (Cambridge, Cambridge University Press, 1997)

Samuels D, *Ambition, Federalism, and Legislative Politics in Brazil* (Cambridge, Cambridge University Press, 2003)

Souza C, 'Federal Republic of Brazil' in J Kincaid and GA Tarr (eds), *Constitutional Origins, Structure, and Change in Federal Countries* (McGill-Queen's University Press, 2005)

[35] Decree 9288/2018.

8

Law-Making Process and Constitutional Reform

Ordinary Legislation – Provisional Decrees – Constitutional Reform – Eternal Clauses

Brazil has a bicameral legislative body: the National Congress is composed of the Chamber of Deputies and the Federal Senate. In the legislative process, the Chamber of Deputies and the Federal Senate have almost exactly the same powers. Proposed bills must be approved in both chambers to become law. The legislative process within the National Congress begins in the Chamber of Deputies[1] unless the bill is proposed by a Senator. According to Art 59, in addition to ordinary laws, the legislative process includes the passage of constitutional amendments, complementary legislation, delegated legislation, provisional decrees, legislative decrees, and resolutions.

The presentation of the details of each main stage of the legislative process – introduction, deliberation, voting, presidential approval or veto, promulgation and publication – is not only a matter of describing a formal procedure but also a way to explain how the core of the Brazilian presidential system works. To understand the powers of the major players in this process and how they are exercised is an important key to understanding the balance of powers between the legislative and the executive branches.

[1] For this reason, the details about the several stages of the legislative process presented in the following subsections are based on the internal rules of the Chamber of Deputies (*Regimento Interno da Câmara dos Deputados*, hereafter also RICD).

I. ORDINARY LEGISLATION

A. Introduction of Bills

Bills may be introduced by any member or committee of the Chamber of Deputies or Federal Senate, the President of the Republic, the STF and other superior and high courts, the Federal Procurator-General and citizens. Although the Constitution is not always explicit in this matter, some of these individuals or groups may only introduce bills within the subject matters related to their activities. Courts, for instance, may only propose bills related to the judiciary.[2]

One important feature of the legislative process in Brazil is the that the President not only has the power to introduce bills but also, in some domains, is the only one who has this power. According to Art 61, § 1, the President has the exclusive power to introduce bills that, *inter alia*, modify the number of Armed Forces troops, create public offices and positions in the direct administration and in autonomous government agencies, and change the organisation of the Federal Public Ministry and Federal Public Defender's Office. Even more important is the exclusive powers of the President in budgetary matters.[3] According to Art 165, bills concerning the multi-year plan, budgetary directives and annual budgets may only be introduced by the President.

Although the bills introduced by the President of the Republic within his or her exclusive powers may be amended in the Chamber of Deputies and the Federal Senate, those bodies' discretion is constrained by Art 63, I, which provides that no amendment may result in an increase in the expenditures originally proposed in the bill. This constraint does not fully apply to the bill on the annual budget, but in this realm the members of Congress are nevertheless subject to restrictions in their discretion, because any amendment in those bills must: (a) be compatible with the multi-year plan and the budgetary directives; (b) specify the necessary funds, which may only arise out of the annulment of other expenditures; and (c) be related either to the correction of errors or omissions or to the provisions of the text of the bill of law.

The exclusive powers granted to the President to introduce bills within certain domains are pivotal to the Brazilian presidential system,

[2] See, for instance, Arts 93 and 99.

[3] On the matter, see Carlos Pereira and Bernardo Mueller, 'The Cost of Governing: Strategic Behavior of the President and Legislators in Brazil's Budgetary' (2004) 37 *Comparative Political Studies* 781.

because among other things, they increase the agenda-setting power of the President, who decides if and when a given bill should be introduced and even at what speed a given bill should be discussed.[4] Presidents have used this agenda-setting power to obtain wider support to their bills.

Finally, the Constitution also grants citizens the power to introduce so-called 'popular bills'. However, this is not an easy task, since popular bills must be subscribed by a large number of citizens, namely, by 'at least one percent of the national electorate, distributed throughout at least five states, with no less than three-tenths of one percent of the voters of each of these states'.[5]

B. Deliberation

Every introduced bill is referred to at least one of the standing committees and afterwards necessarily to the *Committee on Constitution, Justice and Citizenship*, which analyses the compatibility of bills with the Constitution. In many cases, the decision of the committees on a proposed bill may be final. For instance, if all committees to which a bill had been referred decide against its approval, it should be considered rejected. Moreover, in some cases, a bill may be considered definitely approved even without being discussed and voted on the floor by all deputies, unless an appeal is filed by one-tenth of the members of the appropriate House. Thus, if the RICD allows[6] and no appeal is filed, a draft may be considered approved without having been discussed and voted on by all deputies.

C. Voting

There is more than one voting procedure in the Chamber of Deputies (and in the Senate). The most common procedure is so-called symbolic voting. Symbolic voting dispenses with nominal (roll-call) voting, and a bill is considered approved if a clear majority of the deputies remain

[4] The President may request urgent consideration of the bills that he or she introduces (Art 64, § 1).

[5] Art 14, III and 61, § 2. Since the number of registered voters in Brazil in 2014 was 142,822,046, a popular bill must be endorsed by at least 1,428,220 voters.

[6] According to Art 24, II, of the RICD, some types of drafts must be discussed on the floor, including drafts of complementary law, codes, popular bills, among others.

seated when the voting procedure begins. If the result is unclear (and in other cases established by the RICD[7]), the decision must be made through a roll-call vote. An ordinary statute is approved in the Chamber of Deputies if it receives the plurality of votes in a session in which at least a majority of the deputies are present.

If a bill is approved in the Chamber of Deputies, it goes to the Federal Senate, where the legislative procedures follow very similar steps. If the bill is approved in the Senate without changes, it goes to the President for approval or veto. If the bill is rejected in the Senate, it is archived.[8] Finally, if the bill is amended in the Senate, it is sent back to the Chamber of Deputies, where those changes may be accepted or rejected. In any case, after approval – with or without the Senate's changes – the bill is sent to the President of the Republic. Thus, it is important to emphasise that although both houses have similar powers in the Brazilian bicameral system, the Chamber of Deputies, because it is the chamber in which the vast majority of the bills are introduced, has a slight predominance, since it may overrule changes introduced to a bill in the Senate.

D. Presidential Approval and Veto

Bills approved in both houses of the National Congress are sent to the President of the Republic for approval. According to Arts 66, § 1 and 84, V, the President may accept or reject the bill either partially or entirely. This means that unlike in the case of many other presidential systems, a line-item veto (partial veto) is allowed in Brazil, which considerably increases the power of the President vis-à-vis the Legislature. The power of a partial veto, however, may only be exercised upon full texts of provisions, that is, articles, paragraphs, clauses or subclauses. The President cannot strike out words, numbers, and punctuation; even full sentences cannot be struck out if they do not comprise the entire text of the provision. Approval may be explicit or tacit (if the President does not sign the bill within 15 working days, it is considered approved). This precludes the possibility of so-called pocket veto: after the period of 15 days has elapsed, the silence on the part of the President shall operate as approval. A veto must always

[7] All types of legislation requiring a qualified majority (absolute, 3/5 or 2/3 majorities) must be decided through a roll-call vote (RICD, Art 186, I). Additionally, if any deputy requires a roll-call vote, the plenary session must decide upon it (Art 186, II).

[8] The subject of an archived bill cannot be discussed again in the same year unless the absolute majority of both chambers of the National Congress so requests (Constitution, Art 67).

be explicit and justified. The Constitution mentions two reasons for a presidential veto: the President of the Republic may consider the bill either unconstitutional or contrary to the public interest.

A presidential veto may be overridden by the Legislature. For this to happen, the absolute majority of the National Congress in a joint session is required. Until 2013, decisions about the presidential veto were made by secret ballot. EC 76/2013 altered Art 66, § 4, and ever since then, the decision is to be made through an open vote.

E. Promulgation and Publication

The approved bill is promulgated by the President within 48 hours. If the President refuses to promulgate a statute, the President of the Federal Senate should do it. Promulgation seems to be a rather formal procedure without controversial implications – but it is not. In reality, it is another important piece of the Brazilian presidentialism machinery. Although the Constitution has no provision allowing it, in the event of a partial veto, the President may promulgate only the part of the law to which he or she agreed, that is, without waiting for Congress' decision on the vetoed part (which frequently takes much longer to occur than the 30 days established by the Constitution). Depending on the content of what had been approved and vetoed, the fact that part of the law has already entered into force when the Congress finally deliberates on the vetoed part may create a *fait accompli* that poses additional hurdles for overriding the vetoes.

Promulgation does not make the law valid and binding. The newly approved and promulgated law must be published in the official gazette,[9] which usually occurs a few days later. Ordinary legislation is numbered sequentially, beginning with Federal Law 1, from 1946.

II. PROVISIONAL DECREES

Provisional decrees (*medidas provisórias*) involve a completely different construction process. Its important role within the Brazilian presidential system, especially in the relationship between the President of the Republic and the National Congress, was emphasised in chapter three.

[9] On 30 November 2017, the printed version of the official gazette (*Diário Oficial da União*) was published for the last time. Since 1 December 2017, it has been published in electronic form only.

According to Art 62, in relevant and urgent cases, the President may issue provisional decrees 'with immediate force of law'. These provisional decrees are immediately submitted to the National Congress. The most important difference between a provisional decree and the introduction of a bill is that the first goes into effect immediately, while an introduced bill only produces the desired effects if and when approved by the National Congress.

Until 2001, the issuance of provisional decrees was not regulated in detail by the Constitution. Consequently, presidents who served prior to 2001 used provisional decrees as a central instrument for advancing their political goals. Provisional decrees, which under the Constitution were valid for a period of 30 days, were repeatedly reissued. In 2001, the Constitution was amended to limit the use of provisional decrees, particularly with respect to reissuance. In addition, the subjects that may be regulated by provisional decrees were limited.

Although the amendment extended the period of validity of provisional decrees to 60 days, it explicitly stated that such decrees could be reissued only once. Additionally, and partially based on the case law of the STF, some subject matters – such as political rights, electoral law, criminal law, criminal procedure, and civil procedure – cannot be regulated by provisional decrees. After the period of provisional validity, the National Congress must decide whether to convert a provisional decree into an ordinary law or reject it.

III. COMPLEMENTARY LEGISLATION

Despite its name, complementary legislation does not complement anything, whether it be the Constitution or other types of laws. At the least, it does not complement the Constitution or other types of laws more or less than any ordinary law does. In almost every respect, a complementary law is a piece of legislation like any other. It possesses only two relevant and distinct features: (1) unlike ordinary laws, which require only a plurality, complementary laws require an absolute majority of each house of the Congress for approval; and (2) they may regulate only those subjects that the Constitution itself explicitly reserved for complementary legislation.

Thus, a complementary law is only needed when the Constitution explicitly requires it. Conversely, if the Constitution does not explicitly require complementary legislation for regulating a given subject matter, then a complementary law cannot be used.

IV. CONSTITUTIONAL REFORM

A. Amendment Process

The procedure for amending the Constitution is defined in a single article: Art 60 defines who may introduce amendment proposals, the legislative procedure to be followed and the limits on the amending power. The degree of interpretative dispute on this subject follows the same order: none in relation to whom may introduce amendment proposals, a few on the procedure, and many in relation to limits.

i. Amendment Proposals

The head of Art 60 and its three clauses clearly and strictly define who is entitled to introduce a constitutional amendment proposal:

(a) one-third of the members of the Chamber of Deputies or the Federal Senate;
(b) the President of the Republic; or
(c) more than half of the Legislative Assemblies of units of the federation, each manifesting its decision by a simple majority of its members.[10]

Since 1988, no constitutional amendment has been proposed by a state legislature. It is likely that there will never be such a proposal. Given the national character of Brazil's political parties, the parties with representatives in the National Congress are the same parties that have representatives in the state legislatures, and there would be no reason whatsoever to spend an enormous amount of political and legislative energy to achieve the difficult goal of gathering support from many state deputies throughout Brazil if it is possible (and much easier) to achieve the same goal within the Chamber of Deputies or the Federal Senate.

ii. Procedure

The Constitution is extremely concise in its description of the procedural rules governing its amendment. Art 60, § 2, established that a constitutional amendment proposal 'shall be discussed and voted upon

[10] Unlike the case of ordinary legislation, constitutional amendments cannot be introduced by a popular bill.

in each House of the National Congress, in two rounds, and shall be considered approved if it obtains three-fifths of the votes of the respective members in both rounds'. This is the core of the amendment process. Art 60, § 3, complements § 2 by providing that constitutional amendments shall be promulgated by the directing boards of the Chamber of Deputies and Federal Senate. One important corollary of these provisions is that the President of the Republic has no veto power over constitutional amendments.

The details of the amendment process are laid down – not identically – by the RICD and RISF. The most important controversies surrounding the process of amendment are related to two-round voting and bicameralism.[11]

The Constitution does not stipulate a time interval between first- and second-round voting. The RICD and the RISF regulate the matter differently. The former provides that there should be an 'interstice of five sessions' between the first and second rounds; the latter established an interval of at least 'five business days'.[12] In both cases, it is possible to question whether intervals of five days or five sessions comply with this constitutional provision. The answer depends, of course, on the interpretation of the aim of the constitutional provision that demands two rounds of voting for constitutional amendments. If two rounds of voting should provide time for members of Congress to reflect upon their first vote, five days (or even sessions) will often be inadequate. If the waiting period aims at 'allowing the political public sphere to occasionally take a stand and exert pressure upon institutionalized politics',[13] then the period of five days (or sessions) is definitely insufficient.

Even more controversial is the fact that on some occasions, the Chamber of Deputies and the Federal Senate have not even complied with the five days/sessions rule stipulated by their internal rules. In one case, the two rounds took place on the same day (indeed, in a single night, within less than one hour). Although this may seem a clear case of a constitutional amendment that could (or should) be struck down in court, the STF has a different position on the matter. Despite its activist

[11] For a length analysis of these and other controversies surrounding the process of amending the Brazilian Constitution, see Leonardo Augusto de Andrade Barbosa, 'Legislative Process and Constitutional Change in Brazil: on the pathologies of the procedure for amending the 1988 Constitution' in Richard Albert and others (eds), *Constitutional Change and Transformation in Latin America* (Oxford, Hart 2019).

[12] RICD, Art 202, § 6; RISF, Art 362.

[13] Barbosa (n 11).

profile, which encompasses (among other things) a self-attributed power to exercise judicial review of constitutional amendments,[14] the Court has traditionally refrained from scrutinising compliance with the internal rules of the houses of the National Congress by arguing that such compliance is an internal matter.[15] In a concrete case in which the Federal Senate held both voting rounds in a single night, the Court decided that since the Constitution does not establish the time interval between the two rounds, whether or not the legislature complies with its internal rules is not a constitutional matter.[16]

Another controversial issue that arises in the process of constitutional amendment in Brazil is related to bicameralism. As stated above, Art 60, § 2, requires that constitutional amendment proposals be approved by both houses of the Congress. To a great extent, this is not different from the requirement that ordinary legislation be approved in both houses. However, there is an important difference. If the Federal Senate alters an ordinary bill that has been introduced and approved in the Chamber of Deputies, the latter may simply overrule the changes introduced to the bill by the Senate and send it to the President of the Republic for approval. Therefore, the first house has the upper hand in the ordinary legislative process. In contrast, both houses have equal power in the procedure for constitutional amendments. This means that a constitutional amendment is only considered approved if both the Chamber of Deputies and the Federal Senate approve exactly the same wording. If the Senate alters a proposal that has already been approved in the Chamber of Deputies, the latter cannot simply overrule those changes: it must either agree with them (and in this case the proposal is considered approved) or reject the changes and stand on its original wording. In the latter case, the proposal is sent back to the Senate. Thus, an indefinite back-and-forth between the two houses might occur.

In 1998, however, the Chamber of Deputies worked out a strategy to circumvent this problem. This strategy may be called the 'partial promulgation' of constitutional amendments. It consists of promulgating only those provisions of a constitutional amendment that both houses agree upon, leaving aside those provisions upon which agreement was not achieved. However, it is very likely that this strategy may have unintended results. Suppose that a constitutional amendment proposal approved in

[14] See ch 4.
[15] See, for instance, MS 25588 (2007) and MS 26062 (2007).
[16] See ADI 4357 (2013). See also ADI 4425 (2013). For a critical account of both this doctrine and this decision, see Barbosa (n 11).

the Chamber of Deputies has two provisions, the first being a general rule for which the second provision establishes an exception. Suppose further that the necessary three-fifths majority was only attained because of the exception established by the second provision, that is, the Chamber would not have approved the proposal if it consisted only of the general rule. The Senate, however, was against the exception (second provision) and approved the proposal without it. Following the strategy of partial promulgation, the amendment could be considered partially approved, since both houses agreed upon the first provision. Nevertheless, promulgating it would misrepresent the opinion of the Chamber of Deputies. In other words, it may be assumed that many deputies would not have voted for the proposal if they had known that ultimately, only the first provision would be promulgated. Notwithstanding these problematic issues, according to Barbosa 'all major constitutional reforms passed [between 1998 and 2016] relied on partial promulgation to succeed',[17] and the STF has confirmed the constitutionality of this strategy.[18] Since presidents and their coalition often depend on amending the Constitution to advance their political agenda, the partial amendment strategy is an essential tool to achieve their goals.

B. Limits to Constitutional Reform

The limits to constitutional reform are established in Art 60, §§ 1, 4 and 5. The Brazilian constitutional literature classifies these limits into three categories: circumstantial, temporal and substantial.

Circumstantial limits. Only three circumstances prevent the enactment of constitutional amendments: during federal intervention into a state and during a state of defence or a state of siege. Until 2018, there had been no federal interventions or declarations of a state of defence or state of siege. Hence, these circumstantial limits had never been enforced. In 2018, the Union ordered federal intervention in the state of Rio de Janeiro. During this period, Art 60, § 1, was enforced and no constitutional amendments were passed.

Temporal limits. The Constitution provides for only one temporal limitation: a defeated constitutional amendment proposal shall not be the subject of another proposal in the same year. Although this provision is rather clear, the issue of exactly what it forbids may nevertheless

[17] ibid.
[18] See ADI 3367 (2005).

be the subject of fierce dispute. The most frequent sources of controversy are proposals that are not identical, but very similar to – and, most important, that have identical effects to – proposals that have already been defeated. Due to the complex details of the legislative process, the floor of both the Chamber of Deputies and the Federal Senate may decide upon an original proposal, a substitute proposal (introduced by the rapporteur), or an agglutinative amendment (a proposal that merges several amendments), among other things. It is not unusual for the presidents of both the Chamber and the Senate to use this procedural complexity so that they can have more than one opportunity to obtain approval of a constitutional amendment.[19] Although this strategy does not seem to be completely compatible with Art 60, § 5, the STF has accepted it.[20]

Substantial limits. The Constitution also establishes that certain matters are excluded from the scope of constitutional reform: they are the so-called eternal clauses, known in Brazil as bedrock clauses (*cláusulas pétreas*). Given their importance and the controversies associated with them, they will be presented and analysed at length in the next section.

C. Eternal Clauses

Brazilian constitutionalism has a long tradition of increasing the rigidity of its constitutions by establishing non-amendable clauses. Except for the 1937 Constitution, every Brazilian constitution since 1891 has been rigid not only in the sense that amendments demand a special procedure but also in the sense that a constitutional core – the so-called eternal clauses – is shielded against amendments. I call this 'constitutional super-rigidity'.[21]

From 1891 to 1988, Brazilian constitutions with eternal clauses had protected only two provisions: the republican regime and the federal

[19] For more details on this type of strategy (with concrete examples), see Barbosa (n 11).

[20] See, for instance, MS 22503 (1996).

[21] Hence, my use of the term 'super-rigidity' has no direct relationship on the debate on degrees of constitutional rigidity. This latter discussion aims at establishing indices and typologies about how difficult it is to amend any given constitution (based on factors such as required majority, approval by state legislatures, popular referendum, bicameralism, among others). Measured according to such indices, the Brazilian Constitution would surely not be among the most rigid. For more details on this distinction, see below.

system. The 1988 Constitution considerably extended the list of eternal clauses. According to Art 60, § 4, no proposed constitutional amendment shall be discussed if it tends to abolish: (I) the federal form of state, (II) the direct, secret, universal, and periodic vote; (III) the separation of powers; and (IV) individual rights and guarantees.

There are several interpretation quarrels regarding the exact meaning of these provisions. The mainstream trend is to interpret them very broadly. The experience of authoritarian rule in Brazil, under which constitutional provisions have been constantly circumvented, has led many to believe that the only way to protect the core of the Constitution is by excluding its content from any discussion. Of course, it is questionable whether this strategy is effective in preventing attacks against the constitutional order and whether it has positive effects on constitutional dynamics. In any case, eternal clauses have been a central element of Brazilian constitutionalism.

The key expression in Art 60, § 4, is surely 'tends to abolish'. At least according to the wording of this article, not every amendment to the eternal clauses is forbidden, only those that tend to abolish them. The exact meaning of this expression remains a puzzle for courts and academia. There are very few studies on this issue and it seems that the constitutional literature accepts that it is not feasible to develop an abstract criterion for defining the meaning of the expression 'if it tends to abolish' and that the only way to resolve this problem is through case-by-case analyses and ad hoc solutions. Still, it can be argued that some differentiations among the four eternal clauses of the Constitution are in order. These differentiations do not solve any controversy in advance, but may help us better understand the challenges that each of these clauses may pose.

The less problematic of these clauses appears to be Art 60, § 4, II: '… if it tends to abolish: … (II) the direct, secret, universal, and periodic vote'. Direct and secret voting are binary expressions. Tending to abolish in this case may be considered synonymous with abolishing. There seems to be no gradation, for example, between a secret and a non-secret ballot. Although there may of course be degrees of publicity within different types of non-secret votes – depending, for instance, on how many people and how easy it is to obtain access to the content of that vote – this fact does not seem to be relevant because in all cases the vote will no longer be secret. The concept of universal voting is perhaps somewhat more problematic, since 'universal' has never meant 'all' (for example, children do not vote) and therefore it is not a binary concept. Still, it seems unproblematic to accept the following rule: electoral franchising cannot be restricted, but it can surely be broadened (ie, become 'more universal') in relation to the franchising set forth by the Constitution in 1988. Thus, it would be unconstitutional to disenfranchise the illiterate, but not to extend voting rights to immigrants.

A second set of eternal clauses has nothing to do with rights, but with institutional design. These are clauses I and III of Art 60, § 4: '... if it tends to abolish: (I) the federal form of state, ... (III) the separation of powers'. Within institutional design, possibilities are virtually countless. There are more and less centralised federal states, just as separation of powers may be designed to foster more collaboration or more competition among branches. Thus, it is not simple to decide in advance what may and may not be changed in Brazilian federalism or the separation of powers. The fact is that both the federal design and the separation of powers have undergone several changes since the enactment of the Constitution.

The last eternal clause is that of Art 60, § 4, IV: '... if it tends to abolish: ... (IV) the individual rights and guarantees'. This is without any doubt the most important and complex of all four eternal clauses. First, individual rights are seldom a matter of all or nothing (either you have full freedom of religion or you have nothing at all). Secondly, individual rights are not a matter of institutional design in which it is widely accepted that even if changing one single feature may affect the design, such a change will seldom compromise the core of federalism or separation of powers.

Art 60, § 4, IV, also gives rise to controversies that the other three clauses clearly do not, controversies that go beyond the interpretation of what is meant by 'if it tends to abolish'. To this day, it is not even clear what the expression 'individual rights and guarantees' encompasses, since this expression is not consistently employed throughout the Constitution. Perhaps the most intense debate in this realm is related to the inclusion of social rights as part of the eternal core of the Constitution. This is a quite polarised debate. On the one hand, those who understand that social rights are an achievement to be preserved clearly stand for the inclusion of social rights within the eternal clauses. In contrast, those who think that social rights, especially workers' rights, are an obstacle to free entrepreneurship generally see in the expression 'individual rights and guarantees' a clear reference to freedom rights, not to social rights. So far, the STF has never been clear about this.

That said, the Court has already ruled on the existence of individual rights that are not enshrined in either Art 5 or Heading II of the

Constitution, that is, rights that are not part of the constitutional Bill of Rights.[22]

Hence, at least based on the case law of the STF, it is possible to assume that the scope of the eternal clause is not limited to the rights set forth in Art 5; other individual rights are also protected. However, whether or not all provisions of the Bill of Rights (including, therefore, social and workers' rights and political and nationality rights) are protected remains an open question. Nevertheless, given the expansive case law of the STF on the eternal clauses, there seems to be no reason to assume that social and workers' rights (or at least many of them) should not be considered individual rights and therefore protected. Even though the Court has never decided that social rights are part of the eternal clauses, it has ruled that political and electoral rights are.[23] Hence, there seems to be at least some evidence that the STF would be prone to place all these categories of rights under the protection of the eternal clause of Art 60, § 4, IV.

Irrespective of the stance of the STF and constitutional scholars in relation to the breadth of the scope of the eternal clauses, in Brazil there is certainly a widespread belief that only what is protected by eternal clauses is actually guaranteed. There is an obvious distrust of the democratic process. This is nothing new. In the Constituent Assembly, the debate on the inclusion or non-inclusion of certain matters into the constitutional text was frequently marked by a distrust of ordinary politics. The rationale during the Constituent Assembly had frequently been that only what is entrenched in the Constitution is truly protected. In the post-constituent period (until today), this idea has also been ubiquitous. However, this approach goes up one level: many think that true protection is only achieved when constitutional provisions are shielded by an eternal clause.

D. Amendment Rate

There is a vast literature on constitutional amendments and the rate of amendments written by both political scientists and constitutional scholars. Among many other things, this literature attempts both to define what is a high amendment rate – since the number of amendments is only one variable in this realm, and sometimes it is not even the most

[22] ADI 939 (1993). See also RE 587008 (2011).
[23] See ADI 3685 (2006).

important – and what are the reasons why some constitutions are much more frequently amended than others. Concerning the first question, one could argue that the amendment rate of the Brazilian Constitution is high irrespective of the criteria used to define it. Almost all of the reasons that are usually cited to explain high amendment rates are present in the Brazilian context. Save for bicameralism, which is usually mentioned as a feature that slows down the amendment rate, everything else seems to favour high amendment rates: (1) The required majority for approving amendments – three-fifths – is lower than the standard two-thirds adopted by many constitutions. (2) No popular referendum is needed. (3) Virtually the entire amendment procedure takes place within the National Congress. (4) There is thus no veto player outside the legislature. (5) The approval of state legislatures is not needed. (6) No elections should be held between proposing and approving an amendment. (7) The Constitution is long and detailed and includes several public policies.[24]

Thus, although the Brazilian Constitution has a core that is extremely rigid, it is rather flexible compared to other constitutions, and the fact that it has been amended more than 100 times between 1988 and 2018 seems to be good evidence of this proposition.

It is important to keep in mind that the amendment rate may not explain much about the constitutional dynamics of a given country. Even though more than 100 amendments within 30 years may be considered a high amendment rate, that number says almost nothing about the extent and impact of those amendments, which may vary considerably. In Brazilian constitutional history, some examples are revealing. In 1834, a single act – the Additional Act – almost converted Brazil from a unitary state into a federal state;[25] the 1967 Constitution was amended only once and the result was a new constitution (the 1969 Constitution).[26]

Under the 1988 Constitution, two constitutional amendments – EC 38/2002 and EC 60/2009 – that contributed to increase the amendment rate did not change anything noteworthy: the first added Art 89 into the ADCT to regulate the military police in the former federal territory of Rondônia; the second made minor changes to this

[24] See, for instance, Cláudio G Couto and Rogério B Arantes, 'Constitution, Government and Democracy in Brazil' (2008) 4 *World Political Science Review*. For an argument that attempts to mitigate the link between the amendment rate and the all-encompassing character of the Brazilian Constitution, see Barbosa (n 11).

[25] See ch 7.

[26] See ch 1.

same Art 89. Another, even more telling example is EC 70/2012: this amendment did not change anything in the Constitution; it merely added a new article to an earlier constitutional amendment. Thus, it may be argued that 'head counting' in this area usually means little.

E. Total Revision of the Brazilian Constitution

Constitutions usually do not provide a procedure for their total revision. Although there are exceptions, constitutions usually have a claim (at least an implicit one) to eternity. The possibility of constitutional amendments aims to strengthen this claim to eternity: the Constitution may and should be altered to cope with new contexts, but it should not be replaced. The 1988 Constitution follows this tradition. It has no clause that provides for constitutional replacement.

Nevertheless, the Constituent Assembly of 1987–88 provided for a constitutional revision to occur five years after its promulgation, that is, in 1993. Article 3 of the ADCT established that the Constitution 'shall be revised after five years, counting from its promulgation, by vote of an absolute majority of members of the National Congress in a unicameral session'. The differences between the constitutional revision and the ordinary amendment process relate to both aim and procedure. While amendments aim to make specific changes to the Constitution, the 1993–94 constitutional revision was intended to be comprehensive. From a procedural point of view, the differences are even clearer: while amendments require three-fifths of the Chamber of Deputies and Federal Senate to be approved, the changes made during the 1993–94 constitutional revision demanded only an absolute majority in unicameral sessions.

At the time of the constitutional revision, an important question arose: was the constitutional revision convention free to change anything in the Constitution or was it subject to the same limits set forth for constitutional amendments? The first case would potentially result in a total revision of the Brazilian Constitution. However, both the constitutional literature and the STF understood that the constitutional revision convention was bound to the same limits that applied to constitutional amendments.[27]

In any case, lowering the required majority did not lead to a comprehensive constitutional revision. Only six amendments were approved,

[27] See ADI 981-MC (1994).

almost all of them with a rather minor impact, except for ECR 5/1994, which reduced the presidential term from five to four years.

Because the Constitution does not provide for a second constitutional revision, since 1994 the ordinary amendment procedure has been the only path for reforming the Constitution. Nevertheless, time and again the summoning of an assembly with the specific aim of revising parts of the Constitution has been brought up as a way to overcome difficulties in making alterations, especially those related to the political and electoral systems. The rationale behind this idea is to take the decision about changing the rules of the political process away from those who have a personal interest in the matter, namely, incumbent federal deputies and senators. There is no consensus on the constitutionality of such a measure. Constitutional scholars are clearly divided on the matter, and since the idea has never materialised,[28] the STF has not decided the issue.

FURTHER READING

Barbosa LA de A, 'Legislative Process and Constitutional Change in Brazil: on the pathologies of the procedure for amending the 1988 Constitution' in R Albert, C Bernal, and JZ Benvindo (eds), *Constitutional Change and Transformation in Latin America* (Oxford, Hart [forthcoming])

Hiroi T, 'The Dynamics of Lawmaking in a Bicameral Legislature: The Case of Brazil' (2008) 41 *Comparative Political Studies* 1583

Paula F de, 'Does Brazil Have a Legislative Policy?' (2016) 4 *The Theory and Practice of Legislation* 329

Silva VA da, 'A Fossilised Constitution?' (2004) 17 *Ratio Juris* 454

[28] After the mass protests of 2013 (see ch 5), President Rousseff went on national TV and stated that she was willing to summon a constituent assembly with the aim of reforming the political system. A few days later, the idea was withdrawn.

Conclusion: Change to Overcome

On 5 October 1988, the President of the National Constituent Assembly, Ulysses Guimarães, delivered one of the most important political speeches in recent Brazilian history, on the occasion of the promulgation of the current Constitution. He finished the speech with the following words: 'The Nation wants to change! The Nation shall change! The Nation will change! The Constitution is meant to be the voice, the word, the political will of a society on its way towards change. May its promulgation be our cry! Change to overcome! Change, Brazil!'

In this book, the enactment of the 1988 Constitution has been depicted several times as a moment of inflexion. None of the seven Brazilian constitutions before 1988 had such transformative potential as the 1988 Constitution does. It is not surprising that 'change' was one of the most important words in Guimarães' speech. And indeed Brazil has changed considerably in the last 30 years, and the Constitution is (at least partially) responsible for many of these changes. Organised civil society, popular movements, the working class, indigenous peoples, as well as big landowners, corporations, public servants, and many others have used the Constitution as argument for advancing their goals in the last 30 years. There is hardly any political and social dispute that does not raise constitutional controversies.

Nevertheless, as stated at the outset of this book, Brazil remains a country marked by the deepest inequalities. Wealth inequalities, racial inequalities, gender inequalities, regional inequalities, as well as inequalities in rights protection, inequalities in access to public goods and services, among many others, are still an inherent part of Brazil's constitutional, political, and social life. It may thus be argued that the recurrence of the word 'change' in Guimarães' speech is still overshadowed by the recurrence of the word 'inequality' in the description of almost all aspects of Brazil's everyday life. In many areas, the Constitution promised more than it could deliver, defined goals without creating means to achieve them, and even maintained some historical inequalities.

These are perhaps one of the reasons why the widespread hope that the Constitution could bring about social change has gradually been dampened and why, after 30 years, many seem to assume that if something has to be changed it is the Constitution itself. The 30th anniversary of the 1988 Constitution coincided with a period of political and institutional crises and, as usual in such moments, several proposals for amending the Constitution in order to completely change the political, party, electoral and government systems have been put forward.

This book has a different tenor, which deserves to be emphasised one last time in this conclusion. It assumes that the 1988 Constitution has transformative potential that is still waiting to be realised. This will hardly happen without strong social and political mobilisation, in every political and institutional arena. Just as the important achievements of the last three decades were to a great extent the result of such a mobilisation, which has almost always aimed at enforcing, and not changing, the Constitution, future transformations will hardly occur should this path be eventually abandoned. Thus, transformation still depends above all else on transformative legislation, transformative policies, as well as transformative constitutional interpretation. It almost never depends on constitutional reform.

The political and social motto '*Change to overcome!*' is thus still as vital and contemporary as it was when the 1988 Constitution was enacted. And its meaning has remained unchanged: 'The Constitution is meant to be the voice, the word, the political will of a society on its way towards change'. Changing the status quo, not the Constitution, has been the real challenge in the last three decades and will continue to be for many years to come.

Index

Introductory Note

References such as '178–79' indicate (not necessarily continuous) discussion of a topic across a range of pages. Wherever possible in the case of topics with many references, these have either been divided into sub-topics or only the most significant discussions of the topic are listed. Because the entire work is about 'Brazil', the use of this term (and certain others which occur constantly throughout the book) as an entry point has been minimised. Information will be found under the corresponding detailed topics.

www.ingramcontent.com/pod-product-compliance
Ingram Content Group UK Ltd.
Pitfield, Milton Keynes, MK11 3LW, UK
UKHW021033150926
475561UK00003B/79

9 781509 935079